Holger Ernst/Stefan Glänzer/Peter Witt (Eds.)

Success Factors of Fast Growing Companies

Bibliographic information published by Die Deutsche Bibliothek
Die Deutsche Bibliothek lists this publication in the Deutsche Nationalbiografie,
detailed bibliographic data is available in the Internet at <http://dnb.ddb.de>.

Prof. Dr. Holger Ernst is a professor of technology and innovation management at the Otto Beisheim Graduate School of Management (WHU).

Dr. Stefan Glänzer is a serial entrepreneur and a lecturer at the WHU.

Prof. Dr. Peter Witt is the Otto Beisheim Professor of Entrepreneurship at the WHU.

1st edition March 2005

All rights reserved
© Betriebswirtschaftlicher Verlag Dr. Th. Gabler/GWV Fachverlage GmbH, Wiesbaden 2005
Softcover reprint of the hardcover 1st edition 2005

Gabler is a company of Springer Science+Business Media.
www.gabler.de

No part of this publication may be reproduced, stored in a retrieval system or transmitted, mechanical, photocopying or otherwise without prior permission of the copyright holder.

Registered and/or industrial names, trade names, trade descriptions etc. cited in this publication are part of the law for trade-mark protection and may not be used free in any form or by any means even if this is not specifically marked.

Cover design: Ulrike Weigel, www.CorporateDesignGroup.de

Printed on acid-free paper

ISBN-13: 978-3-409-12706-6   e-ISBN-13: 978-3-322-84561-0
DOI: 10.1007/978-3-322-84561-0

Holger Ernst/Stefan Glänzer/Peter Witt (Eds.)

Success Factors of Fast Growing Companies

Selected Case Studies

For

Kamini

Uta and Caspar

Hille, Laura, Julia, and Alexandra

Preface

This book contains the stories of multiple fast growing companies. All these case studies were written by our students at the Otto Beisheim Graduate School of Management (WHU), Vallendar, Germany, in consecutive seminars on success factors of fast growing companies. We have been conducting this seminar for graduate students on an annual basis in close cooperation with entrepreneurs and managers from high growth firms since the fall semester of 2001. The idea for such a seminar came up in early 2001, after the downturn of the new economy. We strongly felt that the time for entrepreneurship and successful innovation management in growing companies was not over, it was rather just about to re-start again. We decided to start the academic exercise of a seminar with graduate business students and look for cases of firms from different industries that successfully grew and prospered despite the crisis and despite difficult capital market conditions.

This book covers a broad range of industries, company ages, and company sizes. Most of the case studies in this book were written about German companies. Although they were founded and are now headquartered in Germany, many of them have become international while growing, some nowadays are truly global firms, like Qiagen and SAP. The companies under consideration in this book are active in diverse industries like biotechnology, internet services, nanotechnology, software, food processing and others. While the case studies all share the common characteristic of impressive growth rates, some of them are still in the start-up phase while others are older and can best be described as mature firms today.

The case studies of fast growing firms can be used in different ways. First, they serve as illustrative case examples for teaching courses in entrepreneurship, innovation and technology management or business strategy at the graduate and executive level. Second, we think that the case studies of fast growing firms presented in this book are well suited to be used as illustrations and practical examples in more theoretical courses on new business formation, corporate strategy, and growth management. Finally, we personally use the cases studies of this volume in business plan seminars and graduate courses on entrepreneurship to train students in checking business models, making revenue and cost forecasts, and laying out plans for future growth.

First of all, we thank the authors of the case studies who agreed to have their material published exclusively in this book. Every team of authors had intense conversations with at least one founder or top-manager of the company under investigation, and every team rewrote the case study many times to get the main story line out clearly. Special thanks further go to all the entrepreneurs who gave their precious time to discuss the content and

implications from the case studies with us and the students. Many of them came to attend the case presentations during the seminar at WHU. Most importantly, without these entrepreneurs, there would be no success stories of fast growing firms in this book. Without these entrepreneurs sharing their experiences and knowledge with academics, there would be no opportunity to learn systematically about the success factors of fast growing firms. We also thank Jutta Hauser-Fahr and Renate Schilling, editors at Gabler, for their help in completing this project. Last but not least, we are especially indebted to our research assistants Jan Miczaika and Jan-Henrik Soll for their help in formatting the cases and double-checking all data to be reported in the cases with the respective companies.

Vallendar, January 2005

Holger Ernst, Stefan Glänzer, and Peter Witt

(hernst@whu.edu / stefan.glaenzer@20six.net / pwitt@whu.edu)

Table of Contents

Victor Henning, Julian Raabe and Jan Reichelt
    12snap GmbH 1

Julien Bert, Christopher Daniel and Arne Weinhardth
    Beepworld GmbH 19

Cécile Gouesse, Stefan Heidrich, Marc Koeppe and Anika Radloff
    Dialego AG 35

Robin Baum, Andy Bookas and Christopher Daniel
    DocMorris.com 55

Richard Hahn, René Mauer and Ulrich Ochmann
    European Telecommunication Exchange AG (EUTEX) 73

Fabian Hedderich, Joerg Oestreich and Marc-Oliver Ziegenbein
    forium GmbH 89

Michael Adams, Lydia Rullkötter and Sabina Schnelle
    GenPat77 Pharmacogenetics AG 107

Anna Bassler, Martin Heibel and Simone Sipply
    Getgo 127

Florian Beba, Sebastian Kösters and Tore Meyer
    Guenstiger.de 145

Stefanie Keuler, Fabian Neuen and Julia Reichert
    Jamba! AG 161

Matthias Ehrgott, Peter Herrmannsberger and Felix Reimann
    OnVista AG 183

Jens Bender, Sophie Nietfeld and Philipp Reinke
    Qiagen N.V. 199

Malte Bornemann, Björn Hagemann and Udo Kießlich
    SAP AG 217

Maximilian Niederhofer
    SinnerSchrader AG 239

Eric Adler, Christoph Frehsee, Florian Kreuzer and Tim Kunde
    Sushi Factory 255

Victor Henning, Julian Raabe and Jan Reichelt

12snap GmbH

1 Introduction 3
2 The company 4
3 The mobile marketing industry 12

1 Introduction

On the 24th of June 2002, Dr. Michael Birkel, the young CEO of mobile marketing provider 12snap, sat in his Munich office and thought of the coming Wednesday, which could be crucial for the future of the company. 12snap's venture capitalists, who owned more than 50% of equity, had called in a meeting to discuss the company's current status. According to its initial business plan, 12snap should have been profitable in 2000 already, but it had yet to reach break-even. Even though revised versions of the business plan foresaw 2003 as the year when 12snap would reach profitability, Dr. Birkel was concerned that the investors may become impatient. Still, 12snap's operating figures had been displaying a steady upwards trend, and he was more than confident that profitability was within the company's reach in the months to come.

The previous week, the large Swedish competitor "Lokomobil", which had a reasonable customer base, had run into liquidity problems because of its' failure to gain further financing. 12snap could perhaps acquire Lokomobil for far below its actual value. Dr. Birkel believed it to be a perfect fit to 12snap and a chance to expand its reach in the dynamic European market.

After the dot.com-bubble had burst, it was increasingly hard for start-up companies to set up new financing rounds. Dr. Birkel was aware of this, so he did not expect his VCs to inject new cash into 12snap's operations. Rather, all he needed them to do was keep their confidence in the company's opportunities. Despite their constant involvement with 12snap, he could not count on them knowing the company's strengths as intimately as he did, nor could their vision of the company's future be as clear as his was. Considering all alternatives, Dr. Birkel decided to prepare a presentation for the coming Wednesday, clearly outlining the positive development 12snap had gone through over the last two years. He intended to exhibit how its key success factors were to form the cornerstones of further rapid growth, and how they could effectively be applied to their potential acquisition target in Sweden.

Now, Dr. Birkel had two days until the 26th of June to translate his confidence into a sweeping presentation which would reassure the VCs to maintain their support. He started to recall how 12snap, and the young industry of mobile marketing, had evolved…

2 The company

2.1 The early days

The founding team consisted of five members with complementary skills. Dr. Birkel, Mr. Müller, Mr. Mühlfriedel and Mr. Röding came from McKinsey & Company. Mr. Mühlfriedel and Mr. Röding additionally knew each other from a MBA programme in Georgia, USA. Finally, Mr. Brand, Mr. Müller and Mr. Röding had already met during their studies at the Technical University of Karlsruhe, Germany.

When these five founders decided to become entrepreneurs in early 1999, they had chosen a rather structured approach, which is unsurprising due to their common consulting background. First, they had narrowed down their choices on whether to enter the B2B internet market or the B2C mobile sector, and had opted for the latter. Their understanding was that it constituted a larger market and was less dependent on advertising revenues. Then, when devising their business model, they had consciously chosen a transaction-based design, for it enabled them to quickly build up a brand because of the high interactivity with customers.

In October 1999, they had already raised sufficient funding under the lead investor Viventures and established a strategic alliance with Vodafone. 12snap's first business model made use of a pre-existing, relatively unknown mobile technology called "Cell Broadcasting", which was somewhat of a cross between the Wireless Application Protocol ("WAP") and the Short Messaging Service ("SMS"). In cooperation with Vodafone, the start-up now began to develop the transaction platform which would enable consumers to participate in auctions via a standard mobile phone.

A massive advertising campaign was launched, with humorous TV spots showing people that won auctions through their mobile phones while being in remote or unexpected places (a public toilet, for example). Pushed by the campaign, 12snap's auction platform went live nationwide in January 2000. Besides building a national brand, a second financing round in spring 2000 enabled an early expansion abroad, with 12snap setting up offices in Rome/Italy and London/UK, with entirely local staff. Dr. Birkel remembered that "bubble pressure" had placed growth before profitability, meaning international expansion even before the business model had been tried and tested.

In summer 2000, according to plan, further applications were rolled out to expand the business model. Fixed-prize sale of goods was introduced, followed by entertainment content such as jokes and horoscopes sent out via SMS.

2.2 Turbulences and the burst of the dot.com-bubble

A few months later, in fall 2000, 12snap expanded its business model. Based on their direct access to a wide base of consumers, the founders saw potential for B2B services. More importantly, the millions of mobile phone users in the database had given 12snap permission to address them through SMS messages. 12snap had previously conducted mobile marketing, i.e. using mobile phones as a marketing channel, for its own purposes. Why not offer the gathered know-how to other firms? After all, the mobile phone offered the opportunity of direct interaction and targeted campaigns, and most people constantly carried their phones with them.

The founders' extensive network proved valuable when acquiring their first customer for this new service. Through their investors' connections they received the chance to meet the Marketing Director of McDonald's Germany and convinced him to take a chance on the start-up's concept. Of course, the importance of this "big name" on the young company's resume could not be underestimated when it came to the acquisition of new clients. However, as Dr. Birkel recalled, most major projects had indeed come to the company through the many business contacts the founders had made in their consulting days. Ads in the advertising trade paper "Werben & Verkaufen" as well as press coverage helped building business as well. The founders' plan estimated mobile marketing to contribute about 10-15% of company revenues.

12snap was lucky enough to complete a third round of financing in October 2000, which the founders knew to be the last because the dot.com-bubble had burst and markets crashed. Dr. Birkel had felt that, with this money in the bank, 12snap would have to achieve profitability because there would be no further cash injections. He also had been aware of the fact that, without this third round of financing, 12snap would have been likely to join the ranks of the many start-up companies that went bankrupt during that time.

In early 2001, the founders gradually realized that neither mobile transactions nor entertainment content could sustain 12snap's business. While growth rates had been stunning and 12snap had actually become one of the leading mobile entertainment content providers in Europe, revenues and profits lagged far behind expectations. In addition, Dr. Birkel anticipated the mobile telecommunication providers such as T-Mobile, D2 Vodafone, Viag Interkom, and E-Plus to aggressively move into transactions, commerce, and content to claim these businesses as their domain.

2.3 A change of direction

While the external pressure pushed 12snap to rely more on the mobile marketing segment of its business model, it took the will, daring, and flexibility of the founders to give up their prime position in transactions and content once it was not deemed economical any more. Other factors sweetened the move towards mobile marketing for the founding team: its economics were favorable compared to those of transactions. No sustained investments in warehousing and the maintenance of an auction platform were required, and margins for the B2B marketing service were higher. Thus, when 12snap finally decided to abandon all other activity and focus solely on mobile marketing, it only gave up on minor revenue, but excessive cost. Until today, Dr. Birkel considered himself flexible enough to exit from an established business model at any time when a more promising one emerged, notwithstanding sunk costs and opportunity costs.

From spring 2001 onwards, 12snap emerged as the leading mobile marketing company in Germany, serving prestigious clients such as Adidas, L'Oréal, Coca Cola, Nestlé, Microsoft, Columbia TriStar, 20th Century Fox, and MTV Networks. For its clients, 12snap combined classic advertising creation, on-pack tie-ins, and mobile phones in one marketing mix. Overall, 2001 turned out to be a successful year, as revenue grew by about 120% to reach €2.4 million. As far as 2002 had proceeded, Dr. Birkel thought it well possible to maintain this growth rate.

2.4 The value proposition and campaign examples

By June 2002, 12snap's database contained close to 18 million European mobile phone users who had all given the permission (by "opt-in") to be contacted for promotional purposes. Most of them belonged to the commercially attractive segment of 14-39-year-olds, with further demographic and psychographic data such as gender, location, residence, and interests available for cost-efficient, well-targeted campaigns with high response rates.

Sometimes, 12snap would design advertising campaigns from scratch, but most often, it worked with the respective ad agency of its clients (the Rome office had meanwhile been relocated to Milan because of this). In any case, 12snap offered the complete solution to port the campaign onto the mobile channel: in-house, it created logos, ringtones, images, videos, voice messages and MMS, and any other content needed for the mobile campaign. 12snap was proud of its' deep understanding of what consumers wanted on their mobile phones and what not, so that the "feel" of a brand would not get lost when it entered the mobile world. Furthermore, 12snap took over project man-

agement and devised the "on-pack messages" on the product packages which would animate consumers to actively participate in the campaign. Then, it provided scalable software and hardware solutions which needed to be able to receive, process, and respond to the tens of thousands of SMS sent by consumers after a TV spot had been aired – and all within a few seconds, because consumers expected something to happen immediately when they had sent a message. Finally, 12snap implemented and carried out the campaign by sending out initial messages and message responses.

A prime example was the McDonald's/Disney "Txt a Monster" campaign which 12snap had conducted in the UK earlier in 2002. Designed as a promotion both for McDonald's and Disney's animated film "Monsters Inc.", it was used in 1,200 McDonald's restaurants. All medium- and large-sized French fries-packages contained a little fold-open window, beneath which one of six "Monsters"-characters and a "Monstercode" was hidden. Via mobile phone or the webpage www.textamonster.co.uk, consumers could send in the Monstercode. Within seconds, they would receive a message from "Monsters Inc." to notify them whether they had won one of many prizes worth a total of several million Euro, including 500 flatscreen TVs, 2,000 DVD players, 5,000 mp3/CD players, 1,000 Disney DVD sets, and 370,000 mobile phone ringtones and logos.

Collaborating with Microsoft's ad agency Bartle Bogle Hagerty on a European-wide campaign, 12snap helped supporting the launch of the Xbox in 2002. The campaign was distinguished by being the first one ever to make use of multimedia-MMS. While few phone models supported this new messaging format, its owners were thought to be early adopters – exactly the clientele which Microsoft wanted to reach. The messages were sent to all the users which had previously registered on Microsoft's onlinegaming site www.playmore.com, in addition to tens of thousands carefully selected users, which had shown an interest in gaming, from 12snap's database. Every recipient was given an Xbox mobile phone display logo for free, as well as being directed to a video on the playmore.com-site.

For the 2002 soccer world championships, 12snap and Adidas' ad agency "180" set up a campaign for Adidas which contained the world's first mobile phone real-time betting game. Humorous "Footballitis" TV spots asked viewers to send in their predictions for top soccer matches, with highly attractive prizes (e.g. an original jersey worn by French national player Zinedine Zidane or a meeting with the German national team).

12snap's mobile marketing campaigns were superior to traditional direct marketing campaigns in many ways. E-mail ads were often dismissed as "spam" by its recipients, while direct mailings were cost-intensive and not very targeted. In some cases, other forms of direct marketing even entailed negative effects for the brand: many consumers were angered by the waste caused by AOL and their millions of internet access CDs, most of which went into the trash. Mobile marketing, on the other hand, seemed to be welcomed by consumers: in 12snap's Nestlé and Esprit campaigns, about 60% of

participants had entered based on recommendations by friends. Free logos and ringtones were forwarded to friends, causing network externalities free of charge for the advertiser. Response rates were exorbitant: when digital vouchers for perfume samples were sent out in the Esprit campaign, 33% of recipients redeemed them in stores. But campaigns were not only beneficial for sales, but also for the brand: in a follow-up study to the Esprit case, 64% of recipients stated that they intended to buy the new perfume that had been advertised, and 77% of recipients felt that the campaign rendered the brand more likeable. Similar results were achieved in the Nestlé campaign.

Because of its success with Esprit, mobile couponing was considered an area of lucrative growth by Dr. Birkel. 12snap had started to develop a back-end solution that would enable it to send out coupon "barcodes" to mobile devices – these barcodes, which then appeared on the device's display, could in turn be scanned right at the point of sale, with direct feedback about the coupon's usage being transmitted back from the vendor to 12snap. This way, a once-used coupon would be voided so that it could not be used again even if forwarded to another mobile phone. Additionally, it allowed for personalization and tracking to gather valuable data regarding consumer behavior.

2.5 Financing structure

For the first few weeks, when the business plan was written, the company had been running on the founders own savings. Shortly after its inception however, the young company needed external money to build up business. Especially the infrastructure to handle the thousands of page calls per day had been extremely capital intensive. Additionally, 12snap had been looking for strategic partners who could provide either knowledge or contacts (see table 1).

Table 1:   *Investors*

About Viventures

Viventures is a venture capital fund based in Paris with a presence in the US, Europe and Asia. The fund was established to provide capital for innovative telecommunications and Internet businesses. Created by the Vivendi Group it now counts 18 corporations with substantial interests in the high-tech industry as investors, such as British Telecom, Mannesmann, Siemens Venture Capital, Nokia, Cisco, SG Asset Management, la Compagnie Nationale à Portefeuille, Audiofina, Compagnie Financière et Industrielle Gaz & Eaux, Sojecci Ltée, Donaldson, Lufkin & Jenrette, EDB-Singapore funds, Viel & Cie, Europatech, Net Fund Europe, and

others. Viventures is currently launching Viventures 2, a $500m fund.

About Nokia Ventures

Based in Menlo Park, Nokia Ventures L.P. is a US $150 million venture capital fund formed in 1998 to invest in early stage, high-growth companies in the areas of e-commerce, information technology and communications. Nokia Corporation has invested in the fund with the express intent to gain exposure to new markets, business models, and technologies beyond the reach of Nokia's current business unit strategies. Nokia Ventures seeks partnerships with leading-edge companies attacking high-growth market opportunities that will benefit from the combined resources, experience and contacts of the Nokia Ventures team and from the association with a world-class brand.

About Apax Partners & Co

Apax Partners & Co advicies investment pools exceeding a total volume of $5,5 billion under management. With offices in Munich, London, Paris, Madrid, Tel Aviv, New York, Palo Alto and Tokio, it's one of the largest and most global players in the private equity arena. Apax focuses on six industries, the internet being core to each of these sectors' investment strategies. Mobile commerce is one of those "hot spots". The Apax portfolio encompasses service providers like Webraska Mobile Technologies and infrastructure providers like Argo Interactive. Apax is one of the most active investors in the Internet economy with investments in companies like Clicksure, beenz, iMediation, PaperX, PecuNet, ENBA, NetDoktor, eDreams, QXL and many others.

About Argo Global Capital LLC

Argo Global Capital is a U.S. Venture Capital firm with more than US$460 million of committed capital. Co-founded in 1997 by its CEO, H.H. Haight and by Telesystem, a private equity company in the digital economy, Argo is a leading international firm dedicated to the wireless industry and the convergence of wireless and the Internet. Argo's two funds, GSM Capital Limited Partnership and ARGO II-The Wireless Internet Fund Limited Partnership, have made more than 38 investments in the wireless sector in Europe, North America and Asia from its offices in Boston, Montréal, London and Hong Kong. Major wireless operators around the World – including France Telecom, Deutsche Telekom, KPN, ESAT, Singapore Telecom, SmarTone, VoiceStream, Microcell Telecommunications and TIW – contribute capital and ongoing support to Argo's funds and its portfolio companies.

About Goldman Sachs

Goldman Sachs is a leading international investment banking firm and has been active in the private equity business since 1986. Goldman Sachs is currently expanding its activities in this area in Europe with a special focus on technology

> companies. In the U.S., Goldman Sachs is already one of the leading investors in the technology sector. 12snap is Goldman Sachs' 7th investment in Germany in the last 12 months.

1st finance round:

The capital of the first finance round in October 1999 came from Viventures, a well-known French investor headquartered in Paris. The round was also supported by the state via the "Deutsche Beteiligungsgesellschaft tbg" and "Bayernkapital", who only acted as silent investment partners. The capital raised enabled 12snap to enter the mobile transaction market and survive until its required second finance round.

2nd finance round:

Led by Nokia Ventures as the main investor, the second round in March 2000 was closed at DM 13 (€ 6.6) million. This capital permitted the European expansion in summer 2000 with the intention to build a pan-European mobile shopping service. In addition, Nokia and especially the co-investors became strategic partners for the young company. In a press release issued back then, Bernd Mühlfriedel, the Chief Financial Officer (CFO), had commented: "We feel that Nokia Ventures can add a lot of value to our operation through its experience, good industry contacts and technical and marketing insight." The other investors included again Viventures, Apax Europe IV, an investment pool advised by Apax Partners & Co, and Goldman Sachs.

3rd finance round:

For the third and last finance round Apax Europe IV took over the lead in cooperation with Argo II. This round closed at €37.2 million. Utilizing the capital, further technology developments and enhancements of the provided service were accelerated. Moreover, new investors such as telecommunication and new venture specialists Sirios Capital Management, CDB Web Tech and Broadband Capital brought valuable knowledge and networks into the equation.

With the closure of this third round, a little more than 50% of the company belonged to the investors named above, a further 10% was controlled by the company, and the remaining equity was held by private investors, the founders, and the employees.

In the financial press, 12snap was praised for having picked its investors very wisely even under the pressure to survive. "We chose our partners systematically", Mühlfriedel explained. The criteria had been "good connections, coaching, strategic assis-

tance, and in particular with regard to going public soon: much experience". Even after the times had changed and an early public offering had become very unlikely, the partners were able to contribute strongly to the success of 12snap.

2.6 The organization

Since the foundation in 1999 the organizational structure of 12snap has changed dramatically. This transformation was primarily driven by the strong growth in the first two years, the changes in the business model that had resulted in the company closing down an entire business unit, and finally by procedures to compensate for the diminishing start-up spirit.

The start-up phase had been characterized by strong growth and a portfolio of different business models. At that point in time the hierarchy had been very flat and all important issues were discussed in the team. Arguments and discussions, not titles on a business card, were key to decision making. Qualified work force was a scarce resource, and in a very short period of time a lot of people were hired, mostly via network contacts, but also via job offers in newspapers. Key to the success of this modus operandi was the fact that all founders had a common professional background in consulting and corresponding common values. Nevertheless, accelerated growth established the need for clearly defined procedures.

Accordingly, over time, the approach was altered. Driven by the awareness that the people were one of the key assets of 12snap, and by the experience that it was preferable to leave a position open instead of accepting a "second-best solution", the company's organizational and personal structure was changed. As the size of the team grew, decision-making processes became more formalized. Discussions were still paramount, but as the start-up spirit was gradually replaced by the feeling of being an established company, Dr. Birkel and the founding team assumed a more authoritative leadership style to increase professionalism. Furthermore, it became obvious that the company not only needed ambitious people, but also specialists and assistants to cope with everyday work. Processes were put in place that standardized procedures and prevented 12snap to "re-invent the wheel day after day", as Dr. Birkel thought of it.

However, 12snap did not create a dedicated knowledge management system. There was an archive of all projects and campaigns to be found in the company intranet, but overall, knowledge was very much tied to people and their experience. 12snap did not hold any patents, as the process of registering them was deemed too costly and time-consuming. Notwithstanding a slight increase in formality, the core values were kept alive. Despite the processes, the hierarchy was still very lean. Moreover, the incentive system – consisting of bonuses and stock options – was still available for the entire work force and not only for the top management. Finally, the founders had managed

to maintain a positive atmosphere of flexibility, self-realization, family flair, and identification with the company.

In June 2003, three of the five founders were still with 12snap. Alexander Brand and Andreas Müller had left amicably to pursue a career with Siemens AG. Distributed over its three locations in Munich, London, and Milan, 12snap employed 45 people, 25 of which were working at the Munich headquarters. These were mainly marketing and technology experts, as well as some creative staff recruited from advertising agencies. The different country offices were managed rather independently by the locals who had set them up in the early days (see figure 1).

Figure 1: Organizational chart as of June 2002

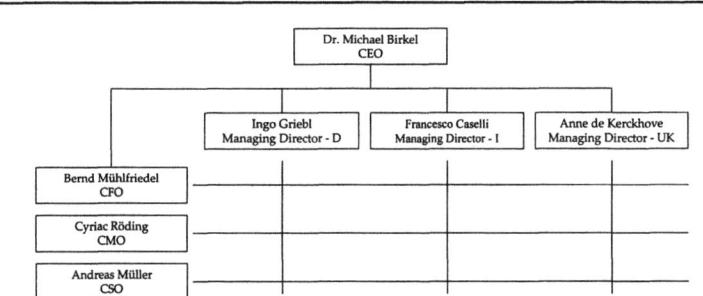

3 The mobile marketing industry

3.1 Industry forecasts and value chain

Most mobile telecommunications forecasts refer to the wireless advertising market. Research companies like Kelsey Group, Ovum, and Durlacher project this market to reach $16-23 billion by 2005. Western Europe is expected to capture the largest share with a potential reach of more than 280 million consumers, an average mobile phone penetration rate of 75%, and text messaging already generating more than 10% of mobile operator revenue. Text messaging is increasingly adopted especially by teenagers: in some European countries, they account for up to 83% of all SMS ("Short Message Service") sent, with about three messages per teenager per day (see table 2 and figure 2).

Table 2: SMS usage in Europe

UK	Germany	France	Spain	Italy	Scandinavia
1.2 Billion SMS per month	2.2 Billion SMS per month	0.4 Billion SMS per month	~0.9 Billion SMS per month	1.0 Billion SMS per month	~0.4 Billion SMS per month

Source: Frost & Sullivan (2001), Modell Data Association

Figure 2: The phenomenon of SMS

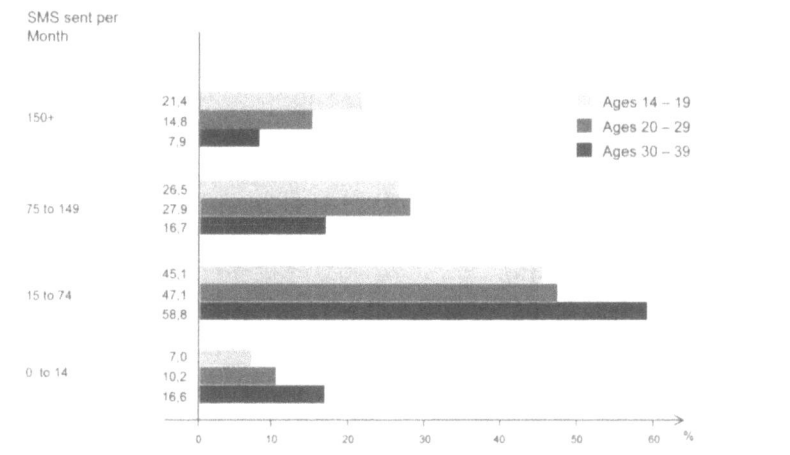

Of course, the $16-23 billion represent the overall advertising value created along the entire mobile communication value chain. The relevant market for 12snap and its peers is the one for mobile marketing services, which Forrester Research estimates to represent about €600 million in Western Europe by 2006. The countries leading the advancement of mobile marketing are the UK, Germany, Italy, Sweden, and Finland. The value chain (see figure 3) could generally be described as containing at least five distinct types of entities, which will be described in the following.

Figure 3: Value chain of advertising and mobile marketing

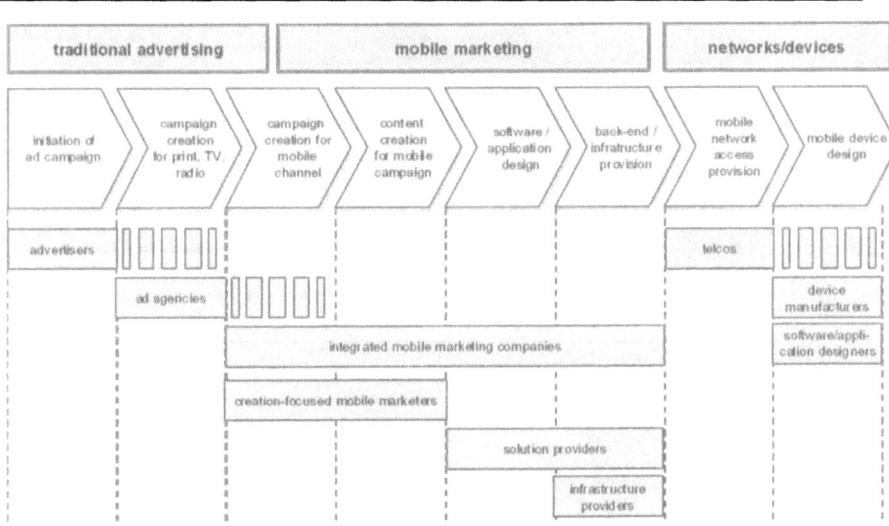

3.2 Advertisers

The advertiser is any company that wants to use mobile devices as a marketing channel, thus becoming a client of advertising agencies and mobile marketing companies. For an advertiser, the benefits of mobile marketing campaigns are multifaceted:

- Immediacy: mobile campaigns can be planned and executed within days, whereas setting up a traditional direct mailing campaign takes weeks.

- Contextual personalization: the message can be adapted to a consumer's behavioral and demographic profile, as well as to a consumer's current location and the time of day at reception.

- Impact: because of the highly personal nature of the mobile phone, nearly every message is read, and response rates are impressive (see figure 4).

- Direct response: consumers' reactions to a campaign become visible within minutes.

- Cost effectiveness : broken down to an equal number of responses, a mobile marketing campaign is one-fifth the cost of direct mail and one-twentieth the cost of call-center interaction.

More and more companies become aware of these advantages, and Dr. Birkel estimates that about two thirds of all major brands are using the mobile marketing channel already. On the other hand, there is sufficient room for growth, as only about 1% of marketing budgets are currently being spent on mobile marketing.

Figure 4: Response rates to different methods of targeted marketing

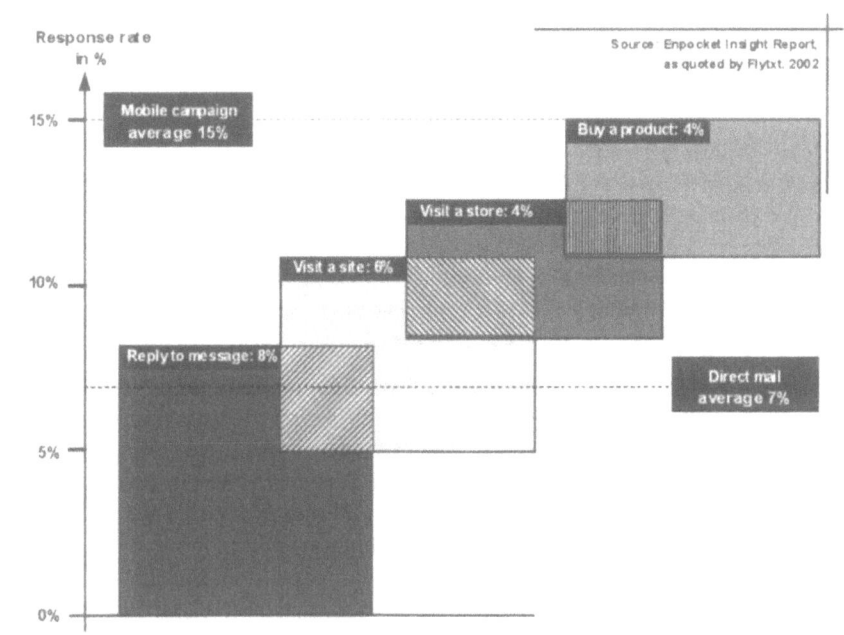

3.3 Advertising agencies

Traditional advertising agencies focus on classic creations for print, TV, and radio, as well as providing media buying services. Even though they lag behind in creation for the mobile channel, they "own" the client relationships: advertisers place their budgets with advertising agencies for long periods of time, and agencies work closely with the marketing managers of their clients. Thus, advertising agencies often act as an intermediary between the advertiser and the mobile marketing company.

Dr. Birkel hopes that more traditional agencies will enter the mobile marketing business soon. He reasons that this will make 12snap's life easier: if traditional agencies also engage in the creation of ad campaigns for the mobile channel, his company could focus on its core competency of mobile content creation, provision of permission-based access to the mobile phone users in its database, and project management including the software and hardware solutions. Furthermore, the mobile marketing business would attain higher significance in marketing agendas.

3.4 Mobile marketing companies

Most of 12snap's competitors also offer content creation for mobile advertising campaigns, as 12snap does. The mobile marketing companies' value proposition, however, is their technological know-how: they develop the back-end solutions, platforms, and applications required to carry out the campaigns. Over the coming years, a host of new technologies such as streaming media and "3G" (3rd generation broadband) will be introduced, so that mobile marketing companies have an even better chance to differentiate themselves from traditional ad agencies.

12snap is the market leader in terms of sales in Germany and Italy, but faces one or two major competitors in each of its markets. In the UK, 12snap competes head-to-head with Flytxt, which had been founded in 2000 as well. Like 12snap, it relies on marketing expertise together with technological leadership. Flytxt has recently entered the German market. In Germany, the second-largest player behind 12snap is Mindmatics. Mindmatics' profile is slightly different, as they lean more towards providing the technology, and less towards content creation. Furthermore, their mobile phone user database contains less than three million entries. Munich-based Apollis Interactive has chosen a similar approach as Mindmatics. However it does not maintain its own customer database for campaigns, using advertiser's pre-existing databases instead. Completing the picture, there were pure infrastructure providers, the largest in Europe being mBlox. They don't offer any marketing services, nor undertake application programming, but focus solely on simple, reliable, and cost-effective SMS transfer.

3.5 Telecommunications companies

The largest telcos in Europe are the British company Vodafone and the German-based T-Mobile. They „own" the relationship to mobile phone users by providing them with devices and network access. Despite long-running efforts to build other sources of revenue through additional services, their business model is mainly establishing phone connections and messaging. Only recently, Vodafone has introduced its "Voda-

fone Live" concept. Adoption rates look promising: instead of focusing on the technical merits and concepts such as WAP and GPRS ("General Packet Radio Service"), the value proposition has been based on fun, entertainment, and a sense of community. Multimedia messages and camera-phones are at the center of the campaign.

Telcos are likely to look at the mobile marketing growth with mixed feelings: on the one hand, they benefit through the use of their networks, and by owning the consumer relationships, they possess considerable leverage. However, churn rates – their biggest problem – already hovers around 30%. If consumers perceive marketing messages as spam, this could backlash into even higher churn rates. Telcos will therefore have to generate strategic options to limit aggressive solicitation if necessary.

3.6 Device manufacturers

So far, the major device manufacturers such as Nokia and Motorola have been content with creating value through their latest collection of high-tech devices. Yet, a future power struggle between them and the telcos is a possibility: most telcos already insist on having their logos printed on the devices prominently, and in some cases (especially in Asia), the manufacturer logo has been replaced by the telco logo in its entirety. Industry experts wonder when manufacturers will begin to fight back, and whether they possess the power to do so: insiders argue that this is the case since many consumers often just choose their telco based on the mobile phone model they desire. In this setting, Nokia could thus simply threaten to withhold its devices and give them to competing telcos exclusively.

Turmoil in the value chain can mean tremendous opportunities for software, content, and service providers: AOL, for example, has forged contracts with device manufacturers allowing it to pre-install its AOL Instant Messenger on mobile devices, much to the dismay of telcos: the Instant Messenger will still use their networks, but using it costs the consumer far less than sending an SMS. Other rumors have MTV preparing a deal with Motorola that will threaten the telcos' claim to be the consumers' sole source of mobile entertainment content. In a similar vein, software company Real Networks is preparing a version of its wide-spread Real Player that can run on mobile phones, enabling other content players aside from the telcos to tap into mobile entertainment revenue.

What will all these developments mean to 12snap and its business model, and will the success factors that have spurred 12snap's growth so far still be the factors driving its growth in the future? Having gone over the facts, Dr. Birkel has found plenty of reasons to look ahead confidently. All he has to do now is breathe life into them for the presentation on Wednesday.

Julien Bert, Christopher Daniel and Arne Weinhardth

Beepworld GmbH

1	Beepworld	21
2	Company Background	21
3	Business Model	24
4	Current Situation	27
5	Industry Analysis	29
6	Issues at Hand	30
7	Future Prospects	32
	Appendix	33

1 Beepworld

Dr. Thomas Finkenstädt took the paper out of the fax machine and threw a quick glance at it. Already the first look gave him a pretty good impression about what kind of work was coming to him. The fax was sent by a lawyer, and the company had been receiving more and more letters and faxes from these people. By now, they did not scare Dr. Finkenstädt any more, as he had – involuntarily - gained a lot of experience in dealing with these situations. Still, they represented a major nuisance, as the four legal complaints Beepworld received in an average week ate up a large part of his work time.

On the way back to his desk in the brand new office in Düsseldorf, he started to think about the development of the company after he had joined his son David in 2000.

2 Company Background

Idea

In fact, it was by coincidence that Dr. Thomas Finkenstädt first became aware of his son's activities. Already in 1999, David, then age 16, had created the first homepage for a friend. As he had been interested in computers, especially software and programming ever since he first saw a computer, building a private homepage did not represent a major challenge for him. The friend however, completely thrilled by the result, spread the word, so that more and more people wanted him to construct their private homepages as well. In exchange, friends would invite him over for dinner, whereas people he did not know that well would pay him a humble fee.

Pretty soon he became popular within the entire school for programming elaborate homepages. Due to this snowball effect in combination with the growing popularity of the Internet, David could soon no longer satisfy the growing demand. It was at that point of time that he had the revolutionary idea that would become the basis of Beepworld's business model.

David decided to design a software tool, with the help of which Internet users could construct their homepages like a kid could build a house out of a box of bricks. This would enable less experienced users to create individual homepages on their own, and would allow him to satisfy all demand.

Initial Phase

With the initial easy-to-use modular system for creating private homepages, David could address an even larger target group. However, he offered the tool for free and wanted to come up with a solution how to promote his idea. Being an active Internet user, David knew ways to use the Internet for his purpose.

He visited different communities, panels and chat rooms and posted his offer under the name "Beepworld". This increased traffic at Beepworld's website, and subsequently attracted companies who wanted to put banner ads on this site. Pretty soon, David could charge up to DM 3,000 for a banner ad. Step by step, his software tool started to turn into a business model.

On the other hand, David also incurred significant costs. Software and finished homepages had to be stored somewhere, the customers had to be provided with fast and reliable upload opportunities and needed to be able to access their homepages on a 24/7 basis. These requirements obliged David to rent an adequate amount of storage capacity from an external provider. All in all, Beepworld's revenues were sufficiently large to cover all expenses, but did not allow for high profits.

In mid 2000, David seemed to have run out of luck and feared that he would have to close down Beepworld. One of his banner ad customers defaulted on a DM 2,500 contract at the same time as Beepworld was due to pay the server bill. At that time, David's budget did not offer him any way out of this liquidity crisis. Facing this solvency issue, David turned to his father for help.

Startup Phase

However, what first looked like bad luck soon turned out to be a blessing in disguise. Dr. Thomas Finkenstädt unconsciously smiled when he thought back to the day in 2000 when his son addressed him with his problem. Of course, he knew that David was running something on the Internet, and he also knew that some smaller monetary transactions were involved, as he had to give his agreement when David had applied for a trade license. But he had never even bothered to understand what exactly David was doing. On the occasion of David's financial problems, Dr. Finkenstädt first sat down with his son and made him explain exactly what Beepworld was doing and how the software tool worked.

David could prove that Beepworld was financially viable and that there was sufficient demand in the market for his software system for modular homepages. At that point, Dr. Thomas Finkenstädt took two decisions. First, he would provide his son with enough money to pay for the outstanding bill. Second, he would help him to exploit the potential he believed to see within his son's idea. The new Beepworld was born.

Founders

Even if he did not dispose of a classical managerial education - he had studied biophysics and psychology – Dr. Finkenstädt felt confident that he could cope with all upcoming challenges. After all, he had worked in several executive positions with Schering, an experience which had allowed him to become acquainted with most managerial activities. As far as programming was concerned he was not as skilled as his son. Still, he had already developed special interest in computers, while working as a scientific assistant in an artificial intelligence research team. All in all, Dr. Thomas Finkenstädt knew he could support his son. By putting Beepworld's management on a sound basis, he hoped to be able to reach a point where considerable profits could be extracted within a limited period of time.

In 2000, David, his oldest son, was attending high school. Up to that date, most of his customers had been from his age group, so that he was well aware of what they wanted. As Dr. Finkenstädt wanted his son to successfully pass the A-levels, he knew that the school would put a time constraint on David's availability. Still, he was sure that David would manage to cope with the workload. However, he was aware of another kind of challenge that he would have to face. As he was divorced with both sons living with him, he would have to carefully watch out, so that his younger son Tim would not feel neglected. The best way to do so would be to integrate him within the Beepworld activities.

Growth Phase

The first few weeks after Dr. Thomas Finkenstädt had joined the company, he and his son had come up with a number of ideas they wanted to introduce into the Beepworld concept. He thought back to the way they went about this, and how much in fact he liked those intense discussions. Normally, his son would come to his room and talk to him about a new idea, something he had heard of, or simply something he had seen elsewhere. Then they would start to discuss, consider advantages and disadvantages and try to test different argumentation chains. Once they had agreed on doing something, either he – for business matters – or David – for technological issues – would implement it. He admired his son for the programming skills and technological understanding and was truly impressed, as David managed to put all their ideas into practice on his own. Both of them were proud of this creative process, which could take place at any time of the day or the night, and did not believe in the time-wasting process of planning things out on paper.

One of Dr. Thomas Finkenstädt's first insights was that he realized that Beepworld was largely dependent on the banner advertising budgets of their business partners. He expected a sharp decline in banner ads, as the dot.com bubble had just bursted and e-

commerce related business models seemed to suffer from acceptance problems. Subsequently, he wanted to diversify their revenue sources.

This, in turn, would only be possible if Beepworld was able to reach even more users. Admittedly, they already had quite a number of users at that point of time, but they were by far not yet large enough to catch enough attention for their business model on their own.

David's personal relations with Netzquadrat, an Internet service provider, should prove helpful, as they explained to him the rules of the game of running an online business. Some of Beepworld's first business contacts resulted from this acquaintance. Based on Netzquadrat's guidance, the two founders learned about the importance of newsletters or the possibility of banner exchanges. As both tools did not have any negative effects on liquidity, they could easily be used to promote Beepworld in the market.

The combination of word of mouth and banner exchange seemed sufficient to attract an increasing number of users to Beepworld, and business continued to grow at high rates. More and more customers made use of the company's services and David's latest developments found great acceptance. He had provided users with the possibility of joining each other in chat rooms and panels on Beepworld's homepage (see Appendix Figure 1). News of the latest developments was spread through a bi-weekly newsletter.

Still, sheer size did not yet mean a diversification of revenue sources. However, it gave the founders more leeway for action.

3 Business Model

Administrators

By the end of 2000, the company had reached a size which made it very difficult for David and Dr. Thomas Finkenstädt to control Beepworld's website. The different chat rooms and panels had to be monitored so that no topics would evolve that could harm the company's reputation. Another point that needed supervision was the private homepages. Beepworld, although only providing links, could be held responsible for the contents under specific circumstances.

Some of Beepworld's users had brought forth the idea of creating the position of administrators, and the founders liked the idea. An administrator would be in charge of controlling, guiding and monitoring chat rooms and homepages, and in turn receive

specific rights that a normal user would not have. Administrators could, for example, ban users from Beepworld or block homepages should they be offensive. Although the daily time exposure amounted to 3 to 4 hours, Beepworld received up to 30 applications for one of the 39 administrator positions per day. Users were so proud of belonging to the Beepworld community and of obtaining the responsibility that they were keen on that position, even if it was unpaid.

Change of Paradigm

The importance of this group became apparent when Dr. Thomas Finkenstädt wanted to introduce a new revenue source for Beepworld. So far, all of Beepworld's services had been for free, and he had agreed with his son that the company should try to charge fees from the customers in order to compensate the decline in banner ad revenues. As both of them were aware that this change represented a major breach of paradigm, they realized that the group of administrators could be of great help with the introduction of this new concept.

David and Dr. Thomas Finkenstädt invited all of them to a personal meeting and carefully explained their situation. They were relieved to find acceptance for the new concept with the administrators, and prepared argumentation chains how the fee could be explained to the users. The basic homepage was still for free, as Thomas and David Finkenstädt assumed that their customers would not pay for a service they had not experienced before. This featured up to 20 sub-pages and some music and picture galleries with limited memory capacity. But add-ons, such as extra storage space, visitor counters, flash applications, guest books or secured pages were subject to a charge.

The administrators agreed to the pricing scheme and promised their support. In his next newsletter, Dr. Thomas Finkenstädt introduced the new concept, and with the help of the administrators, most of the Beepworld community members accepted the change. The administrators showed increased presence in the chat rooms and panels, were available for questions on a 24/7 basis and even increased promotion efforts by posting news in various communities.

At his desk in Düsseldorf, Dr. Thomas Finkenstädt looked out of the window. In hindsight, he realized that the familiar notion he and his son had established within the Beepworld community was another factor that had greatly contributed to the successful change. In his regular newsletters, Dr. Finkenstädt kept the users informed about Tim, David and himself, and after the first meeting with the administrators, it had become tradition to meet up twice a year and exchange information. Additionally, Tim himself was heavily involved in taking care of the community and handling customer requests.

By this move from indirect revenue generation, through advertisement, to fee-based revenues, Beepworld was finally able to diversify its revenue basis. And as experience should show, it had just been at the right point of time. Only shortly after this change, the demand for online advertisement collapsed, prices plummeted and exclusively advertising-financed business models went bankrupt. From being the only source of income, the importance of banner advertisements for Beepworld had decreased considerably. In 2003, only 10% of revenues depended on online ads, with a slightly increasing tendency.

Payment System

However, before the customers could be charged for additional services, Beepworld had to develop a new payment system. Dr. Thomas Finkenstädt and his son came up with the idea of developing the system of Beepcodes. A Beepcode was a code number, which Beepworld users could purchase and then use to acquire add-on features for their homepages or any of the other services Beepworld offered. The Beepcode thus represented a virtual currency for the Beepworld community.

In the beginning, users could exclusively acquire their Beepcodes via a fee-based premium rate phone number. The customer would receive the Beepcode at the end of a phone call. He would thereby spend the amount of money equivalent to the price of a Beepcode on that phone call and be charged via his phone bill. The phone company would directly deduct a commission of around 40% and then transfer the remainder to Beepworld. This system did not require any administration and was default proof. However, the high commission fees reduced Beepworld's profit margin considerably.

In 2001, Beepworld introduced a second billing method via Firstgate, a global payment system. In this case, a user had to open an account with Firstgate and transfer money to them. This enabled Internet service providers to ensure the correct billing of their offers. Once Firstgate had confirmed the payment, Beepworld sent out a Beepcode to the user by email. In comparison to the premium rate phone number, Firstgate was less expensive, charging only 5% commission fee, but fraud risk averaged 10% and the money transfer to Beepworld took longer.

In 2001, 95% of the revenues were collected via the phone number system. This share had decreased to 60% by 2003, whereas Firstgate had gained popularity in turn. The main reasons for this trend had lain in the bad image premium rate phone numbers had developed in the public combined with the customers' desire to use trustworthy payment methods.

4 Current Situation

Based on these concepts, Beepworld has become the biggest homepage generator in the German speaking market, which also includes Switzerland and Austria apart from Germany. These cross-border activities are considerable, as they made up 15% of Beepworld's total revenues. In 2003, a total of 1.65 million users were currently registered with Beepworld, and between 1,000 and 2,000 people decided to become a member every day (see Figure 2). Dr. Thomas Finkenstädt was proud when he thought what they had achieved without ever investing in any sumptuous promotion campaign.

Out of all registered users, approximately 700,000 subscribe to the bi-weekly newsletter. This equals the number of users Dr. Thomas and David Finkenstädt consider as active "Beepers". Those users communicate with each other and discuss different topics. They engage in chat rooms or panels, ranging from very specific technological subjects to more general questions.

Revenues

The active Beepers are also the group of people spending money on Beepworld's homepage add-on features. In 2003, the best-selling service was additional memory capacity. Some add-ons, like storage space or visitor counters, are at the customer's disposal ad infinitum after purchase, others have to be renewed every 6 months. They are priced between € 2 and € 4, according to what the founders have estimated as a suitable price, and represent 63% of total revenues (see **Fehler! Verweisquelle konnte nicht gefunden werden.** 3). On average, as Dr. Thomas Finkenstädt has calculated, one in six registered users spends exactly € 3 with Beepworld. In total, apart from the infinitely extendable memory capacity, one customer could spend up to € 18 for a homepage and thus individually combine different modules to adapt it to his personal needs.

Still, next to banner ads and add-on features, the company tries to further tap new revenue sources. In early 2003, a big Asian consumer electronics manufacturer approached Beepworld via a well-known US-based international survey company and asked whether they were interested in conducting a survey within their user group, which the Asian company considered as representative for its targeted customers. David and Dr. Thomas Finkenstädt agreed to this project and rewarded their users with Beepcodes for their participation. This example shows another significant advantage of their virtual currency. The founders could use the Beepcodes like a money press without incurring high cost.

As this experiment worked out well, the Finkenstädts decided to extend the cooperation with corporate clients. Subsequently, they have happily accepted more requests for surveys. All in all, six surveys accounted for approximately 15% of 2003's revenues and are expected to grow in volume and weight. The Finkenstädts hope to achieve an annual contract with the above-mentioned agency in order to get into regular contact with other potential survey clients.

Only a minor part of revenues consists of commission-based sales. With the recently launched merchandising product range, Beepworld offers interested users options to buy shirts, cups, puzzles, bags, stickers, or key fobs and have their homepage's URL written on them. All the founders have to do is display the offers on Beepworld's homepage, and an external company takes care of production, delivery and billing. In exchange, Beepworld receives a commission. From the start onward, daily sales have amounted for approximately 15 to 30 products and contributed about 2% to annual revenues. However, in addition to the small positive cash flow, Beepworld also profits from a promotional effect through increased dissemination of the company's name and advances the community feeling.

Beepworld furthermore offers special features for mobile phones, such as ring tones and display logos, on a commission basis to its users. Mobile phone upgrades, however, are not in the main focus of Beepworld's managers. They are sourced from third parties and provide only small margins. However, since the typical Beeper generally shows interest in modern technologies such as the Internet, it is very likely that he is also interested in mobile phone upgrades. Thus, this offer is mainly used as an attention-catcher and for customer retention purposes. Consequently, Beepworld does not offer a large variety of choices in comparison to other providers.

Cost

Despite Dr. Thomas Finkenstädt's efforts to diversify Beepworld's revenue sources, he has not forgotten to keep a close eye on costs. He has been determined to never let expenses exceed revenues so that Beepworld remains independent from any external capital. This policy is mirrored in his preference for commission deals as well as in his tendency to outsource anything that he does not consider to be Beepworld's core competence.

The major cost driver, accounting for approximately 60% of total cost, is technological equipment. Modern and reliable hardware has its price, and especially information technology products show very short product life cycles and frequent innovations. For this reason, Beepworld prefers renting rather than buying such equipment. Beepworld has negotiated a contract with a service provider that includes storage space, hardware support and technical helpdesk for a monthly flat fee of € 20,000. The storage space

that this contract provides is sufficient even if Beepworld's growth is to continue at a similar pace for the next few years.

Further costs arise from four technical assistants, which have been employed on a mini-job basis of € 400 per month. These jobs have the advantage of reduced social security charges. Their task is to take care of customer service issues and to solve minor technical problems. Office furniture and software amount to approximately 10% of total cost.

5 Industry Analysis

Whenever Dr. Thomas and David Finkenstädt wonder how their company has been able to grow so fast in only four years, they inevitably come to the conclusion that their business model has successfully covered a niche in the market.

Beepworld is operating in the Internet service industry. From a general perspective, every company offering homepage creation and hosting services could be considered as a potential competitor. However, an inconspicuous smile came to Dr. Thomas Finkenstädt's face when he thought about companies such as 1&1 Webhosting, Tripod/Lycos or Host Europe. At first glance, they are offering homepage services just like Beepworld. The important difference, however, is that these companies focus on the more experienced and technology-refined customers who already possesses basic programming skills. All these companies, although they have been in the market much longer than Beepworld, have neglected the large group of interested but technologically unskilled users.

By offering this user group the opportunity to experiment with the modular system and to build a basic homepage for free, Beepworld managed to overcome their customers' fear of contact with creating private homepages. In the second step, when the user wants to upgrade storage space, Beepworld charges considerably higher prices than other service providers in the market. At that point of time, customers either lack the necessary experience to compare prices on the market or are already tied up in the Beepworld community so that they would not mind paying a premium.

In fact, the Finkenstädts judge the Beepworld community to play a major role in their success. They have been able to create a feeling of social affiliation among their members and to communicate the notion of "all Beepers together against the anonymous big companies". None of the companies like 1&1, Tripod or Host Europe have succeeded in establishing such a cohesive community.

Still, there is an important drawback of their system. The more Beepworld's users take interest in their own homepages, the more likely they are to spend more money on

add-on features. At the same time, however, they become more Internet literate and are thus likely to switch to a cheaper provider, who does not offer Beepworld's modular system. Beepworld therefore believes that the average user would stay with them for 2.5 to 3 years.

Nonetheless, the fact that their strategy targets a specific customer group allows Beepworld to successfully differentiate itself from the "big players". Following this strain of thought, the Finkenstädts do not consider these companies to be their direct competitors and evaluate their market position as consistent, durable and promising.

Of course, there are some copycats of their business model within the market. However, none of them has succeeded in attracting more than 30,000 users at a time. As the Finkenstädts consider this amount as too far away from the critical user mass, which they estimate to be around 500,000 users, they do not to consider them as competitive threats so far.

6 Issues at Hand

Dr. Thomas Finkenstädt looked back at the fax, which had been lying in front of him for the entire time he had spent wrapped up in his own thoughts. While the competitive situation did not seem to give any reason to complain, Beepworld was facing other concerns.

Legal Complaints

The company has received more and more legal complaints, as a number of lawyers have tried to hold them responsible for content violation matters. Current legal terms do not exactly clarify whether Beepworld is partly in charge of controlling the content of the private homepages that could be accessed via links from the Beepworld website. The first thing David and he had decided to do after receiving the first complaint was to turn Beepworld's legal form of a GbR into a GmbH in order to reduce their personal risk resulting from potential liability claims.

In most cases, either Dr. Finkenstädt or his lawyer has succeeded in turning down the legal complaints. So far, they only once had to settle a complaint out of court. Dr. Finkenstädt felt comfortable that the legal complaints could also be dealt with in future. However, he was rather annoyed by the time and the money he had to spend with his lawyer for taking care of all these issues. Every hour spent on these matters is an hour lost for Beepworld. As much as he wished the German legislation to create

legal security for online businesses, he feared any new law. What would happen to Beepworld if the government passed a law that prohibited Beepworld from addressing its own users?

Market Saturation

Currently, the legal issues are one of Dr. Finkenstädt's minor worries. He admits that Beepworld has experienced a slowdown of its community's growth rate and he has wondered about the reasons. Is this a temporary or a permanent effect? Is there anything going wrong within the community, have they overseen any recent changes in the market, or is the German market simply saturated? Having experienced a nearly exponential growth during the first 2 years of their business, the founders currently observe only linear growth rates. What would be the effect on their business model if the growth rates would further decline? Neither he nor his son knows enough about their own customer base to correctly answer this question. Although the users have to provide personal data in the registration process, Beepworld does not have any possibility to verify the details. They estimate that about 60% of their users are younger than 21 years and contribute up to 40% of Beepworld's total revenues.

Recent Changes

In fact, the most recent changes have led to the situation that Dr. Finkenstädt was now sitting behind a brand new desk. David, now aged 20, has decided to study biology in Düsseldorf after he finishes high school and completes public service. Tim has decided to study medicine. Subsequently, the Finkenstädts moved from Herdecke, where they had been living, to Düsseldorf. Here, they have set up a proper office rather than continuing to run Beepworld from their private home. This step had become necessary, as they had decided to move into different apartments, David closer to university, Dr. Finkenstädt closer to the city center. Furthermore, they planned to employ a programmer who would take over a number of David's tasks to free up some time for his studies.

Julien Bert, Christopher Daniel and Arne Weinhardth

7 Future Prospects

Dr. Thomas Finkenstädt turned his eyes back to the computer. Finally, after all these thoughts, he had to return to work. He was about to finish drafting a newsletter where he wanted to introduce their idea of expanding to the United States to the Beepworld community. They planned to enter this market the same way they had succeeded in Germany. Alliance conversations with Firstgate were already underway, and he had already recruited some administrators whose English was good enough to handle the awaiting challenges.

Beepworld GmbH

Appendix

Figure 1: The chat portal of beepworld

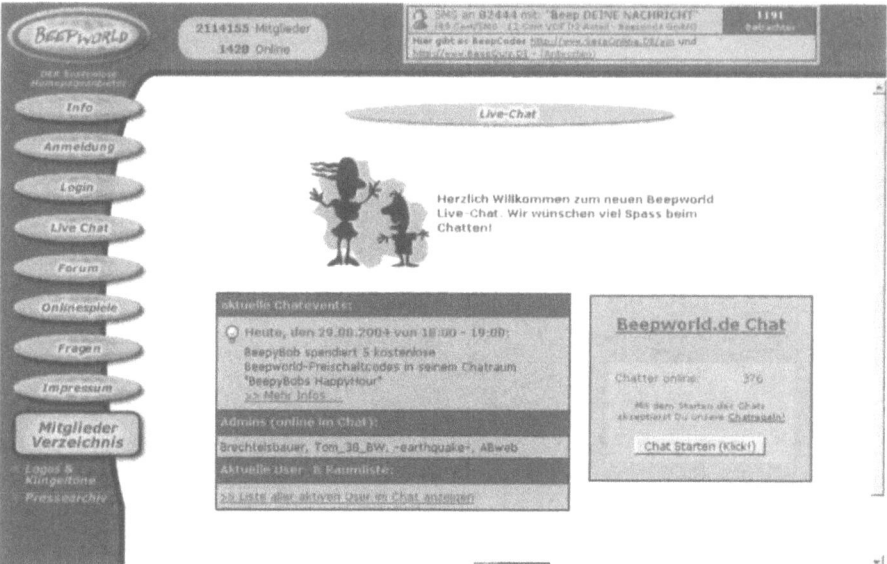

Figure 2: Growth of the Beepworld Community

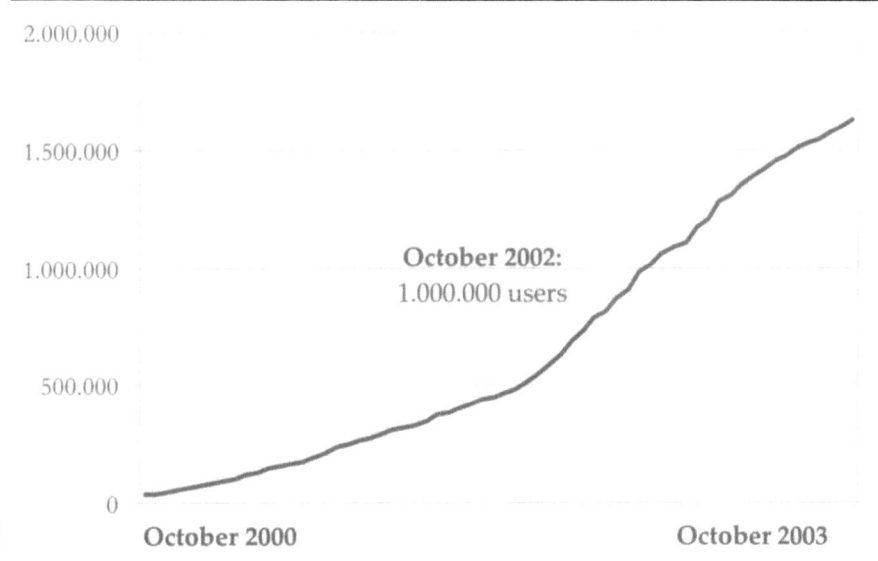

Figure 3: Revenue Split

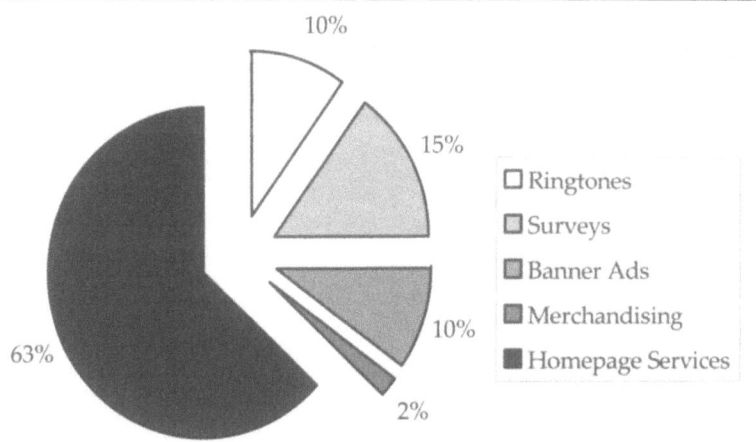

Cécile Gouesse, Stefan Heidrich, Marc Koeppe and Anika Radloff

Dialego AG

1   Introduction 37
2   History 37
3   Market Characteristics 38
4   Competitors 39
5   Analysis of Competitive Situation 40
6   The Business Model 41
7   Analysis of Key Success Factors 44
8   Outlook 50
    Appendix 51

„Dialego is always ahead"

(Dr. Hans-Willi Schroiff - Vice President of Market Research/Business Intelligence at Henkel)

1 Introduction

Andera Gadeib, 34, founder and CEO of Dialego AG, one of Germany's leading institutes for online market research, entered the modern office located in the heart of Europe in Aachen, Germany. She wondered about how to further establish the company in the market and how to foster its growth. Sitting down at her desk, she smiled and reflected upon the turbulent times the company recently had gone through in the course of the bursting stock market bubble, which especially hurt the companies in the new economy.

Gadeib was aware of the necessity for Dialego to stay on the competitive edge. She assessed different alternatives for the company, including internalising certain services Dialego so far had to purchase from external suppliers (e.g. addresses for its international market panels), further expansion of its own service offering and increasing the company's customer base.

2 History

Dialego was founded in March 1999. Unlike many other dot.coms at that time, this start-up was not driven by the internet hype of that period. Rather, Gadeib had already developed the business idea during her studies in the US in 1996, where she had written her diploma thesis about purchasing patterns on the internet. There, she had realized the potential to enhance the existing service offering in this so far underdeveloped sector. Gadeib first founded an internet-based marketing consultancy, but more and more developed the idea of founding a company offering online market research.

In March 1999, Gadeib founded the company "Dialego", which is Greek and means "I choose". The core service offering at that time was the planning and implementation of market surveys via the internet.

Originally founded with less than EUR 5,000 start-up capital, Dialego only shortly thereafter received funding by one of the most regarded venture capitalists, 3i (which, after the second round of founding, owned 27% of the company's capital). With 3i aboard, demanding rapid growth rates in terms of turnover, and the help from the internet hype at that time, Dialego experienced an accelerated growth. In 2000, Dialego was given the 'European Award for the Spirit of Enterprise' for being the most innovative European company in that year.

However, in retrospect, Dialego's growth had come too fast. The company's internal structures had not yet been sufficiently developed. With the economic downturn starting in 2001, Dialego consequently decided to downsize to an economically reasonable level, resulting in 40% of its employees at that time being laid off. Since then, sustained growth has been the new guideline. The fundamental change in strategy worked out, and today, Dialego is one of the most renowned and successful companies within its industry within Europe.

3 Market Characteristics

Market research can be described as the "systematic design, collection, analysis and reporting of data and findings relevant to a specific marketing situation facing the company" (Kotler, P., Marketing Management, p. 129, 2002).

As the world in 2001 showed signs of stagnation with a growth rate of only 1.4%, the market research sector was unable to come away unscathed and was seriously affected. Industry, retail, the media and the service sector spent an estimated EUR 17.3 billion worldwide on information services provided by market research companies. In 2001, the market for online market research had experienced a growth rate of 30%, whereas the traditional market research sector grew only modestly by 5%. Nevertheless, the overall sector still grew faster than the global economy due to the dependency of all companies on market research (see figure 1): Regardless of the trend in the global economy, the various industries needed to have updated information about consumers´ needs.

The specificity of online market research is that it uses the internet as a means to survey consumers about their opinions. Every time a survey is carried out, online market researchers typically choose among their registered users to select a representative sample. Among those, using a random process or quota samples, the final panelists are chosen and informed via e-mail asking them to fill out the respective questionnaire. As answering the questionnaire is voluntary, the panelists are given incentives (in the form of web-points) for doing so. These save either as a virtual currency that can be

redeemed at over 140 shops, e.g. at Amazon.de or at Body Shop, paid out directly to the panelist's bank account or can be donated to charity.

A core issue for online market research companies is to secure the information provided by the panelists during the registration process and the completion of a survey. As most of its competitors, Dialego uses the SSL-encryption system to protect the personal data of their panelists when data is transmitted over the World Wide Web. A lack of data confidentiality is devastating to the company as this leads to a loss of panelists, a very critical resource for online market research companies. A further challenge online companies are facing is to ensure the quality of their surveys. Here, the focus lies especially on the offline recruitment via telephone or on the street of new panel members apart from online recruitment to enlarge the scope of the panel. The goal is to further increase the coverage of the panel. With international surveys becoming more and more important, online market researchers additionally have to increase the international coverage of their panels.

The traditional market research companies have realized the boom of the online market too. Their reaction has been to develop internal online departments like eSolution (GfK group) or eMind@EMNID (Taylor Nelson Sofres plc). Their presence has increased the necessity for newly established online market research companies to prove their superiority even more.

However, the biggest challenge for the online market research industry so far has been to convince potential clients of the quality and utility of their service offering. The main question is the reliability of the survey (representativeness etc.). Online market research companies have to differentiate themselves from traditional market research companies, e.g. in the dimensions of quality, new methods and to a lesser extent price and time. Dialego puts great emphasis on the fact that many of its proprietary methods provide insights which cannot be obtained through traditional market research.

4 Competitors

Online Market Research Companies

The existing main competitors are all roughly comparable in terms of number of employees, panel size and years of existence (Dialego was founded in 1999, EARSandEYES in 1998 and MediaTransfer in 1996). The management usually has a Marketing and IT background and possesses an extensive personal network. The client base is generally diverse, varying from small to large companies such as Henkel and Audi (Dialego), Lever Faberge and Microsoft (EARSandEYES) or BMW and T-Online (Me-

diaTransfer). All competitors offer basic services like website evaluation or customer satisfaction measurement. However, each company owns its self-developed proprietary software tools like the virtual supermarket of Dialego or MediaTransfer's e-millieus, the latter only being licensed. All competitors try to leverage their specialist know-how being focused on internet-research methods and their flexibility to differentiate themselves from their online as well as traditional competitors.

Traditional Market Research Companies

In response to the huge growth rates for market research online, the traditional market research companies developed internal departments offering online solutions.

In 2001, the market leader in traditional market research in Germany was the GfK Group. Back then, they generated a turnover of 531.6 million Euros in their 90 subsidiaries and associated companies located in 42 countries worldwide. Lately GfK developed an online department named eSolution. The online division is a part of the "Ad hoc Research Services", which account for 42% of GfK's revenues.

TNS' online department is named Emind@emnid and offers online and offline market research for companies of the New Economy. TNS possesses a large German offline panel called askX@emnid with 80,000 members.

Advantages of well-established companies such as GfK or TNS are their financial capability, their economies of scale and their panel size that ensure a higher validity of any survey carried out. However, in certain cases these companies might lack specific online research related know-how and could be tempted to merely carry out carbon copies of their traditional offline methods. Thus, these companies might forgo the opportunity to exploit the methodological advantages online market research offers.

5 Analysis of Competitive Situation

In 2002, the market for online market research was not yet highly competitive. So far, the market has offered annual growth rates of around 30% and an attractive profit potential. Each online company has its own niche and specialty. However, necessity for consolidation is expected for the future, so reaching a critical size is regarded as crucial for the players in the market.

Threats are created by traditional market research companies due to their bigger size (economies of scale) and their financial strength. Additionally, traditional market re-

search is regarded as being more reliable and less biased. Furthermore, modern software offers customers the possibility to carry out market research on their own. But as these tools require a certain level of experience, the threat from "do-it-yourself" software is only moderate. Additionally, customers typically lack manpower and time to undertake studies on their own.

Traditional market research companies are expected to enter the market, intending to leverage their knowledge and their superior capacities. But there is the possibility of emerging new competitors as well, as they could be attracted by the huge growth rates and profit potential of the online market research industry. Barriers to entry are imposed by the experience base built up during prior studies, methodological knowledge specific to online market research, process capabilities, a commitment to maintaining high research standards and the necessary IT knowledge.

In the case of Dialego, bargaining power of suppliers is mainly a concern with regard to international panel service providers. These firms charge fees for allowing access to their panels. However, with the decline of the dot.coms, these panel service providers have struggled to survive in the market, too. Recently, strong new players have entered into the market of panel service providers. This in turn led to increased competition, strengthening Dialego's bargaining power compared to the situation in 2000. In addition, Dialego has been pursuing a strategy of buiding up proprietary panels in most important European markets, which further limits its exposure to potentially unfavourable developments on the supply side.

Dependency on few big, institutional clients is high as those account for a major part of the overall annual turnover. However, dependency can be mitigated by increasing the customer base and also by clear differentiation from the competitors (e.g. in terms of prices charged or service offered).

6 The Business Model

Dialego defines itself as a market research institute providing full service in the area of internet based market research. 'Full service' means that its offers include the planning and implementation of online market research studies as well as their analysis and deriving strategic recommendations based on the results. 'Internet based' indicates that the data collection is done exclusively online. Dialego develops software and hardware systems for the data collection online, in particular for inquiries over the World Wide Web and tests in virtual online worlds. All research tools are based on the basic technology SMAN®, a system for market research in the internet and intranet developed by Dialego. SMAN® enables Dialego to provide their customers with the latest online analysis of multimedia questionnaires and virtual realities.

Cécile Gouesse, Stefan Heidrich, Marc Koeppe and Anika Radloff

For online studies in Germany and the UK, Dialego is able to offer an established access-pool, which contains over 80,000 registered, mainly actively recruited users. The recruiting of participants for an inquiry is done via telephone using computer aided telephone interviews (CATI) as well as face-to-face and online. For international studies, especially in Western Europe, Asia and the United States, recruitment of participants is done in cooperation with other research institutes, but sometimes panel resources have to be bought, and are fairly expensive. Therefore, Dialego is currently building up proprietary panels in key markets which limited the dependency on external resources.

The advantages of online market research are said to be a higher quality of data, higher speed, the possibility to carry out the same survey in parallel across different countries and the potential to enter into a dialogue with consumers. These characteristics have led to the development of new online research methods, which specifically make use of these advantages. This way, a new class of consumer insights can be obtained. Furthermore, online surveys are sometimes less expensive than face-to-face or telephone interviews, and they can achieve a higher coverage of the sample population (see Figure 2).

However, there are possible drawbacks, too. One problem is linked to the fact that not everybody uses the internet. Older people are less likely to use the internet than younger ones, and therefore it is harder to get a good sample of these people for online research. Furthermore, somebody who is willing to learn how to use the internet at the age of, let us say, 60, is likely to be of a different opinion towards technology than other people of his age. For some surveys this may create a strong bias. This especially applies to Internet- and technology-related studies. If the aim is, for example, to estimate the degree of utilization of MP3 players, the fact that the sample contains only people who use the internet could distort the result, as the probability that somebody uses a MP3 player if he also uses the internet may be higher than for someone who does not use the internet. However, for most consumer goods, this bias does not exist anymore.

Another problem for online market research comes from the methodology, i.e. the survey technique itself, as it is not possible to transfer mimic and gestures over the internet from the interviewee to the interviewer, making it impossible to record these data. This is why it is not recommended to conduct focus groups on the Internet.

Because of these problems, it is very important for Dialego to advise their customers whether online market research is appropriate or not in each single case. This openness seems to be essential to keep a good reputation with the customers.

For the customers, the main reasons to commission Dialego to do market research as opposed to doing it internally are the complexity of the market research method, the quality of the research, and the required resources. In comparison to other providers of online market research services, Dialego is confident that its competitive edge re-

sults from being more focused than others, especially than the classic market research institutes. The company believes that it has a sustainable advantage thanks to its vast experience, being one of the online-research pioneers in Germany, and its profound process capabilities, leading in turn to a superior quality level of analyses.

Dialego's product portfolio contains classic analytical instruments such as advertising pre-/post-tests, product/concept tests, brand/image analysis, website-tests and customer satisfaction studies. Hence, the basis for online market research is mainly the same as for traditional market research. The methods have been adopted, but the implementation is different; in combination with the internet, the questionnaires can be expanded with videos and sounds, and they can also include more plausibility tests to ensure a better quality of the results (see Figure 3).

The most important products offered by Dialego rely on the SMAN® basic technology: It provided the basis for Dialego's online research tools. It is used to generate questionnaires, first trend analyses, samples and includes a number of applications for analytical purposes, e.g. for statistical analysis of sociodemographic characteristics. In 1997, the software was registered at the patent office, but only in 2001 Dialego induced the examination process. Before that, there had been no possibility to get a patent for software in Germany. The decision of the patent office was still due at the time this case was written. The technology makes it possible to integrate TV-spots as videos in a questionnaire, or to include virtual products as stereoscopic, interactive models for a packaging test. Virtual presentations may diminish a cognitive strain of the test person and thereby facilitate an evaluation of the object close to reality. SMAN® also permits adaptive testing, giving the test person the possibility to examine and judge online all alternatives that had to be tested.

The product range includes FutureMarket© ShopTest and FutureMarket© ShelfTest©. These two products come within the limits of virtual test environments. Gadeib claims that these tools are real innovations in the online market research area. The FutureMarket© ShopTest allows one to observe the customer and his buying pattern in a virtual supermarket, i.e. in a competitive environment with real products and shelves. To reproduce a purchase experience close to reality, the test person can add a product with a mouse click to his shopping cart. This tool makes it possible to analyze the quantity purchased, the brands, the decision rate (i.e. the decision certainty) and the sequence of choice (prioritization). After the virtual purchase, the test person is asked some qualitative questions regarding his product choice. The goal of the FutureMarket© ShopTest is to estimate the success of new products, packaging sizes or new designs, unnoticed by competitors. The principle of the FutureMarket© ShelfTest© is almost the same. But in this case, the objective is to analyze the effects of a placing of a new product in a shelf, a variation in the assortment (new prices, new packaging) or a new positioning (change in shelf level). Tests for the configuration of preferred positions are also feasible. The advantages of these virtual test designs are again the speed of the survey implementation and the eventually lower costs compared to a classical

shelf test. This can be combined with tools supporting product development activities such as ConceptFit, PackageFit and ProductFit which help assist marketing managers in decision making during the product development process. Pricing research, e.g. based on conjoint studies support the pricing decision. Similarly, Dialego has developed tools providing insights into different questions market positing and communication policy such as copy tests.

R&D is done by the Dialego Research Center, partly in cooperation with scientific institutions such as the RWTH Aachen (Technical University of Aachen). Dialego's research center deals with application-oriented methodological and methodic questions of online market research. Through the research center, Dialego created a strong link between practice and science.

Dialego usually segments its customer base according to the clients' product needs: product tests account for roughly 40%, research of advertising for 30% and others make up the remaining 30%. A segmentation according to industrial sectors leads to shares of 50% for consumer goods, 20% for telecommunication and IT, 10% for media, and 20% for other industries. Its customer base was comprised of well-known companies like Henkel, Bayer, DaimlerChrysler, Microsoft, Volkswagen, Vodafone etc. Dialego obtains about 50% of its revenues from sustainable business (see figures 4 and 5).

7 Analysis of Key Success Factors

While Gadeib was thinking about how to strategically position Dialego in the future, she started wondering about the key success factors that had allowed her company to become as successful as it was. She had already identified a set of seven categories of generic success factors. Any decision on the company's strategy needed to be based on a detailed evaluation on how the company had managed these generic success factors in the past and what influence they would have on its future performance.

The start-up phase

- <u>Location and network.</u> Critics often asked Gadeib how she had made the choice to situate Dialego in Aachen and New York. Dialego was not in Berlin, at the prestigious Potsdamer Platz, the new economic centre of Germany's capital, nor in Munich or Hamburg, where many start-up companies had found a home. For Gadeib, the advantage of Aachen lay at hand; it was the extensive network of people she

could rely on, because Aachen was her home town. Also, from a logistic point of view, Aachen was not such a bad choice – the three airports of Cologne/Bonn, Dusseldorf and Brussels were within reach of the office. Additionally, New York had been chosen as the place for a representation office, because Gadeib had ties to this city due to her studies in the United States. Additionally, she had identified a partner which helped to enter the North American market. She believed that the product range FutureMarket© was a real innovation in the US market, creating addition growth potential Therefore, she chose to open a small office in New York.

Reputation of the Venture Capitalist (VC). Helpful as it had been, some public financial aid only had covered a very limited part of the necessary start-up capital. Therefore, Gadeib had also looked for a venture capitalist to invest in Dialego. She managed to fill the well-known venture capitalist 3i with enthusiasm. The reputation of this venture capitalist was an important success factor, as his commitment resulted in a positive perception of Dialego in the media and with potential clients. But on the other hand, the company partially suffered from the influence of 3i, as the VC was permanently challenging Dialego with milestones and higher turnover targets that were not reachable. The pressure to fulfil these milestones led to a couple of management decisions that were disadvantageous for the company. In a first consolidation phase after market growth stagnated, Dialego had to lay off 40% of employees in order to adapt to market developments.

Reference clients. Having started her business, it had been more than difficult for Gadeib to acquire the first clients for numerous reasons: Potential customers were either reluctant to try out online market research methods or simply did not know Dialego at all. With the help of her personal network, Gadeib managed to acquire some top customers from the German industry, such as the car manufacturer Audi and the German consumer goods producer Henkel. Quickly, these customers became "reference clients" and facilitated the acquisition of others.

External consultants. Ambitious as she was, Gadeib had at first not wanted to see the need to rely on external consultants in order to get her business going. However, especially with regard to specific questions that were not within her area of expertise, she had relied on consultants who did a good job for her, giving her advice on questions regarding taxes, law issues and strategic development of her company. Reviewing the start-up phase of her company, she considered herself lucky to have had identified the business opportunity.

Human resources

Top-down management approach. With regard to her leadership and management approach, Gadeib applies a top-down management style that includes cooperative

aspects. She is always open for new ideas and inputs from her employees, but has always made it clear that she is the one responsible for the final decision. By doing so, she avoids the dilution of decisions and made sure that the company could respond quickly to market requirements.

- Employee satisfaction. A company's success is always based on hard and soft factors and it is crucial to have a well-balanced mix of these different factors. Employee satisfaction is among the soft factors. Gadeib is proud of having a high level of employee satisfaction within the company, resulting in highly motivated and committed employees. Dialego is only able to provide high quality services as long as the employees see the need to perform above average. But they are only willing to perform in that way as long as they are satisfied with their working conditions.

- Employee training instead of new hiring. Gadeib knows that in order to be able to sustain a pole position within the market of online market research, Dialego does not only have to be flexible with regard to the latest trends in the market, but also maintain this flexibility in its human resource policy. It is the company's philosophy not to recruit outsiders to react to a new market trend, but rather to educate and train current staff to respond to these changes. By doing so, Dialego guarantees the availability of the necessary know-how. Additionally, it is difficult to find excellently trained people in the market that can provide this know-how for the company.

- Continuous training, education and incentives. All employees are permanently given the opportunity to carry on with their education. This turns the idea of "lifelong learning" into reality. As an example, employees are provided with newspapers and magazines containing the latest market research trends, and the company offers seminars. This approach is facilitated since every project manager is intrinsically motivated to keep himself up-to-date with regard to his area of expertise. If it were not for this constant approach of further training and education, Gadeib doubts that the company can keep up with the quickly changing work environment. Dialego does not offer stock options to its employees, but their salaries include variable incentive schemes in order to foster motivation.

- (In)dependence of external service providers. Though being generally very satisfied with the company's internal organisation and its human resource policy, Gadeib has been concerned about Dialego's dependence on external service providers. The company has to buy such services as international panels, if necessary, and translations to other languages from external service providers. Gadeib is concerned for two reasons: on the one hand, external providers charge a high fee for their services and she is not willing to pay these huge amounts of money. On the other hand, she prefers to be independent of these external service providers, as (volatile as the business is) she can never be sure that the service provider satisfies the quality levels expected by Dialego. Therefore, the company has been trying to

build up its own resources in this field to save costs and limits its dependency on external service providers.

Internal organization

- Interface coordination issues. Internally, Dialego is well organized. It is important to have an efficient coordination of interfaces in the company in order to avoid mistakes and to constantly assure services with high quality. Employees attend numerous workshops throughout the year. Additionally, external consultants are hired to maximize the quality and efficiency of the internal organization. For each relevant business process, standard procedures as well as check lists, standards and filing structures have been developed.

- Separation of sales and project management. Gadeib always considers it to be important to strictly separate project management and sales: "Market researchers are very bad sales persons. They are way too oriented towards methodological issues, therefore we have to keep these two functions separated in our company". Until now, this policy which is relatively unique in the market has done the company a good service.

- Internal communication. For Gadeib, it is important to have close contacts to her employees. Internal communication is always done on a very personal basis in order to be in touch with employees and the latest developments in the company.

Technical Know How

- Data security management. Data security is one of the most important issues for online market research. It is a top priority to secure panel participants' personal data, which is stored on the company's server. Employees are explicitly in charge of data security in order to insure that no hacker can access the system. Gadeib knows: "Client data is only once lost to the market by accident. Because afterwards, the company will no longer be in the market!". She is proud that Dialego had successfully managed its clients' data thus far.

- Motivation of panel participants. Dialego offers so called 'panel points' with a value of EUR 0.1 each, as an incentive to register (40 points) and to fill out the questionnaire. As soon as 300 panel points are collected, these points can be used for purchases with cooperation partners, such as the book store Amazon.de or ChateauOnline, a wine grocer. Once a participant collects 500 points, the corresponding amount is transferred to his bank account. For Gadeib, it is important to pro-

vide these kinds of incentives for the business model to work and to attract panel participants. Of course, this incentive is not allowed to be too high to avoid that participants take advantage of the system and register more than once. However, many participants also seem to be intrinsically motivated which is demonstrated by the fact that many panelists chose to donate their points to charity.

Gadeib is satisfied with the way Dialego manages its portfolio of panel participants. Dialego checks panel participant's authenticity by their phone number and bank account coordinates, among many other plausibility checks. By doing so, Dialego minimizes misuse of its panel.

- Availability of company website. When Dialego assesses the availability of its website, the company has to differentiate between two websites: The official company website (http://www.dialego.de) serves as the brochure and contact place for press releases and general information about the company. Theoretically, this website should always be available, but there is no major issue in case the website should be offline temporarily. More crucial is the accessibility and availability of the company's online market research website, the panel website where panel participants have to log in to fill out a questionnaire. Dialego spends a lot of resources on the availability of these websites, because the company's reputation and the success of an online survey depend on this factor.

Marketing, Public Relations and Reputation

- Build-up of reputation (company and founder). Marketing activities are extremely important in the online market research business – market research is a people business. With a certain feeling of pride, Gadeib remembers comments comparing her to Dr. Elisabeth Noelle-Neumann. Dr. Noelle-Neumann and her husband were the founders of the "Institut für Demoskopie" at Allensbach, a private opinion research organization, which managed to achieve a high reputation in Germany after the second-world war and served as the primary polling service and public communication advisor for Germany's Christian Democratic Party. Gadeib is believed to have the potential to become for online market research what Dr. Noelle-Neumann had been for the traditional market research business.

- Lobbying. Extensive and efficient lobbying is an area where Dialego has always been very active. The company has never missed any opportunity to send employees to give talks and to interact with influential decision makers in favour of online market research.

- Focused, limited marketing expenses. Gadeib had to smile when she remembered how much money she had spent for marketing during the first years of Dialego's operations. This money, she was convinced, could well have been spent more effi-

ciently. Currently, the company's marketing budget is significantly less than 5% of overall sales. This money is handled very restrictively. During the start-up phase, money had been more or less wasted and consequently, the marketing budget has been sharply cut.

Reputation. Industry experts and customers perceive Dialego as the expert in the area of online market research. This reputation has helped to create a very positive brand image in the industry.

Prizes. Market research is all about marketing, public relations and reputation. It is crucial to be omni-present in the market. Dialego has managed to win many prizes in the years 2000 and 2001, which came hand in hand with a lot of media support: in 2000, the company won the 1st prize on the German 'start up competition' on the regional and the county level (Bundesland) and made it to the 8th position on the federal level. In the 'Best of Internet World' challenge, Dialego was awarded the prize for the best service offering. Additionally, the company also won the 1st prize for the best female entrepreneur in the 'vision competition' and was given the 'European Award for the Spirit of Enterprise' for being the most innovative European company in that year. In 2001, Dialego again won the 'European Award for the Spirit of Enterprise'. This time, the prize was explicitly awarded to Andera Gadeib, being the best recent European, female entrepreneur. These prizes and the media interest that was connected to them helped to build up the reputation of the brand name Dialego.

Industry Specific Success Factors

Manage the relationship to the client. If she was asked to identify the main key success factor of her business, Gadeib would definitely know the answer: market research for sure is a "people's business". In order to create a sustainable competitive advantage, it is imperative to create and foster a long lasting relationship with the customer. Long ago, Gadeib had realized this need. The low customer churn rate is an indication for her success. At Dialego, everything is about the customer and how to manage the relationship with him. With a smile on her face, she thought about Dialego's extensive customer data base. Every employee being in contact with customers has to understand this database, so that in case an employee were not available, a colleague could utilize and access these data.

Focus, quality, flexibility, technology orientation and short time-to-market. Dialego needs to be focused on online market research. Gadeib does not esteem competitors who position themselves on a very broad basis, diluting their profile. Her company always has been and continues to be a focused company, concentrating on its core competence online market research. Focus and quality come hand in

hand. Dialego is known for the high-quality of its market research service. The company claims to provide zero-defect-work. Clients value this approach and trust the company's service. It is even more important to be able to quickly react to market changes. Dialego has successfully managed to keep a flat hierarchy, allowing the company to be as flexible as possible to react to market changes and market requirements, as it is the market leader. And to sustain this position, Dialego always has been very fast in adopting new technologies. To sum it up, Dialego is positioned as a highly competent company, claiming to always be ahead of the competition and to be the technology leader, introducing innovations first to the market.

Talents/Versatility. Gadeib knows that, to a large extent, Dialego's success depends on her talents, her versatility and her personality. With her strong vision of online market research, she has taken her company to the current position at the top of the German online research market.

8 Outlook

Looking back at the success factors, Gadeib wondered how these success factors could help her with the decision on the company's strategic development in the future. The market for online research is in a growth phase while classic market research is facing stagnation. Dialego needs a clear strategy for the future as there would be fewer entrants into the online research market and a phase of further consolidation awaits in the days to come. Gadeib wondered how to react to the threat of large research companies that are currently trying to establish their online departments within the market. How should Dialego grow in the future, how well had the company managed its generic success factors in the past, and what role would these success factors play with regard to the company's future development?

Dialego AG

Appendix

Figure 1: Comparison of annual growth rates

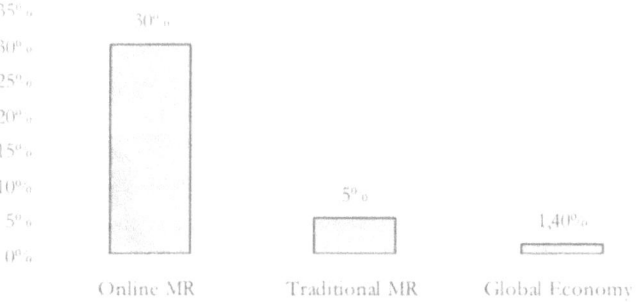

Source: Interview Andera Gadeib and internet research

Figure 2: Online market research compared to traditional market research

Advantages	Disadvantages
Capabilities of the Internet permit the application of new methods	Representativeness of panel for some analyses questionable
More plausibility checks possible, leading to higher quality data	Some population groups are difficult to recruit for an online panel (e.g. people older than 60 years)
Visualization of prototypes e.g. for concept tests Panelists are easily accessible	Lower acceptance with some customers
New insights about consumers through a true dialogue	Data loss: mimic, gesture, intonation cannot be transferred via Internet
Rich personal data about panelists	
Better coverage	

Source: Team analysis, November 2002

Figure 3: Overview of Dialego's current product offering

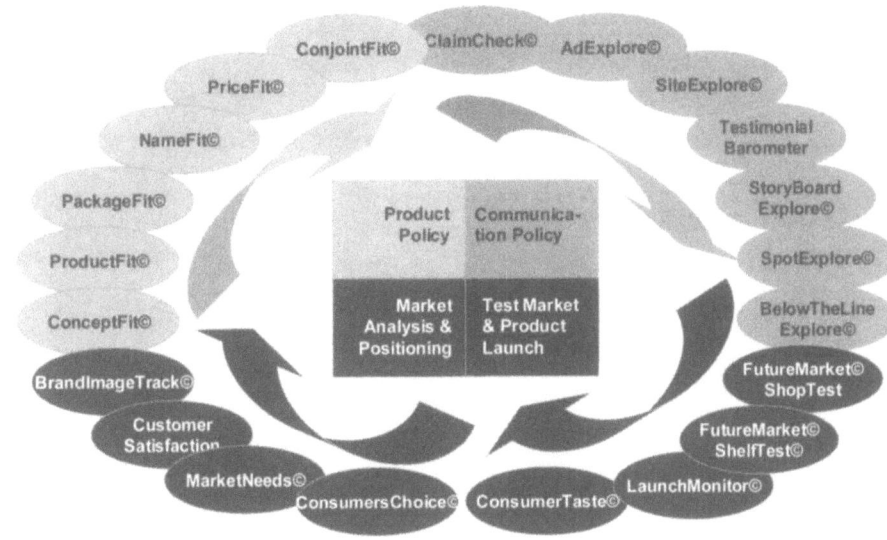

Source: Dialego AG

Figure 4: Customer segmentation by industrial sector

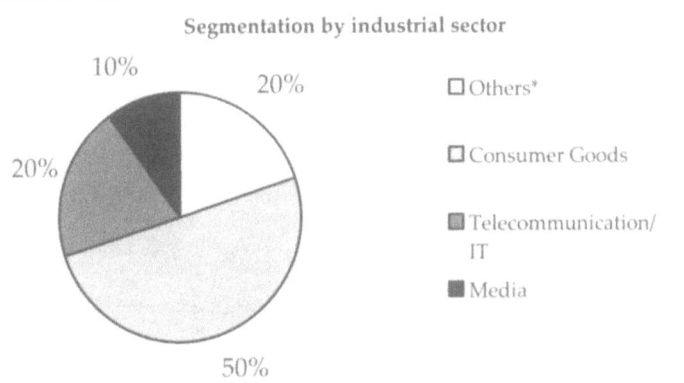

*other sectors are automotive, pharmaceutics, financial services, energy and e-business

Dialego AG

Figure 5: Customer segmentation by type of product requested

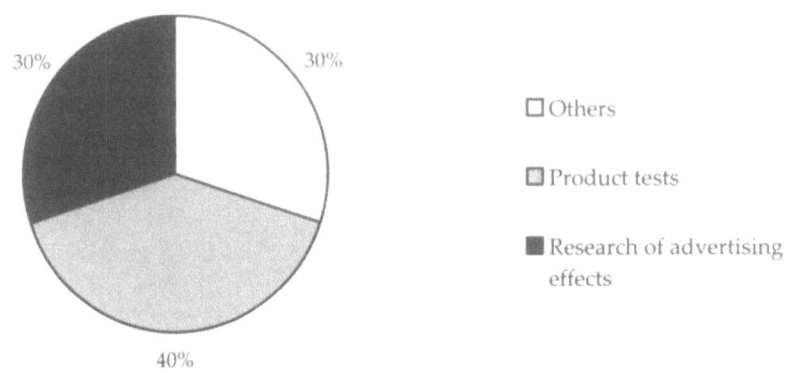

Source: Interview with Andera Gadeib

Robin Baum, Andy Bookas and Christopher Daniel
DocMorris.com

1 Introduction 57
2 German Health System 57
3 Market Information 59
4 DocMorris 62
5 Business Model 63
6 Company Structure 65
7 Competitors 68
8 Outlook 68
Appendix 69

1 Introduction

On August 5, 2004, Mr. Ralf Däinghaus sat at his desk in Heerlen in the Netherlands and looked at the papers that contained the new company structure. About five years earlier, he had founded DocMorris, the first European online pharmacy, together with his friend Jacques Waterval. During this period, the company had experienced highly controversial feelings. On the one hand, there were a number of trials, the last one decided at the European Court in December 2003. On the other hand, revenues had grown from zero to EUR 140 mn and the number of employees from 5 to over 300 in the same time. DocMorris had now reached a size where it had become unavoidable to set up a company structure. They had decided to install a matrix structure in order to cope with the requirements of a fast growing company in a dynamic environment. Still, Mr. Däinghaus wondered when it would become necessary again to undertake the next changes. As DocMorris operated within the German health system, their company was highly subject to political influences.

2 German Health System

The health system is part of the German social system. It is built on the principle of solidarity, i.e. all people living in Germany are entitled to have access to specific health standards regardless of their income, age or gender. For this reason, a majority of the expenses incurred in case of illness are reimbursed, starting from the visit to a general practitioner (GP) or a dentist, a stay in hospital or rehabilitation center, as well as expenses for drugs or medicines.

Compulsory Health Insurance

At the core of the German health system is the health insurance. By law, health insurance coverage is compulsory in Germany. Still, a person can choose among different options with regards to his or her health insurance. The most important differentiation criterion is the gross salary. If the person earns a gross salary in excess of EUR 45,900 per year, he can decide whether he wants to become a member of a private medical insurance (PMI) company or a statutory health insurance (SHI) company. All employees grossing less are automatically members of SHI companies. The next choice option exists within the different SHI or PMI companies, with offered treatments and price as main decision criteria.

The main difference between the PMI and SHI companies are the different kinds of treatments and reimbursements that are covered, with the PMI coverage in general exceeding the SHI coverage. Whereas the price of a health insurance with a SHI company is a percentage rate of the salary, the PMI insurance price does not depend on the income. It is rather a combination of age, known illnesses and desired services and treatments. Under certain conditions, the health insurance is free for family members and children of SHI members, whereas PMIs do not know this rule. SHI is, in general, less expensive than PMI for retired people, whereas it is often the case that PMI is cheaper for younger persons with high incomes. In most cases, it is rather easy to change from SHI to PMI, but it is hardly possible to change back to SHI.

In 2000, 71.815 mn people or 87.4% of the German population were insured with a SHI company. Out of these, 29.327 mn were employees with yearly gross salaries less than EUR 45.900. About 6.563 mn persons were entitled to choose a PMI, but decided to stay with a SHI nonetheless. 15.310 mn SHI members were retired people, 20.614 mn persons belonged to the family of SHI members. In 2003, the biggest SHI companies were AOK, DBK and Barmer, with more than 30 mn insured people among them. Due to market liberalization and privatization tendencies in the SHI market, the number of SHI companies has decreased drastically. Between 1993 and 2003, 1,221 SHI companies consolidated to 324.

About 10.368 mn Germans were PMI members in 2000. The biggest PMIs were Debeka, DKV and Allianz with 13.18%, 13.17% and 12.41% market share in 2002.

Fees

The insurance fee of SHI members lay between 13.7% and 15.7% of their gross income in 2003, depending on the SHI company. 50% of the insurance fees were paid by the employee, the other 50% by the employer. Due to the different tariffs, it is not possible to make a similar statement for PMIs. In total, EUR 226.14 bn were spent for the different components of the German health system in 2001.

Medical Aid

In Germany, there is a strict differentiation between primary and secondary medical aid. Each person can freely choose a General Practitioner (GP) and a dentist, and should, in case of illness, see this GP. The GP will then, depending on the illness, treat the patient or send him to a specialist. All self-employed GPs, specialists and dentists belong to the level of primary medical aid. Only when the GP or the specialist esteems it unavoidable, the patient will be sent to hospital, the secondary level of medical aid.

The hospital is either a general hospital situated rather close to the patient's home, or a specialized hospital. The GP or specialist is entitled to choose the hospital in accordance with the patient. In case of special illnesses, the patient needs to visit a rehabilitation centre. In general, the visit of a rehabilitation centre is only possible after a hospital stay. In 2003, there were about 40.000 self-employed GPs and specialists in Germany, 2.250 hospitals and 1.000 rehabilitation centres.

Pharmacies

A pharmacy supplies a number of different products and services, and in most cases a combination of them.

3 Market Information

In 2003, there were 21.569 pharmacies in Germany, employing 137.148 persons. Out of these, 46.140 were pharmacists, of which 2/3 were women. The remaining 91.008 were pharmaceutical support staff, namely pharmaceutical-technical assistants (PTA) or pharmaceutical aids (PA). With slightly more than 80 mn inhabitants in Germany, there was one pharmacy for 3.810 Germans.

Product Classification

All European countries classify saleable products in a very similar way into five different schedules (see figure 1). In general, a pharmacy is allowed to sell products from schedules two to five, but it is obliged to follow specific conventions for purchasing, processing and supplying. Consequently, the pharmacy has to set up a store layout that allows for meeting regulations, product delivery and service provision. The store layout depends on the pharmacy's business emphasis. A pharmacy accentuating schedule four and five drugs will prefer a larger front-office than a prescription-oriented pharmacy emphasizing schedule two and three drugs, where the dispensary area or back-office will be bigger.

Robin Baum, Andy Bookas and Christopher Daniel

Products and Services

A person can enter a pharmacy for two reasons. Either the person wants to see the pharmacist for personal advice or the person wants to collect medicine as prescribed by a GP or a specialist.

In the first case, the advice can concern a specific medicine or drug, but also an illness. The pharmacist or the PA/PTA is obliged to give the required advice or information free of charge and is entitled to recommend schedule four or five drugs. In case of doubt, however, the pharmacist has to ask the person to see a doctor.

In the second case, the person has already been to a GP or specialist, and received a prescription for schedule three drugs, or in very rare cases for schedule two drugs. The patient hands the prescription to the pharmacist or his staff and receives his drugs in exchange. The pharmacist or the PTA/PA are obliged to find out whether there are any potential side effects with the patients' drug history and to inform him about the way the drug is applied.

Payment

The payment process depends on the drug schedule as well as on the patient's health insurance. The pharmacist finds all information required for a correct payment process printed on the prescription.

If the patient is member of a PMI, he is entitled to reimbursement of schedule two, three and four drugs. He will pay the price of the drug to the pharmacist, receive a receipt, send it to his PMI company and be fully reimbursed.

If the patient is member of a SHI, the payment procedure is more complicated. The patient has to pay a part of the drug's price to the pharmacist, depending on the value of the drugs. For drugs costing less than EUR 50, he has to pay EUR 5, for drugs costing more than EUR 100, he has to pay EUR 10, and for all drugs in between, he has to pay 10% of the price. This rule applies to all drugs on the prescription. This payment scheme is applicable to all SHI patients, but is limited to a maximum of 2% of their gross income, or up to 1% if they have chronic diseases. Once this limit is achieved, the patient is freed from medical payments for the rest of the calendar year. Schedule four products are not reimbursed. None of the health insurances refund schedule five products.

By law, the price of all schedule two, three and four drugs is fixed in Germany, so that the pharmacist cannot gain an advantage over his competitors by selling at lower prices. This is only possible for schedule five products. Consequently, most pharma-

cies can be found in pedestrian zones with high customer traffic, close to medical centers, or in houses with a large number of GPs.

Revenues

The pharmacist's revenues depend on the schedule the sold drug is from. For each drug sold from schedule two and three, the pharmacist receives a fixed fee of EUR 8.10 and 3% of the sales price from the patient's PMI or SHI. He advances the expenses for schedule two and three products for the PMI and SHI companies and is refunded in exchange for the original prescription.

As the pharmacist's gain is fixed for these products, he does not display much interest in cheap procurement of these drugs. The pharmacist is more interested in obtaining a good price for schedule four and five products, as his profit depends on the difference between sales and purchase price. On average, a German pharmacy generates revenues of EUR 1.529 mn per year, with an EBIT margin of 6%.

Drug Supply

The drug supply consists of the drug supply to the end user, but also of the drug supply to the pharmacy.

Supply Chain

Traditionally, a pharmacy supply chain is rather simple. Drug manufacturers supply wholesalers, which, in turn, supply the pharmacy (see figure 2). In Germany, there are 16 wholesalers with nearly identical product ranges, which receive deliveries from more than 200 different drug manufacturers. As prices are only fixed for the end user, the wholesalers can compete with different prices. This, however, is only of interest for schedule four and five products, as the pharmacist receives a fixed payment for schedule two and three products. Consequently, the pharmacist can choose whether he prefers to order his products with a small number of wholesalers and obtain more favorable prices due to a larger order volume, or whether he wants to hunt for the cheapest price on the market.

End User

A pharmacy is obliged to guarantee the required drug supply to the end user. Patients are entitled to have access to at least one pharmacy at any time of the day within a 20 kilometer radius. Consequently, pharmacies establish alternating schedules for night- or weekend availability. Furthermore, all pharmacies should provide the patient with his drugs within a minimum timeframe. This implies that all pharmacies run an inventory of the most frequently demanded drugs, but also need wholesalers that supply the out of stock drugs within a short period. Most wholesalers provide the pharmacy with two or three deliveries per day.

Legal Restrictions

In addition to the fixed sales price for the end user for drugs from schedule two to four, there are some important legal constraints that influence the pharmacy's business in Germany. The most important rule is that a pharmacy has to be owned by a pharmacist. It is, for example, not possible that a businessman owns the pharmacy and only employs a pharmacist. Furthermore, a pharmacist can only own up to a maximum of four pharmacies. Finally, it is not allowed to undertake advertisement for drugs from schedule two to five.

4 DocMorris

DocMorris was founded on October 4, 1999 in the Netherlands by the German Ralf Däinghaus and the Dutch pharmacist Jacques Waterval and started operations in June 2000. The business idea was rather simple, namely to start an Internet pharmacy. A normal pharmacy should be put online, so that patients could obtain information about the available products via Internet, order online, by phone or fax, and receive the desired products by mail.

The pharmacy was founded in the Netherlands for two main reasons. First, only in Great Britain and the Netherlands (which are a neighbour to Germany) mail order was allowed. Second, the sales price for the end user for drugs is, unlike in Germany, not fixed by the government.

The foundation of DocMorris, however, was highly dependent on one small, but highly important feature. There was a high degree of uncertainty, whether it was legally possible to send drugs by mail.

On June 8, 2000, DocMorris started its online presence. The initial team consisted of five persons, and daily product turnover hardly exceeded ten items. In November 2000, the German Association of Pharmacists sued DocMorris, requiring the company to stop their business. The association went to court because they feared that an online pharmacy might decrease revenue potential for normal pharmacies and based the process on the belief that it was not allowed to send drugs by mail.

The process was initially started at the High Court in Frankfurt, but transferred to the European Court on August 10, 2001. This transfer was based on a number of reasons. First, DocMorris had its seat in the Netherlands, while the Pharmacists` association was headquartered in Frankfurt. Second, drugs were sent from the Netherlands to Germany, which implied that any verdict would automatically impact trade flows between European countries. Third, as the EU plans to introduce comparable health systems across the different countries in the long run, a trial including important aspects of the health system appeared to be of supra-national interest. As such a transfer is rather uncommon, DocMorris was of high public interest and highly present in all types of media.

On December 10, 2002, the trial was held in Luxemburg. DocMorris was represented by Prof. Dr. Koenig, director of the Center for Research on European Integration in Bonn. Due to the high public interest, it only took one year and one day before the judges announced a ruling, rather than the more common three to five years. Again, the fast process implied a lot of media attention.

On December 11, 2003, it was decided that there are no limits imposed on drugs and medicines from schedule three to five with regards to mail delivery. This ruling classified drugs and medicines from these schedules as belonging to the free traffic flow within the European Union and thus lay a firm foundation for the future existence of DocMorris`s business model. At the same time, drugs from schedule two could not be included in the product range of DocMorris.

5 Business Model

Although DocMorris is most frequently referred to as online pharmacy, it would be more precise to see it as a pharmacy with focus on mail delivery of drug orders. Al-

though the online presence plays a central role, it is not the most important feature of the business model.

Order Process

If a customer decides that he wants to purchase a product from DocMorris, he has several possibilities how to proceed, depending on what kind of product he wants. In general, the order process differs between prescribed drugs and medicines and those that are purchased without a prescription.

Prescribed Drugs

The customer disposes of four different possibilities of contacting DocMorris if he has a prescription from his GP or specialist and wants to obtain a drug or medicine. First, the patient can go online, select the products he needs and order them. Second, if the patient decides to use the telephone, he will reach a call center and can place his order there. Furthermore, he can place his order via fax or mail. Still, regardless whether he chooses mail, fax, telephone or internet, the patient is obliged to send the original prescription to DocMorris before they start processing the order. This is the case because it is illegal to despatch medicine without original prescription and DocMorris will only be refunded by the SHIs when delivering the original prescriptions.

The customer order follows a standard process. Once the patient has placed his order, all data is inserted in a data base in case of a new client, or cross-checked with the existing data otherwise. Should any uncertainties arise at this point, the call-center of 0800.DocMorris.com will contact the customer. The data is then transferred to a pharmacist, who will check the newly ordered drugs with regard to side- or cross-effects with already prescribed drugs. Again, should there be any problems, the call center will contact the patient.

In the next step, the ordered drugs are collected from stock or ordered if they are not available in inventory. One pharmacist checks the prescription, another one checks if the medicine in the parcel is identical to the medicine indicated on the precontrolled prescription. As DocMorris keeps an inventory of approximately 15,000 different products, the entire process can be completed within two days after the customer's prescription is received.

As SHI members have to pay a fee for the prescribed drugs or medicines, and as PMI members have to advance the expenses before they are refunded, DocMorris needs to receive money from its clients. This either happens via invoice, which is sent out to-

gether with the parcel, or via direct debit. In 2004, less than 0.5% of invoices were left outstanding.

Purchased Drugs

Drugs that are purchased without prescription follow an easier and thus generally faster process, as they can be assembled and sent out before the prescription is received. Still, the quality control with regard to parcel content and cross-effects are kept up.

If a customer orders two or more prescribed drugs, or purchases drugs for more than EUR 40, delivery is free of charge. Otherwise, he has to pay EUR 5 for parcel and postage. In 2004, only 20% of the customers ordered online. 80% preferred the more traditional ways of mail or telephone. 80% of revenues originated from schedule three drugs.

6 Company Structure

The company structure follows a matrix design with three main functional areas, namely finance, operations, and marketing/sales. In 2004, DocMorris had about 300 employees. Among these were 10 pharmacists and around 100 PA/PTAs. About half of the employees were of Dutch, the other half of German origin.

The finance section covers, in addition to all financial issues, also HR, strategic purchasing and accounting and employed about 30 persons in 2004. About 250 employees worked in operations, where they had to deal with order reception, order processing, logistics and customer support. Customer support was conducted by approximately 50 call center employees, of which about half were PA/PTAs, and half were normal call center staff. In total, 70% of the effort went into order processing, and 30% into logistics. 20 employees worked in the marketing/sales department. Their task was mainly to increase market awareness of DocMorris.

In 2003, shortly before the European Court ruling was announced, GfK, a German market research company, conducted a brand awareness study for Doc Morris, asking two different questions. These questions were: "Of which online pharmacy are you currently aware?" and "Have you ever heard of DocMorris?" About 4.4% of the interviewees were able to name DocMorris in the first question, and about 17.0% answered the second question positively. The same study was repeated in 2004, shortly after the

European Court ruling. This time, about 7.8% answered question one with "DocMorris", and 28.3% question two with "yes".

Competitive Advantage

From EUR 1 mn in 2000, revenues grew to EUR 140 mn in 2004 (see figure 3). Break-even was achieved in October 2003. This enormous success was achieved by offering a distinct combination of advantages both to patients and to health insurance companies.

Patients

At first glance, DocMorris provides the same products and services a standard pharmacy offers. Advice and information can be obtained by using the call center, products are sent out after the prescription is received. Still, the business model allows for a number of additional advantages. The first one is discretion. As many persons find it hard to talk freely about their illness face to face with a pharmacist in his store, patients enjoy the anonymity of telephone or online contact. Second, it is more comfortable to have the drugs delivered, rather than going out to see the pharmacist.

The most important customer advantage, however, lies in DocMorris's bonus system. This bonus system differentiates between two different cases. The first case covers all members of PMI companies or SHI members that do not have to comply with the payment scheme due to the 1% or 2% rule. These patients receive a bonus of EUR 3 for each prescribed drug ordered. Once a customer has collected EUR 30 in bonuses, the money is transferred to his bank account. The second case deals with all the remaining SHI members. They receive a bonus of 50% of the payment for the drug, i.e. EUR 1.25 if the drug or medicine costs less than EUR 50, between EUR 1.25 and EUR 2.50 if the drug costs between EUR 50 and EUR 100, and EUR 5 if the drug costs more than EUR 100.

In 2004, DocMorris had more than 500,000 customers registered in its data base (see figure 4).

DocMorris hardly delivers any drugs or medicines for acute illnesses, such as flu or cough. As the patient needs the drug as soon as possible, mail delivery is not attractive in these cases. For this reason, the mail delivery market is estimated to be limited to 8% of the total pharmacy market in Germany. For chronic diseases, however, the combination of mail delivery and the bonus system seems to attract patients (see figure 5). On average, a patient suffering from diabetes ordered 6.5 drugs and medicines from DocMorris per order process in 2004.

DocMorris is able to offer this bonus program due to three main factors. First, as the company is headquartered in the Netherlands, it is not obliged to follow the fixed price rule for Germany. Consequently, DocMorris is able to offer schedule four and five drugs and medicines cheaper to the end user than any German pharmacy could do.

Second, the high number of customers gives DocMorris a strong bargaining power towards the wholesalers or drug manufacturers. Their customer base of 500,000 clients as compared to the average of 3,810 per standard pharmacy gives them a negotiating leverage, so that DocMorris can obtain more favorable prices than standard pharmacies. DocMorris cooperates with three different wholesalers, but also receives about 30% of their products directly from the drug manufacturers and can thereby eliminate the wholesalers' margin of about 6%. As the German SHIs and PMIs reimburse the standard German end user prices, DocMorris can split a part of its margin with the customers and still remains profitable.

Third, DocMorris disposes of very detailed customer data and can sell marketing services to the drug manufacturers. Although there is a lot of quantitative data available on the market, DocMorris can offer direct access to specific patient groups and undertake marketing actions for the drug manufacturers. Projects exist for example with Lilly, Pfizer, MSD, Hoffmann-La Roche and others. When a customer calls, he can be informed about potential drugs or medicines that would be a complementary product to his existing medication. The same is also possible via e-mail.

Health Insurance Companies

DocMorris offers a cooperation contract for all German SHIs and PMIs. The core of the contract is a quid pro quo agreement.

As DocMorris is not bound to follow the fixed price agreement, they can offer the health insurances a discount on the prescriptions. In exchange, the health insurance companies promote DocMorris to their clients. This can happen in direct mailings or phone calls, with the help of flyers or with simple ads in the insurance members magazines.

About 200 SHIs and PMIs have already entered such a cooperation contract. With the help of these contracts, DocMorris was able to win between 25,000 and 40,000 new customers per month in 2004. Most of these customers suffered from chronic diseases.

7 Competitors

Since the European Court had announced that drugs and medicines were part of the free product traffic, a number of online pharmacies with mail delivery had started business in Germany. About five privately run pharmacies had soon gained public attention and started to deliver within Germany. The German Association of Pharmacists had also taken up an online pharmacy and even guaranteed delivery within the same day free of charge in 2004. This could be achieved with the help of the local pharmacy, which would be contacted by the association and would deliver the product and collect the prescription. At the same time, eBay had announced to open its internet auction platform for drugs.

8 Outlook

Mr. Däinghaus finished the inspection of the company structure. He was convinced that they had found a good solution and started to think about further strategic ideas for DocMorris.

As the company was founded in the form of a Dutch company, an IPO could be possible in the near future. Growth figures seemed convincing enough to stimulate the fantasy of stock markets. Or should DocMorris start opening up new business fields, e.g. delivery to hospitals and GPs? Would it be feasible to transfer the business model to other countries, and could the young company cope with the arising challenges? In order to be able to better decide which long-term targets he should set for the company, he first wanted to think about the most important success factors of DocMorris.

Appendix

Figure 1: Standard Classification of Saleable Products

Schedule	Meaning	Requirements	Storage Restrictions	Examples
1	Mostly restricted drugs	Can only be supplied or possessed for research or other special purposes by people licensed by the Home Office. Not available for normal medical uses and cannot be prescribed by doctors who do not have a licence.	Not applicable	LSD
2	Medical use but can be open to misuse	Subject to the full controlled drug requirement relating to prescriptions, safe custody, the need to keep records.	To be kept in a locked safe	Diamorphine (heroin), morphine, pethidine, cocaine
3	Prescriptional medicines	Subject to special prescription requirement, but not necessarily to safe custody requirements and registry.	To be kept away from customers separated by a wall.	Buprenorphine, the tranquilisers nitrazepam, flunitrazepam
4	Pharmaceutical medicines	Controlled drug prescription requirements do not apply as also no safe custody.	To be kept behind the counter	Benzodiazepines and anabolic steroids
5	General sales products including own preparations	Are exempt from virtually all controlled drug requirements other than retention of invoices for 2 years.	No particular restrictions apply	Everyday retail products

Figure 2: Pharmacy supply chain

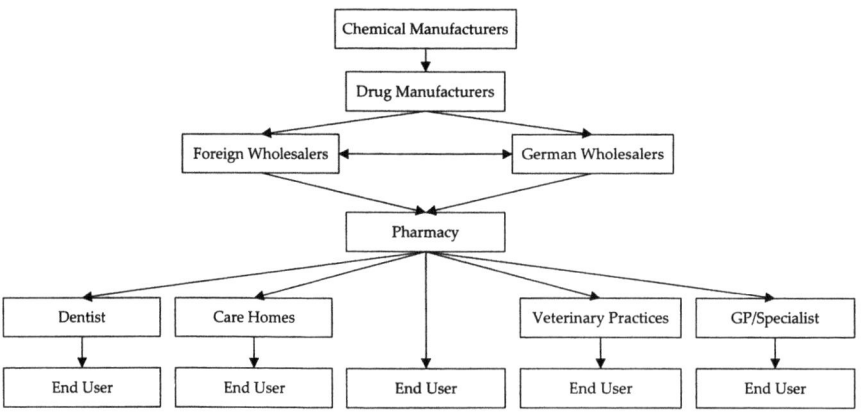

Figure 3: Revenue Development between 2000 and 2004

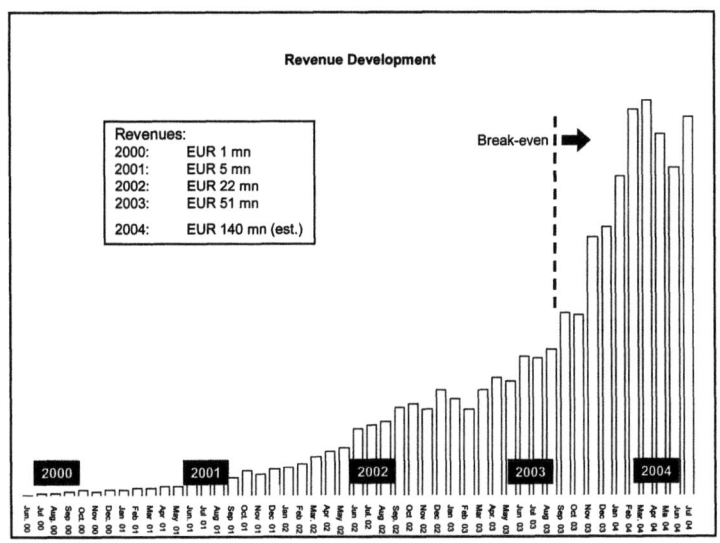

Figure 4: Age Structure of Customers in 2004

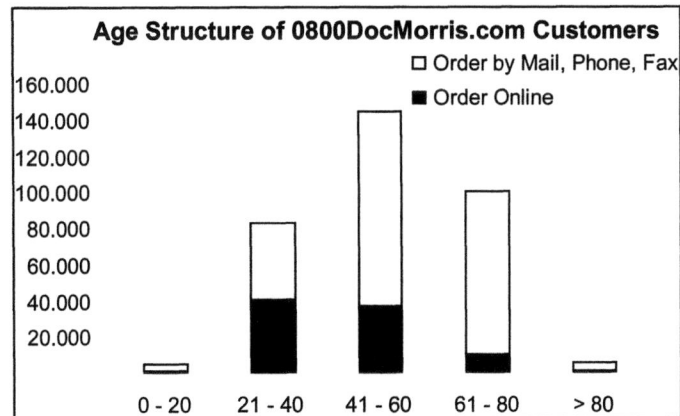

Figure 5: Number of Patients per Indication in 2004

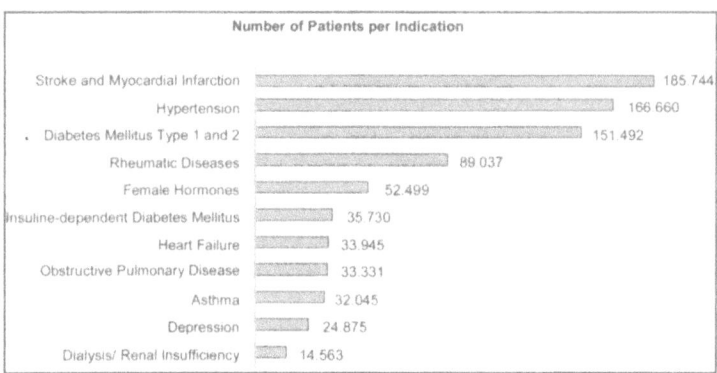

Richard Hahn, René Mauer and Ulrich Ochmann

European Telecommunication Exchange AG (EUTEX)

1 Introduction 75
2 Foundation and Development 75
3 Telecommunication in Germany 76
4 The Company 77
5 Competition 82
6 What Makes This Company Click? 84
Appendix 85

1 Introduction

"Any questions?" Professor Witt finished his lecture on "Introduction to Entrepreneurship" with his usual words. The students packed their bags and Uli quickly left the lecture hall, heading for his car. Two hours later, he would meet Dirk Reupke, co-founder and current CEO of European Telecommunication Exchange AG (EUTEX) in Düsseldorf. Professor Ernst – expert for technology and innovation management – had initiated the contact in order to help Uli with developing his business idea, an internet marketplace for a special interest group.

As usual, the Autobahn to Düsseldorf was busy. Uli had time to think about the entrepreneurship insights he had got from Witt's lecture: "Marketplaces are network products" and "Employees in start-ups have to cope with high uncertainty" were two of his key new insights. Would they prove true in the interview? Business studies at the WHU had always been pragmatic and hands-on, but Uli – 6th semester student and quite interested in entrepreneurship – really wanted to preach what was prayed. EUTEX was quite similar to Uli's own idea, and so the CEO was the right person to ask for some experiences.

"How do you treat your employees? Is technology a key success factor? How did the market look like when you entered? Do I have to be the first mover? Where did you raise capital?" Uli's questions were numerous, and so he hoped Reupke's answers to be as well. He had not spent a single thought about the place where he would meet the EUTEX CEO. Hence, he was even more surprised when he had to pull right into a narrow avenue, slowly approaching an old manor that turned out to house the EUTEX offices. Climbing up the stairs, Uli wondered if the outer appearance could already be taken as a proof of success.

2 Foundation and Development

Reupke had been chief controller in one of the world's largest telecommuniaction companies, Deutsche Telecom AG, before becoming CFO and later on CEO in one of the German service-provider companies in the telecommunication business, Talkline GmbH. Then after his time at Talkline, he co-founded Eutex AG and then went on to build up the company in the position as CEO.

The insides Reupke had gained in his professional life had finally driven the idea to serve the wholesale market of talking minutes as an intermediary. He was convinced that from the big telecommunication companies' point of view, there was room for a

market place in order to push down transaction costs they had experienced when relying on the old method of bilateral contracts with the other players.

In the eyes of Reupke, another important factor to force the trading business was the volatility of the prices of telephone minutes. Furthermore, he was fascinated by the scaling possibilities of a technological trading platform that mainly remains on a block of fix costs and therefore could serve an additional client at marginal costs near zero. Besides the market opportunities, Reupke had the desire to work in an environment with higher degrees of freedom than in the complex hierarchy of big companies.

At the end of the year 1999, the company was legally founded. From thereon, the conceptual framework of the business was developed and worked out in every detail, so that the technological implementation of the system could finally get started. In August 2001, the system went online and carriers could connect to it from this point in time. Since the second quarter of 2003, the company already had begun to be profitable (see figures 1 and 2).

3 Telecommunication in Germany

For a long time since the surge of telecommunication products and services, the market in Germany had been highly regulated and customers had been served by a monopolistic, state driven company, the "Deutsche Telekom AG". No earlier than at the end of the 90's, the German government started to realize the advantages of the play of market forces in the telecommunication industry. Consequently, privatisation was enforced and regulations were relaxed.

The end of the 90's happened to also correspond with the hype of the new markets. The internet quickly became a major tool for companies, even the substance of an endless number of business plans. The discussion about globalisation received new aspects and telecommunication was revolutionized by the mobile phone market. Hence, quite a couple of start-ups also went into the telecommunication industry with the idea to be able to exploit the diversity of chances that seemed to open up (see figure 3).

However, trading with telecommunication capacities could and still can be seen as a market niche among all the business plans – only about twenty players worldwide and around three to five competitors in the relevant German respectively European market have moved into this market. They have developed the concept of making the carriers' and service providers' work easier by offering them spaces to trade unused capacities.

The central question was how many of these companies would, after a reasonable time of existence, prove to be profitable and keep on serving the market. This was of special

importance since the boom phase had reached its peak at the end of 2000 and since then had been falling into a deep recession. At the end of 2003, it became clear that old disciplines like quality and risk monitoring, cost controlling, operative excellence, a financially sound strategy, a top management with lots of experience and knowledge about the specific business, unique services and the flexibility to adapt to consumers' needs were more important than just high-flying ideas and fancy marketing concepts. Those had finally led to the burst of the high tech bubble and the rapid descent of the stock market indices.

"What we did not expect was that our model would work even better in a downturn phase like the one we have been experiencing for the last few years. We can offer added value in terms of lower costs and provide the chance to liquidate overcapacities – music to the ears of stressed out telecommunication managers."

Uli was surprised about the chances that had opened up during the last years of the old and the first years of the new millennium. Curiosity took over when Reupke went into detail about his company.

4 The Company

4.1 Business Model

The initial idea of EUTEX was to be a trade exchange for telephone capacity. Customers – i.e. telephone carriers who also serve as operators (buyer and seller) or mere operators (only buyer) – are given the possibility to sell and buy capacity to and from EUTEX. The company itself does not generate any capacity but provides the technology to route capacity to the point where it is required. The routing medium is a "switching point", a big server linking the necessary lines. In order to use EUTEX's service, customers have to be technically interconnected. Installing this interconnection takes about 2-8 weeks and is done by EUTEX employees.

"With our innovative solution we enable a flexible wholesale business and achieve the lowest transaction costs, best delivery qualities and low financial risks."

Confused by the technical terms, Uli's eyes had drifted to a brochure on the desk. Fortunately, he did not have to ask for a suitable explanation.

The operators are connected to the central switch in Frankfurt or to the access facilities in London, respectively. Price offers to and from EUTEX are submitted via price lists that are common in this type of intercarrier-business. Thus, the customers can use the

EUTEX service without any change in operations and systems. Furthermore, EUTEX is able to deliver various qualities according to customer requirements (see figure 4).

It is comprehensible that customers are enabled to benefit from transaction cost savings and broadened sales opportunities. Before EUTEX was founded, each telephone carrier had its own capacity. Naturally, some capacity stayed unused and simply caused capacity cost while at other points, capacity utilisation was close to 100%. Carriers began to work on that problem by trading capacity among each other, but this caused high searching, contracting and connecting cost and was not really a solution.

EUTEX put itself between the telephone carriers and allowed unlimited trading among all interconnected partners. The customers' main benefit is that they only have one contracting and connecting partner being EUTEX. This significantly lowers transaction cost: customers only need technical interconnection to one partner instead of several. Processing supply and demand within one company facilitates billing and accounting. Customers also save administrative costs as they don't have to manage numerous contracts any more.

Generally, EUTEX cumulates the utilisation risk of its customers and delivers economies of scale. Interconnected customers still stay anonymous and do not get to know from which competitors they source capacity.

As the risk of bad debts is immanent in the trading industry, EUTEX is concerned by this, too. When the company was founded, the founders tried to find an appropriate risk management system providing them with additional information about individual debts and thus lowering the unpleasant incidents of bad debt losses. "Indeed, since our foundation, not a single receivable had to be cancelled."

4.2 Product and product differentiation

EUTEX is one of the leading EU European wholesale marketplaces for telecommunications capacities. Its main clients are network operators and service providers who are enabled to trade and deliver switched minutes to more than 900 destinations in about 215 countries. EUTEX's has established a voice trading system that functions as a real-time spot-market.

The company defined the service "Value Route Trading" for many low- to middle-volume destinations and another service called "Choice Trading" for high-volume destinations. It allows the customers from the buyer side as well as from the seller side to trade on an anonymous basis so that they are free in choosing a pricing strategy. By these means, EUTEX promises and delivers a high quality service to its customers. It has installed the latest Ericsson switch in Frankfurt, ensuring optimal quality routing standards, a "near-time" traffic-reporting and billing service and an advanced trading

system. It can also rely on a daily controlling routine for checking ASR ("answer seizure rate"). A permanent control of capacities offered by the clients ensures that EUTEX itself can always comply with its own quality promises (see figure 5).

4.3 Human resources

"When I founded EUTEX, my most valuable asset was my industry experience. I had been working for Talkline AG before, another large player in the German telecommunications industry." Not only the managerial staff was qualified and experienced, but also the average age of Reupke's sales staff was around 40 years old. "These guys are no rookies with just 2 or 3 years of work experience. They were highly qualified, provided an excellent personal network and had shown their efficiency in long track records" (see figure 6).

With a close eye on headcount, EUTEX had consequently sourced out whatever is not core competency to evade high costs induced by an insupportable administrative staff: billing, administration, network operating, accounting – none of these functions were performed by EUTEX employees. "Why should my people do things that others do better?" This strategy was also reflected in the relation of sales and employees: EUTEX generated equal sales as its major competitor while having only one third of staff (see figure 7).

The very first employees were mostly hired from within the management's circles of former colleagues and friends. They also made use of professional recruiting agencies in order to attract key technological specialists. In contrast to big companies with an anonymous atmosphere, EUTEX could offer a working place in an independent environment with a personal touch and a rather flat hierarchical structure.

"Every day, I have a twelve-o'clock-meeting with my managers. We want our people to know how the company is doing. We want to show them what impact their work has on our performance. And it works. We don't need any office hour requirements. Sure, the workload is high, but everything gets done in time."

4.4 Partnerships

Closely related to the outsourcing strategy is the network of partners that EUTEX has to maintain to keep the systems running and the customers satisfied. "We only use top class partners for our technical infrastructure and the services we offer." Ericsson switching systems allowed the disposition of traffic. Living Systems created the online platform that met the economical and ergonomical needs of the market. Tenovis was

EUTEX's strategic partner for node placements in terms of high levels of availability and security for the platform. Ecobill finally offers the infrastructure and experience of experts in billing and traffic reporting. Their service includes customer rating, billing, invoicing and customer care.

"Of course, we are happy to work with these people. Their products were a crucial argument in the first talks with our initial customers. However, our experts have had contact with some smaller companies who really develop amazing technologies. Up to now, we were reluctant, because – just like us – those guys can hardly provide references. We are not sure if we can already take the risk of another technology but when we see something that could really add value, we might think again."

4.5 Innovation

When talking about innovation in the context of a trader, it is important to realize that product and process innovations can hardly be separated from each other because the performance of the trade service is the product itself. However, offering trading possibilities for different telecommunication units such as derivatives or futures can be understood as a product innovation. By means of implementing this new product type, the company would become more similar to a traditional stock market trader.

Uli was proud to have thought about this possible move, even though he seemed not to be the first one thinking into this direction. "This part of the telecommunication business is still a dream of the future. We might jump on that train when it passes by, but until then we prefer to stick to selling minutes, because that is where we earn money."

Nevertheless, a field of steady innovations was also given by the technological equipment the company needed in order to execute the orders. It had been in March 2003 when EUTEX installed the newest Signaling Monitoring System (Nettest) and hence improved the quality of the trading platform.

4.6 Quality

One of EUTEX's strategic goals is to provide the highest quality standards to its customers. Suppliers not matching these quality requirements are consequently removed from the network. A ratio that measures the quality of telecommunication capacity is the ASR standing for the percentage of attempted calls successfully completed. EUTEX measures this ratio daily in order to evaluate quality and to set price levels for the different product segments.

4.7 Marketing

One of the most critical points in getting the business started was undeniably to get the critical mass of costumers. In contrast to companies of the classical industries, there was no need of elevated spending to create a global image. The crux of the matter was how to approach the decision makers of the carriers. Finally, the reputation and experience of the management and also their commitment to strive for high quality standards were the weapons to win their hearts.

It was a risky undertaking for the clients to get involved with EUTEX because projects in length of up to two months were necessary to interconnect and activate the account. This also showed how essential a close team-work approach between marketing and engineering was. As the market only consisted of around 100 potential customers, the possible target was quite clear cut and limited.

On the one hand, the department head of wholesale had to be convinced that joining EUTEX's platform would drive up the utilization ratio of their equipment and therefore enhance the department's performance significantly. On the other hand, the responsible managing director had to be convinced of the strategic fit between EUTEX and the particular company.

"The others all went for a large bulk of operators and carriers. We never saw a perspective there. When we formulated our quality claims we knew that we had to limit ourselves to the quality providers in the market."

4.8 Financing

All members of the EUTEX foundation team had well-paid jobs before and thus were able to contribute to the foundation with a part of their private net worth. Altogether, EUR 1,000,000 was raised among the founders' family members and friends. "That was a lot of money, ..." Reupke explained, "but we needed more." So the team watched out for some venture capital. "We regularly sent out requests, but soon we noticed that our VC had to be specialised in technology. The others didn't seem to know what exactly to do with us."

Yet, finding our way to technology-oriented VCs, EUTEX encountered vivid interest in their company. Dr. Neuhaus Techno Nord, one of Germany's top five technology investors, invited the founders to present their project and evaluated risk and return.

"When we were raising capital, we were evaluated within a pool of several companies. We were competing against smart and motivated youngsters coming directly from university – just like you, Uli. Our ideas maybe were less creative then theirs, but we had the more experienced team. And who got financed? We did – the others didn't."

Reupke presented a report stating that EUTEX was ranked No.1 among 28 different investments. Although Reupke was far away from having attracted the critical mass of customers, EUTEX was equipped with EUR 8,000,000 venture capital. The better part of this money went into further technology development.

"EUTEX also had a hockey stick, but the investor didn't even look at it. He was much more interested in our personal background, our experience and our goals. Then we showed him our cost data for different trade volumes. It is quite expensive to interconnect another customer, but simply raising volumes doesn't significantly influence our cost. That's where we got him."

Although EUTEX had been financed successfully, Reupke regretted some of his prior decisions. "If I could found EUTEX once again, I would take some more time to gather more equity from the founders. It's no good feeling to build up a company and later see that the major share belongs to someone else."

4.9 Financial Accounting

Financial Accounting tasks in the very entrepreneurial, technology-driven environment of a start-up like EUTEX could obviously not be similar to those of an established manufacturing company. As EUTEX is a relatively small company in terms of employees and regular processes and very client-oriented, planning is rather a management than a controlling duty. Yet, financial accounting at EUTEX is especially important for securing the precarious task of collecting receivables. As EUTEX is giving guarantees for payment transactions it had to establish a risk management system to closely monitor cash in and outflows. This has proven well so far, none of the money had to be written off.

Controlling processes on the other hand seemed to be crucial for the quality claim of EUTEX. "If we didn't check quality and divide the products accordingly, we could not fulfill our value promises. Our main measurement is the ASR which stands for answer-seizure rate. Don't worry, it's just an industry ratio, commonly known and accepted as a quality measure."

5 Competition

Having learnt so much about the context of EUTEX's activities and with a close look on the watch, Uli remembered the beginning of the conversation. Having heard so

much about competitive threats, entry barriers, etc. in his classes, he wanted to know one last thing.

5.1 Competitors

Naturally, EUTEX's market is also served by other competitors. "It doesn't matter that we aren't the first mover. The others had entered before us, so we could learn from their mistakes." Even though Reupke seemed to be very confident about his relative position towards competition, it is obvious that among all competitors, at least some are particularly worth discussing (see **Fehler! Verweisquelle konnte nicht gefunden werden.** 7):

Arbinet – This U.S. competitor is maintaining switching points in New York, London, Los Angeles and Frankfurt. Among its 275 members, this network includes 12 of the world market's 15 biggest carriers. In 2002, over 5 billion minutes were traded over arbinet. Over $100,000,000 has been invested in this global company. Arbinet is still focussed on the US market but has started expanding by setting up switching points in Europe.

Band-X – Founded in 1998, this network lists over 40 million minutes traded every month. Over 130 operators are using Band-X's services over its switching point in London, UK.

TradingCom Europa S.A:– This company was founded in 1999. Its three hubs in Paris, London and Frankfurt transfer about 500,000 minutes per year (sales: EUR 30,000,000 per year). Venture capitalists have invested EUR 13,600,000 in TradinCom.

Besides these firms, there is a variety of nationally focussed companies that hardly threat EUTEX's solid position. "Those don't harm us; we entered late but just look at our growth rates. However, nobody really knows how many companies will fit in that world market, and until we do know, we have to defend our position in Europe and try to promote our expansion plans towards other continents."

5.2 Direct Trading

"Direct trading as an alternative to our model? Uli, this wouldn't work. We're not Ebay. When we entered the market, it was exactly like that: all phone companies had contracts with each other and it was impossible to pass unused capacities around the network. Managing all these contacts caused immense costs." Obviously, direct trading would turn EUTEX's customers into competitors. "We fill the gap and I think I can say we do it well. Not a single customer has left us due to dissatisfaction." Customers

profit from EUTEX's services to such an extent that it would be irrational to try direct trading. "Our platform also generates a certain risk diversification. We accumulate the risk of unused capacity and thus deliver a value to every single customer. None of our customers want to bear this risk." The time between meetings for the student was over, but Uli had heard enough to spend the way home in deep thought.

6 What Makes This Company Click?

The Autobahn back to Koblenz was busy again. Uli had asked questions and written down answers for more than three hours. Now, he knew nearly everything about EUTEX, but still nothing about his own idea. It seemed that single classroom theories were unable to explain the success of this company. Uli was confused. Did this interview help him at all? Or was he just too ignorant to draw his lesson from Reupke's answers? How do all those jigsaw pieces fit together? Two hours later, parking his car at the WHU parking lot, he still hadn't found the answer.

European Telecommunication Exchange AG (EUTEX)

Appendix

Figure 1: Key dates of EUTEX's business development

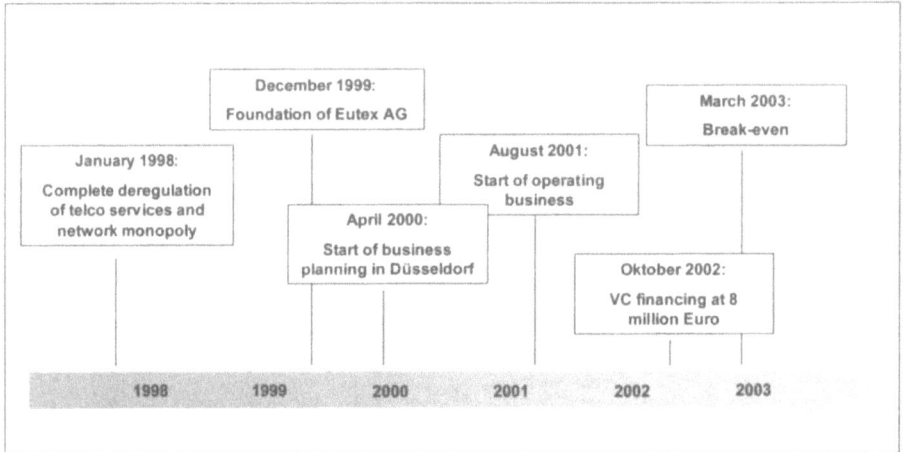

Source: EUTEX AG

Figure 2: EUTEX performance data

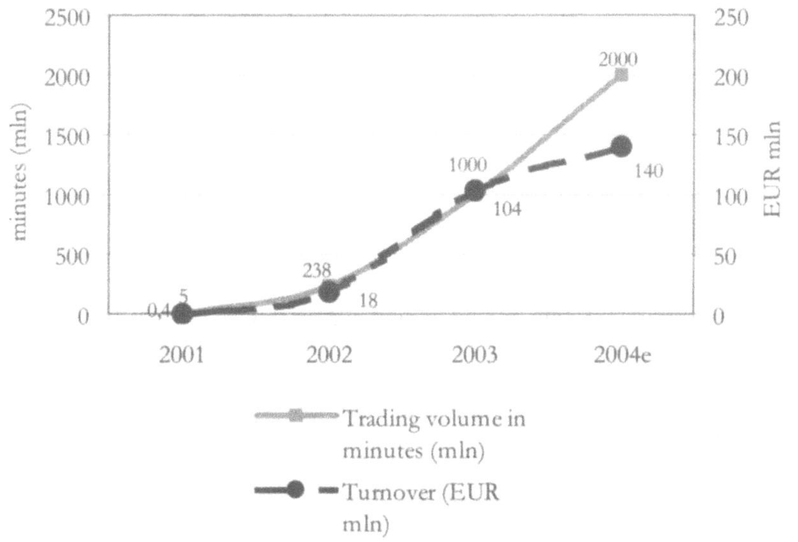

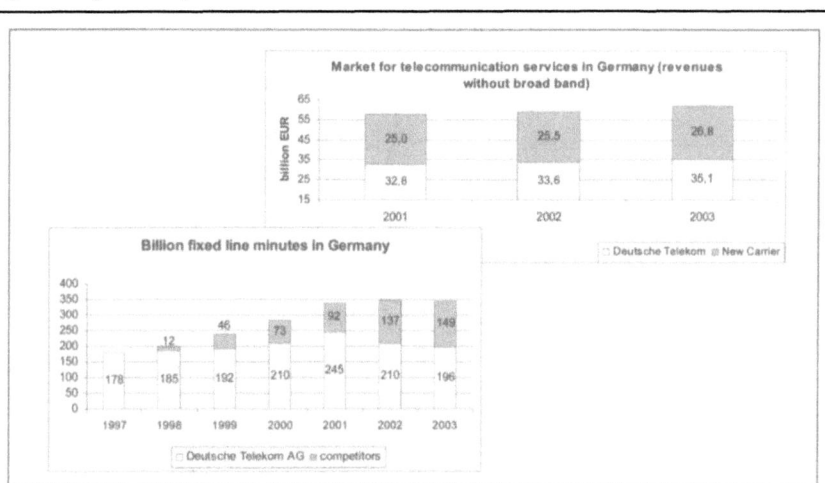

Source: EUTEX AG

Figure 3: Dynamics of German Telecommunication market

Source: VATM (2003); RegTP (2002)

Figure 4: Comparison of product features

Feature	Classic Operator	Marketplace (EUTEX)
Structure	Distributed network, distributed data	Single Hubs, concentrated information sources
	Large and tailored organization	Small and "fractal" organization
Routing decision and implementation	Days to weeks	Max. 2 hours
Interconnection	More than 80 days	10-40 days
Billing and collection	30 to 90 days	2 days (billing)
		7-14 days (collection)
Risk Management	Business only with trusted partners	Flexible for various partners
Network Quality	1st tier operators – high quality	Ability to "blend" several sellers to a good quality
	Niche operators – low quality	

Source: EUTEX AG

Figure 5: The fully automated trading platform and the EUTEX USP:

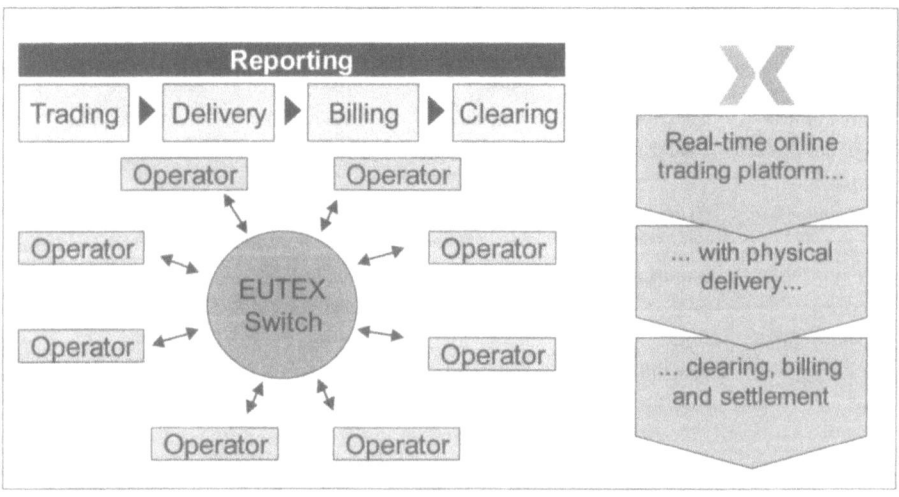

Source: EUTEX AG

87

Figure 6: Management background

Dirk Reupke - CEO. Reupke has over 20 years of experiences in the telecommunication business and has functioned as CFO (four years) and CEO for Talkline before the founding of Eutex.

Horst Westbrock - CTO. Westbrock has extensive experience in the telecommunication and network industry. Before joining the Eutex management he had worked for Ericsson.

Stefan Klebor - CFO. Klebor was assistant to Dirk Reupke at Talkline for three years.

Source: Dirk Reupke, EUTEX AG

Figure 7: Major market players (EUTEX, Arbinet, TradingCom, Band-X)

	Eutex AG	Arbinet–thexchange Inc.	TradingCom Europe SA	Band-X Ltd.
Founded	1999	1994	1999	1997
Delivered traffic/month (mln minutes)	240 (2002) 1000 (2003)	5000 (2002) 8000 (2003	480 (2002)	unknown
Interconnected customers	60 operators (9 out of 10 most important)	275 operators (8 out of 10 most important)	>100 operators	130 operators
Employees	25	90	35	unknown
Financial Rating	BBB	none	none	none
Access facilities	London, Frankfurt (main Ericsson carrier-class TDM-switch)	New York, London, Los Angeles, Frankfurt (virtual)	Paris, London, Frankfurt	London
Invested Capital	EUR 9 mln	USD 123 mln	EUR 14 mln	USD 56 mln
Transaction volume	EUR 100 mln	USD 500 mln	EUR 30 mln	unknown

Source: EUTEX AG, Arbinet, TradingCom, Band-X

Fabian Hedderich, Joerg Oestreich and Marc-Oliver Ziegenbein

forium GmbH

1 forium GmbH 91
2 Business Idea 91
3 Competitive Situation 92
4 Start-up Phase 94
5 Forium Today 96
6 Looking Back and Ahead 99
Appendix 100T

November 21st, 2002, is a cool and foggy day in Berlin, Germany. Felix Bodeewes (29) und Leander Bretschger (32) – managers and founders of forium GmbH (a GmbH is a limited liability company) – spend their lunch break reviewing their company's development since the founding year 1999. They are about to participate in a research project about success factors of fast growing companies and use their time to remember all the obstacles they had to pass in the last years.

1 forium GmbH

Within three years the Berlin-based provider of financial information and services developed from being an ignored "stepchild" of Venture Capital investors into one of the most prominent examples for the successful "new" new economy in Germany.

Forium is positioned as a financial services provider that intermediates between retail customers and financial institutions and service providers.The product and service portfolio is composed of three categories: financial management, the provision of financial information, and the procurement of finance products. These services are offered free of charge to the final customer. Sales are generated mainly through commissions paid to forium by the sellers of financial products. Forium achieves seven digit sales (Euro) with six digit earnings and has become a recognized service company within three years after foundation.

The business situation in November 2002 seemed very promising. Sustainable and profitable growth has enabled Bodeewes and Bretschger to reduce the amount of debt by 75 percent within only one and a half years.

2 Business Idea

Felix Bodeewes and Leander Bretschger got to know each other while working as research assistants at the Swiss Institute for Banking and Finance in St. Gallen, Switzerland. The business idea for forium was strongly influenced by the "provocative" statements of Professor Spremann who had constantly proclaimed the bright future of the idea of one-stop finance – i.e. the idea of offering all kinds of financial services to the customers from one single source. Most banks had ignored his far-reaching vision of customized electronic financial services. Bodeewes and Bretschger however drew their inspiration and motivation from their professor's idea. If traditional financial service providers wanted to ignore this promising segment of

service providers wanted to ignore this promising segment of the financial services market, why should they not try to prove them wrong?

Already during their time at the Institute Bodeewes and Bretschger designed various business models based on the one-stop finance concept. From these days resulted a list of around thirty ideas of how to use the internet to increase the value of financial information and services to the final customer. Bodeewes smiled at the thought that only one of these original ideas had failed in the market so far. This successful selection of appropriate ideas was based on the ability to realistically evaluate the possibilities of a combination of the internet and financial services. This ability was a direct result of the knowledge and experience both founders had with the usage of finance-related software applications and their growing network of personal contacts in both regular and savings banks, which they developed during their time at the institute.

3 Competitive Situation

Providing services of the first two categories – financial management and the provision of financial information – requires collecting and passing on objective and neutral information about all relevant financial products offered by banks and other financial institutions. This also includes providing tools that compare the conditions of different offers and show the savings potential between different alternatives. The third category implies introducing market mechanisms to products that used to be traded "over the counter" (OTC). Based on administrative efficiency, special conditions can be granted to forium customers. Online tools like demand pooling and auctions support the brokerage of finance products. These sales instruments are used for several product groups: Pooling of credit contracts (or bank accounts) leads to an increase in efficiency because of better conditions for the end customer due to scaling effects. Apart from the business fields described above (also see figures 14 and 15) forium acts as a software solution provider selling its services to financial service providers (see figure 2).

Due to the diversified strategic position of forium, several markets need to be taken into account when analysing the company's competitive environment: the market for financial services comparisons and e-commerce (sales), the market for advertising space, the market for software programming, the market for content about private finance. To sum up, forium's market may be called the market for the re-intermediation of financial products.

In the business field with the highest sales – the classic end customer business, i.e. the comparison platform (www.forium.de) – forium's competitors do not come only from the so called new economy, but from the traditional providers of such information:

banks, insurance companies and other financial service providers. However, the forium management regarded internet-based financial service providers to be the most important competitors. Competitive pressure came from companies such as eInsurance, FinanceScout 24 and aspect online, which's business models were quite similar to the one of forium. Potential additional competitors were consumer protection portals or established internet-based operators of financial information portals such as OnVista or Finanztreff. Furthermore, big corporations such as DVAG und AWD, that also followed the idea of providing a one-stop shop solution for financial products needed to be taken into account.

In the business field of software development, the competition was defined by technology. Thus, all software developers were regarded as actual or potential competitors.

The business fields that were built around the ideas of providing content and advertising space can be analysed jointly. As a content provider, forium competed with all service companies that offer information on the internet concerning financial products, including commercial and non-commercial ones. These companies competed for advertisements, which depend on the quality and focus of the content.

Recently, competitive pressure had rather declined than increased. For example, direct competitor Censio (despite of approx. Euro 45 million in venture capital) went bankrupt. Major changes in market structure were not expected for the near future: On the one hand, the number of newly founded companies was decreasing and on the other hand the relatively small niche market in which forium operated was rather unattractive for bigger companies. However, Bodeewes and Bretschger expected this niche to grow as the intensity of usage of the internet for financial services was forecasted to grow by the factor ten within the next five years.

Nevertheless, the service range offered by competitors underwent a more dynamic development. During the start-up phase of forium the services offered by e.g. eInsurance became very specialized and at the same time most competitors broadened service range. The result was a quite similar offer provided by most competitors (see figure 5 to 9). In addition, this broadening of the service range was a phenomenon to be observed also among providers of finance-related internet portals of a different original background and focus. For example OnVista, the biggest German stock market information portal, had just recently included comparisons of insurance and loan contracts into its offer.

Fabian Hedderich, Joerg Oestreich and Marc-Oliver Ziegenbein

4 Start-up Phase

The founding date in the end of 1999 meant that forium came into being in the late phase of the "dot.com boom". Patience and stamina were needed while looking for potential investors. Although Bodeewes and Bretschger had worked out a detailed business plan, nobody seemed to be willing to provide them with the necessary funds to start their business. "The market you plan to enter is already too crowded" was a sentence often heard by the young entrepreneurs during these weeks. The question whether the "simplicity" of the business idea or the realistic and thus comparably conservative business plan were reasons for which investors were put off could still not be answered today. Before the actual foundation, many other issues apart from financing had to be addressed: How could the technological implementation be realised? Who was able to program software according to Bodeewes' and Bretschger's ideas and do so without incurring high cost? Furthermore, the optimal location for the new business had to be found.

In order to undertake the first steps into entrepreneurship in the simplest and cheapest way possible, building up the business was based on the founders' personal network, which was established while working for the Institute, while talking to supposed investors, and by activating private contacts. The main issue was the technological implementation of the concept of comparing financial services developed by Bodeewes and Bretschger. While both founders had broad knowledge in the financial services industry, their programming skills were only scarcely developed at the time. Luckily, the father of Felix Bodeewes knew somebody in his table tennis club, who was a very skilled IT-expert. This had been the starting point for a technology partnership that still played an important role in forium's operations. The Fribourg-based IT company Ixnet GmbH (Ltd.) provided the development and maintenance of the forium finance portal since December 1999. The mainframe computers were located in Fribourg where also the hosting was done. The dynamic contents were created using a combination of Java-Server-Pages (JSP), Java-Servlets and JavaBeans. Until today all "hardcore development" – as Bodeewes liked to call it – was done in Fribourg. The special highlight of the partnership with Ixnet founders Peter Ziras and Martin Bucher was that software development for forium was mainly done by Ixnet programmers for which forium only paid the cost of sales. This arrangement increased the degree of entrepreneurial independence for forium as the necessary but usually expensive IT experts were employed by Ixnet and only "rented" by forium. In return, Ziras and Bucher were offered to buy a share of forium and became its first technology managers. Thus, the first important step had been made: establishing access to a high performing technology at low cost.

Next, an adequate location for the new business had to be found. In the age of the internet, location seemed to lose importance. However, the location decision proved to be an important factor for single aspects of the company's strategy. Choosing Berlin as

the new home for forium was influenced by several factors: Relatively low living cost made Berlin attractive as in the absence of venture capital funding financial constraints were a dominant factor in the start up of the company. Furthermore, Berlin offered the possibility to make use of family-owned premises during the first months of the start up and thus avoid payments for rent. In addition, Berlin was the meeting point of the internet generation and thus offered the opportunity to get in touch with fellow entrepreneurs. Finally, the high number of universities in Berlin created a great "reservoir" of skilled part time workers and interns.

The entrepreneurial and technological foundation was laid. What was still missing at that point in time were partners and customers. Bodeewes and Bretschger still have a very detailed memory of the first twelve moths: Convincing the first partners to cooperate was not only important to generate the cash flows necessary for further growth but also to increase the popularity of the forium services as fast as possible. Cooperating with established internet portals which had an interest in specific contents and services enabled forium to build up a remarkable customer base within the first year of existence while circumventing major marketing expenses. Forium positioned its services according to the design of the partner's website and thus benefited from several 100,000 page impressions per partner per month.

Establishing partnerships and a customer base on the market side proved to be less problematic than dealing with the original suppliers of financial services. According to their conservative nature, banks and other financial institutions were sceptical to work with forium. Bodeewes was not surprised by the banks' reluctance to "buy customers" from forium because "around eighty percent of bank customers are unprofitable for the bank" according to his experience. Smaller financial service providers who had specialized in a specific niche of services proved to be easier to convince of the forium concept. Acquiring supply side partners became easier over time as the list of references grew constantly.

In spring 2000, the first comparison application – i.e. a software that compared offers of different providers of a specific financial service – went online. In the end of 2002, around one hundred customers bought financial services via the forium internet portal each single day. The credit volume processed via forium reached already Euro 108 million in the first full fiscal year (2001) and grew to Euro 201 million in the following year.

Fabian Hedderich, Joerg Oestreich and Marc-Oliver Ziegenbein

5 Forium Today

The strong belief in the potential of the one-stop finance idea motivated Bodeewes and Bretschger to found forium GmbH. The rapid development of the internet had led to profound changes of the sales channels for financial services. The trend towards re-intermediation created new possibilities of designing the relationship between customers and producers of financial services. The absence of large budgets required the founders to position their company in this field carefully and without taking unnecessary risks. Consequently, strategy implementation followed a step-by-step approach that aimed at reducing business risks. One way to reduce risk was the stepwise diversification of the product and service portfolio. After having implemented the first comparison tool for credit loans, new applications for the evaluation of credit card or bank account offers followed soon. In a third step forium enlarged its offer by including services concerning financial investments. This comprised the comparison of investment funds and the conditions for overnight money and fixed-term deposits. The build up of a complete finance portal went on as insurance and tax-related services were added to the offer. The latest service range also contained financial information concerning construction financing, building society savings, car insurances, life insurances and medical insurance. The diversification strategy was not limited to the service range. Bodeewes and Bretschger had decided to use the technological competence to position forium as a software provider. The comparison tools were licensed to third parties, e.g. the comparison tool for credit loans employed by FinanceScout24.

Furthermore, forium sold licences for practical tools such as "cash machine location finder tools" or currency calculators. Finance-related content was not only used on the forium website but sold to customers such as the leading German business magazine "Wirtschaftswoche".

The diversification of products and business fields resulted directly into the creation of new business models. While the majority of sales was still generated by commissions paid by banks and financial institutions to forium other sources of sales were tapped: license fees, revenue sharing agreements, advertising fees, and royalties for content production.

After starting out with tools for information research and product selection the value chain was successfully extended in both directions: towards the end customer and towards institutional customers. In order to provide additional value to end customers, forium pushed forward the integration between the IT-systems of its partners and forium's own systems. By doing so, forium enabled the end customer to not only compare and find the best offer but to directly purchase the offered service or financial product from the original provider. End customers benefited from value-added services such as up-to-date financial information and high quality content, which supported the customers in determining their own demand for financial products.

forium GmbH

The high relevance of partnerships for the sustainable success of forium GmbH was reflected in daily operations and processes: Relationship management for the thirty partnerships has remained a top management task until today. Bodeewes and Bretschger always emphasized the importance of demonstrating their own competence and expertise while not neglecting the role of a good personal relationship. Especially in times of the burst of the internet bubble this approach paid off. The delegation of tasks originally carried out by top management became an important factor in the constantly growing company. However, relationship management remained with Bodewees and Bretschger.

Whenever the founders had to make a strategic decision, they kept one principle in mind: total customer focus. The highest quality and security of the researched and brokered information and products was defined by objectivity and completeness on the one hand and beneficial conditions for the end customers achieved through bundling of demand on the other hand. This consequent positioning as a niche player in info-mediation without an own strong branding was considered as a key element of forium's recipe for success.

Customer focus was further demonstrated by integrating ideas and suggestions of customers into the development of the service range and website. If time was available, Bodeewes replied to customers' phone calls or emails personally: "This way I can walk around my shop and get direct feedback from our customers". For the near future, forium's management had planned to strengthen its competencies in the field of customer relationship management (CRM). During the past years customers were mainly attracted by a "pull strategy". Now, regular customers should be offered special customised offers. They considered their customers' personal financial data to be to sensitive to be saved in a database.

The implementation of the diversification strategy required the founders and employees to develop a lot of new skills in a short time. Bodeewes and Bretschger expect their team and themselves to be extremely competent in all fields of the business: "We want to be capable of carrying out each task in our company. In case of emergency we need to be able to manage the whole company without any employees." The necessity to learn something new every day was an additional motivational factor for the founders in their daily work. Both developed remarkable skills in the usage of several programming languages over time. Bodeewes designed the company website personally, because he believed in the principle of "If you want things done well, do them yourself". Bodeewes added: "We demand a great deal of user friendliness and the "look & feel" of our website has to match our expectations. Why not make it ourselves before spending a lot of money for a 95 percent solution?"

Quality management at forium started with the selection of appropriate employees. The only way to become a full time employee was to work as an intern for the company before. Only such interns who proved exceptional skills and team orientation were offered a part time position with the company. Only who proved his skills again

as a part time worker had the possibility to become a full time employee at forium. Bodeewes and Bretschger paid a lot of attention to putting together a team of employees that have complementary skills. Apart from systematic recruitment, training was used to broaden the set of skills of the team.

Continuous innovation management was another important success factor for forium. Suggestions made by customers were used to support the stepwise process of new product and service development. Because of its specific situation, forium could not afford to take any unnecessary risk. The list of service and product ideas, which had been put together by Bodeewes and Bretschger years ago before founding the company served as the central guideline for this continuous innovation process. Many "new" product ideas were developed by transferring well-known and successful ideas to the internet context.

The lack of venture capitalist support proved to be no disadvantage for the development of forium. Time periods which required extensive cash out flows were overcome by incurring reasonable debt. Bodeewes and Bretschger were looking forward to the coming spring as forium was expected to be "debt-free" by then. The absence of a venture capitalist who would have required extensive management attention and resources (e.g. reporting) or might have tried to impose his or her own ideas for business development also created a certain degree of independence and flexibility that helped forium to grow the way it had done.

Bodeewes and Bretschger regarded the organisational structure of forium as being another important element of forium's success. Until now the management committee was made up of four shareholders. This closed circle of private investors added to the credibility of forium as an independent comparison portal for finance products. Apart from this management committee forium did not have any kind of fixed organisational structure: "We do not need complicated organigrams depicting our organisational structure, yet." stated Bodeewes. However, the young company had experienced difficulties with the integration of additional employees, e.g. when three or more part time employees wanted to work on the same day sufficient technical resources lacked as well as management time to coordinate work steps.

Bodeewes and Bretschger were quite satisfied with forium's progress in achieving competitive advantage. However, they made only little use of measures to protect these advantages – like filing patents or securing secrecy. "Our technology is relatively easy to understand and to copy. We do not consider software patents to be an effective protection mechanism.", Bretschger said. "We protect our competitive advantage by always being ahead of our competitors and being the first ones to introduce new services to the market". Furthermore, the high quality of the internal processes at forium prevented easy imitation. The forium brand had so far not been used extensively to differentiate forium from its competitors. This should change in the future both Bodeewes and Bretschger agreed.

Bodeewes and Bretschger had seen many start ups failing, because of poor management, which often resulted from a lack of information concerning costs and processes within their own organisation. While being aware of the importance of "creative space" for the development of new ideas and relying rather on a shared vision than detailed plans to guide business development, both founders agreed that tight financial management accounting had to take place. Key financial indicators and ratios were calculated and collected to support the decision-making process, which could thus be characterized as being very analytical and fact-based. This "number crunching" included not only cost but also extensive customer information.

6 Looking Back and Ahead

Looking back, Bodeewes and Bretschger evaluate the foundation and the first year of operations as a very instructive period that required a lot of hard work. According to the founders it was also a "very stressful" period marked by a high degree of uncertainty. But the strong belief in their vision of a transparent forum for one-stop finance services fuelled their lasting motivation: "We never had any doubt in our ideas" Bodeewes and Bretschger agreed.

Even with the generation of the first revenues and the relatively soon achievement of break-even the development of forium could never be taken for granted. Which decisions had turned forium into one of the biggest German one-stop finance service providers? What were its specific competencies and competitive advantages? Not only because of the near interview the entrepreneurs decided to analyse the past development of forium. They regarded a profound understanding of their own success as an important starting point for the planning of the future development of the company.

Appendix

Figure 1: Users see the internet as a source of information regarding insurance offerings

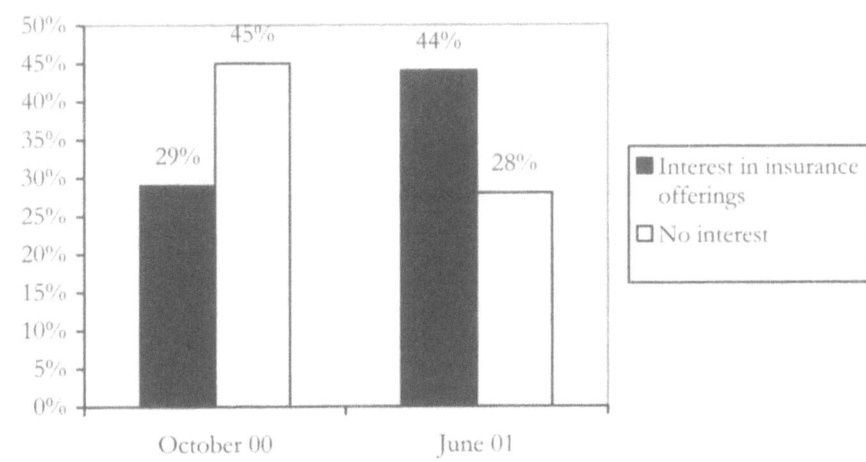

Figure 2: Revenue distribution of forium GmbH

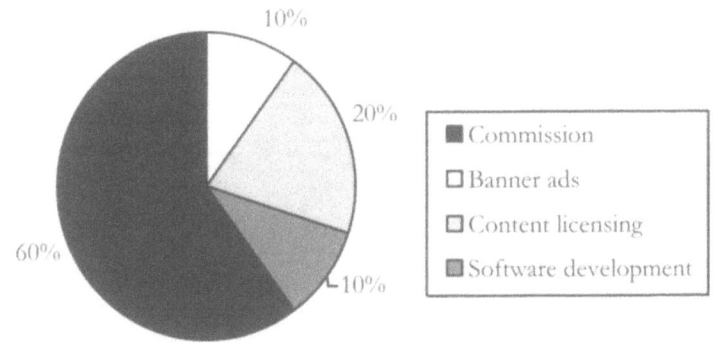

Figure 3: Revenue sources of forium GmbH

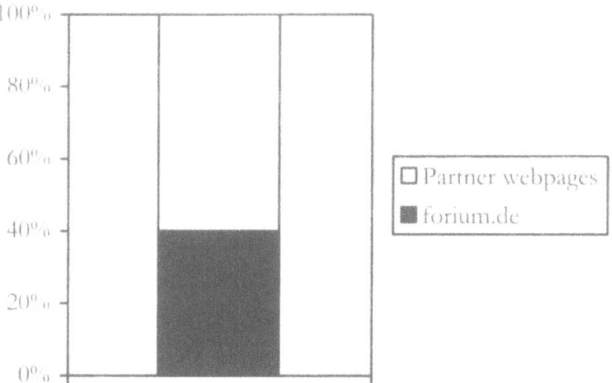

Figure 4: The founders

Felix Bodeewes:
- Born March 17, 1973
- Studies in Economics at London School of Economics (LSE)
- Post Graduate Studies in Business Administration and Economics majoring in finance at HEC Paris (Diplôme HEC, CEMS Diplom)
- PhD studies at University St. Gallen (HSG)
- Work Experience: JP Morgan, London; Morgan Stanley, London; McKinsey & Company, Düsseldorf; Swiss Institute for Banking and Finance

Leander Bretschger:
- Born July 14, 1970
- Trainee at Dresdner Bank
- Studies in Business Administration and Economics majoring in finance and capital market theory at University St. Gallen (HSG), Switzerland,

- PhD studies at University St. Gallen (HSG)
- Work experience: Deutsche Bank, Hong Kong; Bain & Company, München; Swiss Institute for Banking and Finance, St. Gallen,

Martin Bucher:

- Born May 3, 1972
- Studies in Computer Science at Higher School of Applied Sciences Furtwangen and DeMontfort University, Leicester
- Work Experience: Deutsche Post AG, Berlin; Rhône-Poulenc Rhodia AG, Freiburg; GFT AG, St. Georgen; Rautaruukki Oy, Finnland; inxnet GmbH, Freiburg

Peter Ziras:

- Born April 22, 1969
- Vocation training for Spezialist in IT-Distribution
- Studies in Computer Science majoring in artificial intelligence at Higher School of Applied Sciences Furtwangen
- Work experience: Toshiba MRI, San Francisco; Thomas & Partner, Freiburg; Orasis Inc., Irvine,CA; inxnet GmbH, Freiburg

forium GmbH

Figure 5: Screenshot of the webpage www.forium.de

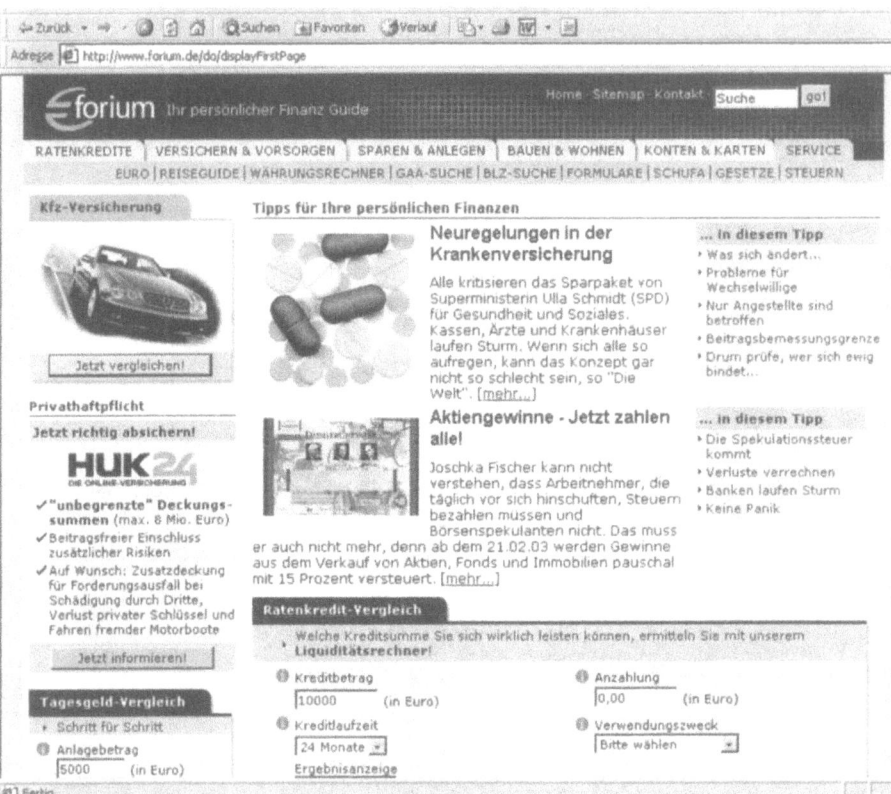

Figure 6: Strategic positioning

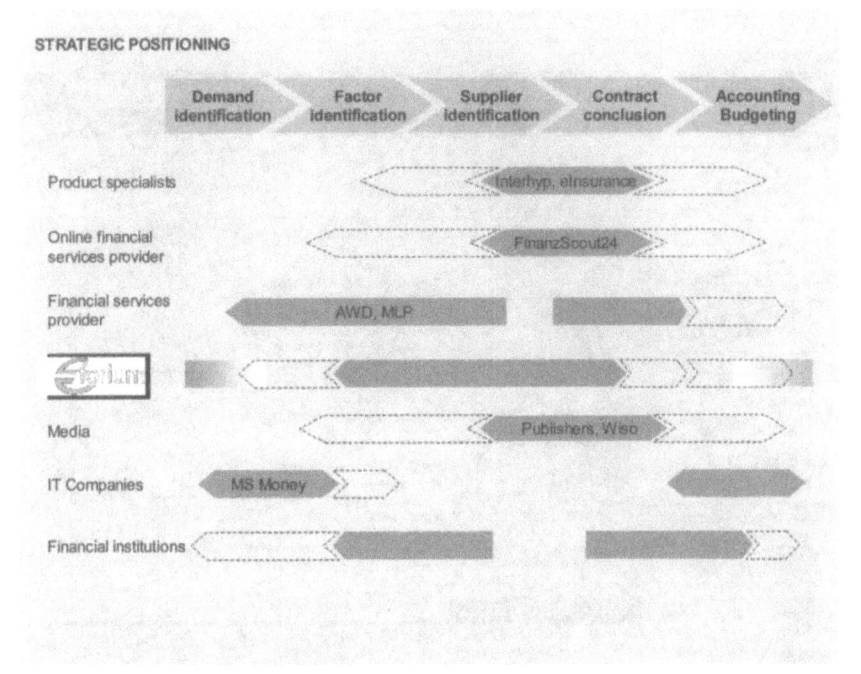

Figure 7: Business model information portal site

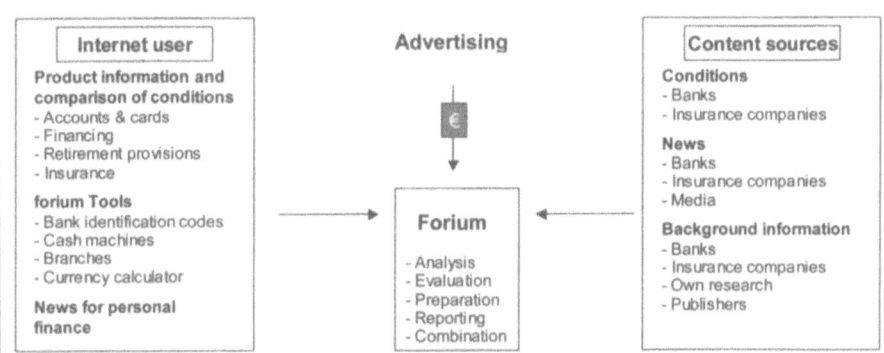

forium GmbH

Figure 8: Business model sales platform

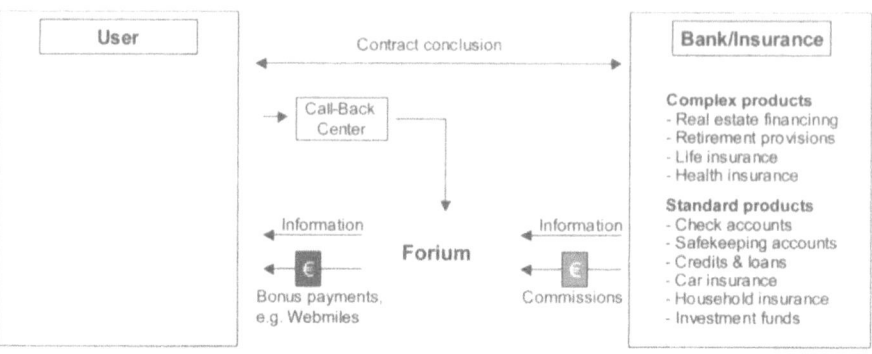

Figure 9: Sales Channels

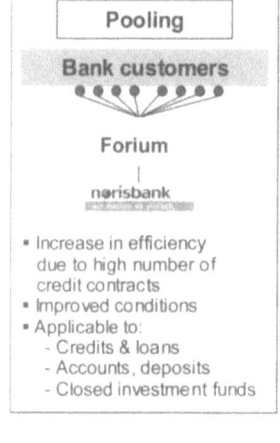
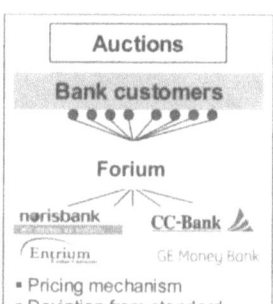
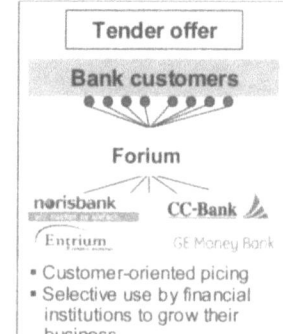

Michael Adams, Lydia Rullkötter and Sabina Schnelle

GenPat77 Pharmacogenetics AG

1 Background 109
2 The Biotech Industry 110
3 Indications 112
4 Company Profile 115
5 Strategic Considerations 117
Appendix 121

On a drizzly fall day in late 2002, Dr. Michael Terhoeven, Chief Business Officer of GenPat77 AG, a rising star of the biopharmaceutical industry, contemplated the challenges of the months ahead. While gazing at the marble monument of Robert Koch just outside his window, he wondered how the fast development of GenPat77's lead product would continue to thrive, how GenPat77's financing needs would be met during the approaching year, and how to leverage the continuing negotiations with big U.S. pharmaceutical companies.

1 Background

GenPat77, a pharmaceutical company located in Berlin, the centre of the European biotech community, develops innovative therapeutics for the treatment of transplanted organ rejection, autoimmune diseases – such as Multiple Sclerosis and Rheumatoid Arthritis – and, potentially, cancer.

Dr. Nalân Utku, Chief Executive Officer and President of Turkish origin, and a graduate of Medicine, discovered "the gene" during her extensive research fellowship at the Brigham and Women's Hospital, an affiliate hospital of the Harvard Medical School in Boston, Massachusetts, in 1993. Four years later, the corresponding protein was identified. In 1998, the excitement of the community and various industry opinion leaders encouraged and triggered Utku to found GenPat77 with the support of two leading business angels: Dr. Metin Colpan, CEO , President and founder of Qiagen, and Dr. Ekkehard Franzke, Vice President at Bain & Company and head of Bainlab in Germany. Today, Utku holds an Associate Professorship at Germany's most renowned medical institution, the Berlin Charité.

Depicting the company's as well as the industry's challenges, 'GenPat77' stands for "Gene expression patterns", elucidating the constant quest for their detection. During various key stages of the process of invention, the figure "7" played a crucial role: the seventh attempt of the experiments proved successful and a seven transmembrane protein, TIRC7, was identified, leading to the lucky number's contribution to the firm's name.

Two years after GenPat77's founding, Fritz Kopitzki, a doctorate in theoretical physics, joined the venture as a Chief Financial Officer. He has a background in management consulting with Bain & Company, focusing on the pharmaceutical industry, financial services and private equity.

At the beginning of 2002, Dr. Michael Terhoeven, the Chief Business Officer joined the triumvirate. Originally a physicist with a doctorate in mathematical physics from the University of Bonn, Germany, Terhoeven gained consulting experience in the Life

Science sector during the six years he worked at Boston Consulting Group. Given his constant quest for intellectual challenges, the persuasiveness of the dynamic and competent team convinced Terhoeven to join in. His vast knowledge of the pharmaceutical industry coupled with his management background made him the perfect fit for leading GenPat77's business development activities.

2 The Biotech Industry

> „The one who controls genes will also rule the 21st century", Jeremy Rifkin, President of the Foundation on Economic Trends.

The discovery of the DNA structure in the middle of the 20th century was the beginning of a revolution in the medical and economical environment with the goal to improve and prolong humans' lives, giving birth to the biotech industry. Over the past decades, research progress, new technologies and new paths of actions opened the way for the foundation of numerous biotech companies as well as the diversification of traditional pharmaceutical companies, causing the biotech industry to grow by tremendous growth rates (see figure 1). In 2000, revenues in the biotech industry stood at USD 27 billion and were forecasted to reach USD 83 billion by 2005. The existing 2600 biotech companies are almost equally spread across the US and Europe. Nonetheless, the US remains the leading biotech nation, not only in terms of the number of companies, but also in terms of industry profitability and maturity (more than 200 US biotech companies are publicly listed, representing a market capitalization of USD 225 billion in 2002; see figure 2). Germany recently gained a strong position as a biotech location due to changes in the regulatory environment, attracting many recent biotech foundations. Biotechnology is one of the most research-intensive industries in the world. The U.S. biotech industry spent $15.6 billion on research and development in 2001.

GenPat77 focuses on red biotechnology, sometimes also referred to as "biopharmaceutical" industry. In this industry, generally one major distinction can be made between two types of business models, namely "product" or "platform technology and service" companies. The latter are focussed on the technology or engineering side in biotech, selling or licensing their proprietary technology or other services to other companies (e.g. Lion Bioscience). This business model is characterised by short (1-3 years) development schedules and thus less risks are involved, but the upside potential remains limited (see figure 3 and figure 4). However, product companies like GenPat77 concentrate on research and development of new agents and products, resulting in very long and risky time frames (8 years or longer), but in case of success then the potential for blockbuster sales are wide open. These companies can be structured according to their contribution to the biotech value chain, which consists typically of the following

phases: bio-informatics, identification of target molecules, search of agent, validation & optimisation, development, production and finally marketing & sales. Companies can either specialize in certain components of the value chain and outsource others or act as an integrated biopharmaceutical company.

When looking at the biopharmaceutical industry, what are the most important characteristics and current trends in this dynamic and exciting environment? The process from the development of a new biopharmaceutical product until its market entry is highly regulated and closely monitored by governmental supervisory institutions (like the FDA – Food and Drug Administration - in the US). This long process can roughly be separated into pre-clinical and clinical (I-III) phases and finally the application for official approval; it involves a high risk of failure and usually lasts up to a decade, costing up to USD 500 million for a single product (see figure 5 for detailed information on requirements and failure rates). This process requires close cooperation between biopharmaceutical companies, research organizations and clinical institutions. Current activities in the biopharmaceutical industry show that there is a trend to shift from targeting rare and highly specialised diseases towards addressing more popular diseases, launching products with the potential of becoming a blockbuster, i.e. having sales of more than USD 1 billion in the US per annum.

One major conclusion one can draw after having understood the biotech (and especially the biopharmaceutical) industry is that a lot of cash is needed and a lot of time goes by until a biotech company perhaps succeeds - starts generating revenues and one day finally generates positive returns on investment. Hence the major financing sources of the biotech industry should be mentioned here: again, the US is leading in terms of financing volume, from 1996 until 2000 the volume rose by more than 200%, reaching USD 38 billion in 2000 (see figure 6), compared to only USD 7 billion in Europe. Moreover, 80% of the worldwide venture capital invested in biotech firms went into American companies. Major sources of financing are seasoned offerings, loans, public subsidies, venture capital, private investors and IPOs. These sources vary over time, especially depending on the capital market environment. In recent times, the wind tends to be tougher for young companies, since venture capital funds hesitate to invest, both due to the high complexity and risk involved in biotech and due to a lack of attractive exit options. Strategic investments, trade sales and co-operations tend to be of increasing importance.

Biopharmaceuticals are based on several new technologies, namely proteins, cell cultures, cloning, recombinant DNA, tissue engineering etc. In the following, we focus on proteins and especially monoclonal antibodies. How do monoclonal antibodies work? Monoclonal antibody (mAb) technology uses immune system cells that make proteins, which are called antibodies. Protein engineering technology will be used, often in conjunction with recombinant DNA techniques, to improve existing proteins, such as enzymes, antibodies and cell receptors, and to create proteins not found in nature. Medical researchers have used protein engineering to design novel proteins that can

bind to and deactivate viruses and tumour-causing genes; create especially effective vaccines; and study the membrane receptor proteins that are so often the targets of pharmaceutical compounds. The research process in order to generate mAb as performed by GenPat77 is typically performed as follows: multiple squirting of increasing concentrations of the proteins into in vivo organisms trigger the development of monoclonal antibodies. By extracting those mAb and transferring them into carcinogenic cells, their progeny is induced. As a consequence, extra-cellular proteins and surface molecules can be identified that do not only bind mAb and do act upon them, but also show profoundly effective behaviour.

3 Indications

Monoclonal antibodies are enabled to encroach upon a variety of human immune responses. GenPat77 currently focuses on three fields of immune mediated diseases (see figure 7):

- undesired autoimmune responses,
- transplanted organ rejection and Graft versus Host Disease (GvHD) after transplantation, and
- cancer (under discussion)

GenPat77 is carrying out intensive research and development in projects aimed at the creation of related drugs.

The first immunomodulatory drug is planned to be in rheumatoid arthritis, the most widespread autoimmune disease, and/or transplanted organ rejection – the initial research objective of GenPat77. Further focus will be on creating diversity in the pipeline-product portfolio.

Compared to older technologies, monoclonal antibodies are a significant improvement: traditional pharmaceutical products are based on small molecules which are chemically synthesised. Since they are not able to exclusively address the affected cells, they usually cause severe side effects.

Transplantations

In order to suppress organ rejection and hinder Graft vs. Host Disease, immunosuppressive drugs constitute an essential tool in transplant medicine. However, currently

available medication has to be taken life-long and causes immense side effects such as infectious diseases, arteriosclerosis and toxic effects, causing death fairly frequently.

Due to these disadvantages of current drugs, GenPat77's research and development focuses on alternatives therapeutics without significant side effects, requiring merely short-term consumption. The first envisaged product will address kidney transplants. It is being developed from a widely characterized gene product, which might have the capacity to fulfil the missing properties of the current immunosuppressive drugs and might replace these in clinical application.

Even though there is a moderately high "unmet need" - approximately 80,000 patients are registered with U.S. transfer lists, waiting for donors - the number of solid organ transplantations performed remained fairly steady over the last decade, growing only by approximately 1,5% per annum. Of the 40,000 transplantations carried out globally per year, 60% are kidney transplants. Specifically for this kind of organ transfers, the drugs Simulect (Novartis), Zenapax (Roche), as well as Thymoglobulin (SangStat) and Atgam (Pharmacia) are well suited. Since its entry in late 1999, the polyclonal Thymoglobulin, which is surprisingly effective but comparably low tech, quickly gained market share and endangered the monoclonal therapeutics.

The future of human organ replacements is considered to be enhanced with the establishment of xenotransplantation, i.e. transferring organs and cells from other species, as well as in those techniques utilising organs newly bred from human stem cells.

Auto-immune diseases

So far, no selective treatments are available for autoimmune diseases such as rheumatoid arthritis, inflammatory bowel disease, psoriasis and multiple sclerosis. The use of current drugs is not only suppressive for the autoimmune reaction, but also interferes with the protective function of the immune system. Patients often face problems with severe side effects such as infectious diseases and tumour formation.

GenPat77 is developing immunomodulatory drugs, which are able to inhibit the immune response towards a specific target in the early stage of immune stimulation. Autoaggressive immune reactions can therefore be selectively modulated at the beginning of the chain reaction without any risk of damaging the immune system as a whole.

The largest segment by disease area within the global autoimmune disease market was the rheumatoid arthritis market, with 55.9% share in 2000. Rheumatoid arthritis is an easily recognizable condition with high prevalence and a variety of products available, therefore this market maintains a high segment market share and is expected to remain the leading segment in 2006 with 55.7% segment market share.

Michael Adams, Lydia Rullkötter and Sabina Schnelle

Between 1 to 2% of the world population suffer from rheumatic arthritis (RA). The total global market for autoimmune disease therapeutics reached an estimated $11.3 billion in 2000. This was an increase of 23.6% over an estimated $4.8 billion in 1996. Key market drivers included products such as Celebrex, Vioxx, Enbrel, Avonex, Betaseron, Rebif, and Synthroid. In 2006, the market is expected to generate estimated revenues of $21.1 billion, reflecting a 15.9% increase from 2000 to 2006.

Pharmacia (28%), Novartis (8%), and Merck (7%) possess large shares of the market. The remainder was taken by various brand and generic manufacturers, both from the pharmaceutical as well as the biopharmaceutical sector.

Cancer

Since cancer constitutes the second most frequent cause of death after heart diseases, the search for effective cancer treatment remains of high concern to the pharmaceutical industry. The need to cure those immune defects is high and yet almost completely unmet. Modern biotechnology has led to the discovery and characterisation of oncogenes and tumour suppressor genes.

Currently, the global market for anti-cancer drugs represents yearly sales of approximately US$ 17 billion. More than 300 new therapies currently undergo clinical testing. Due to this huge market potential, GenPat77 is testing its opportunities of developing products against specific, non-solid types of cancer, but there remains a long way to go until results in this highly complex field of application will be achieved.

Cancer therapeutics entail the development of liposomal anticancer drugs; the worldwide most widely applied product Doxorubicin is highly effective but does have toxic side effects. In the future, major market potential should arise in the fields of prostate and breast as well as skin cancer. The liposomal market segment may well reach sales of over US$1 billion.

Meanwhile, the market for cancer diagnostic products is expected to continue with steady growth. Particularly, the prostate specific antigen (PSA) test market is expected to grow at an annual rate of about five percent. Among the new emerging cancer diagnostic tools, genetic testing for breast cancer will continue to grow in popularity, and thus in market opportunity and size. Given that there are more than 180,000 breast cancer cases annually in the U.S., this stands to be a major market.

4 Company Profile

Organization

Since its foundation in 1998, GenPat77 has gone through a phase of rapid expansion, especially regarding headcount and office space. In fall 2002 the company had 33 employees and had just finished the renovation of further office and laboratory space directly next to GenPat77's existing facilities. Like every typical biotech company, the majority of Gen Pat77's employees were scientists or people with technical backgrounds, while the management and administrative functions were handled by eight employees: Dr. Nalan Utku, the CEO, Dr. Fritz Kopitzki, the CFO, Dr. Michael Terhoeven, the CBO, an employee responsible for project management, another responsible for HR and accounting, another responsible for sourcing and finally 2 secretaries/office managers. Legal advisory accounted for a significant share of GenPat77's cost (the amount spent annually of approx. €50-100k was comparable to one to two full-time employees), but it was handled by external attorneys. Just having hired a Vice President of medical development - who would be responsible for managing contacts to clinical institutions and big pharmaceutical companies – was the last piece of the mosaic of staffing management; Dr. Terhoeven considered the growth phase of the management team to be completed.

GenPat77's scientific group numbered 25 employees, ten of them carrying a PhD, who were organized into four task groups along the value chain. Each one of them was responsible for a dedicated piece of testing/analysis in the long pre-clinical development phase. Dr. Terhoeven considered the four leaders of the groups to be the core of GenPat77's development success. Still, scientists and technicians represented the major cost block for GenPat77, their salaries typically amounting to €30-40k and €20-25k respectively. In order to provide some material motivation and to ensure employee retention, the key scientists' salaries were tied to individual as well as company performance, resulting in a cash bonus. Plans for stock options were in discussion, but the scale and scope were still fairly unclear. Exit clauses were also integrated into contracts to avoid outflow of intellectual property.

What Dr. Terhoeven especially liked about working at GenPat77 was the unique atmosphere among staff, completely opposed to traditional pharmaceutical companies: the culture was very much a family-style, with communication and interaction being widely informal, people usually had lunch together, scientists even listened to their favourite music while working in the lab. Dr. Terhoeven considered this type of culture to be especially important to foster innovation and to manage a fast-growing company, but, on the other hand, he felt that with potential future growth of headcount a more organizational structure might be needed while attempting to maintain such an open-minded and individual culture with 100 employees.

Michael Adams, Lydia Rullkötter and Sabina Schnelle

Products and Patents

As a typical biotech product company, GenPat77's strategic focus is on the development of monoclonal antibodies related to several molecules and different indications. The production, marketing and distribution are not considered to be feasible for such a small company, since those activities require a large amount of capital; hence, GenPat77's strategy is to outsource these processes. Within the development phase, the company sees its core competency in the ability to further specify the targets – based on Dr. Utku's research – and to carry out all pre-clinical trials. Michael Terhoeven was optimistic that phase I of clinical testing for one product could start in the first quarter of 2003. This might be done by either GenPat77 itself or under close supervision by a contract research organization. As opposed to earlier strategic positions, Dr. Terhoeven today is convinced that phase III of clinical testing would be too expensive to be handled by GenPat77 (phase III clinical testing costs can easily amount to high two-digit million dollars); licensing out within or after phase II seems to be the most appropriate solution. When thinking of GenPat77's future product portfolio, Dr. Terhoeven is always confronted with huge uncertainties. He estimates that GenPat77 would be able to have eleven products within a time horizon of ten years (see figure 8 for the current states), addressing different indications within the fields of transplantation, autoimmune diseases and cancer. He hopes that – if all clinical trials go well – GenPat77 could generate its first revenues by licensing in the years 2004 or 2005. Michael Terhoeven is optimistic that some of GenPat77's products had blockbuster potential. Up to now, GenPat77 holds one umbrella-patent on its lead target, the membrane protein TIRC7 (comprising 42 claims and leading to 10 more patents), which grants protection for 20 years from 1997 onwards. For this lead target, GenPat77 has identified two mAb, for a second target, they have already experimented with a fusion protein, and for a third target, another mAb has been identified.

When thinking of competitors searching in the same field or potentially copying GenPat77's mAb, Dr. Terhoeven feels quite confident. The patent protection in cooperation with Harvard Medical School would deter competitors from initiating long and costly lawsuits. In addition, Michael Terhoeven felt that GenPat77's key to success would further lay in the different path of action compared to traditional medications.

Financials

"Saving cash is an entrepreneurial virtue", Michael Terhoeven remembered one of his major lessons from his time at the Boston Consulting Group. How true is this statement for a biotech company?! Up to now, GenPat77 had not generated any revenues, but was confronted with growing expenses. Significant investments had been made in

lab and office equipment, costs of personnel mounted with the growing headcount and costs of ingredient production were very high.

GenPat77's initial financing was provided by Futour, a financing program of bmb+f (Federal German Ministry for Education and Research) for start-up companies in Berlin, constituting one major reason for GenPat77's choice of location. In 2000, the company completed its first venture financing round with 3i Group plc (and tbg as silent partner). In early 2002, a second financing round of € 5 million had just been closed with a VC consortium consisting of the original investor 3i Group plc, PEPPERMINT Financial Partners, Berlin Capital Fund, and IBB Beteiligungsgesellschaft. Dr. Kopitzki was already preparing GenPat77's third financing round, which he envisaged for 2003 in order to provide enough cash for phases I and II of clinical testing.

Due to its venture capital financing, GenPat77 is required to report on a monthly basis to its investors, submitting financials as well as the progress related to agreed milestone achievement. In accordance with common practice, these milestones had been fixed in the VC contracts.

5 Strategic Considerations

Clients and Strategic Alliances

Since 1998, some of the ideas of GenPat77's business model had been under review. Scarce financing sources limited the company's opportunities to cover the whole value chain, incorporating activities from basic research over development of the product to its marketing. Instead, GenPat77 was forced to concentrate on pre-clinical development and the first as well as parts of the second stage of the clinical testing.

Dr. Terhoeven remembered his first meeting with Nalân Utku, and was sure that he would never forget her response when questioning the sustainability of the firm's business model:

> "We are closely networked with the most important centres of immunologic research – this makes us optimistic that we will be able to develop many new approaches to treatment."

One of his first actions in the new position at GenPat77 was to plan and execute a journey to the United States, wanting to meet and build relationships with all of these

significant researchers in order to enable future commercial cooperation. Nalân Utku and her exceptional contacts proved extremely fruitful: for two weeks in a row, CEO and CBO were the guests of reknowned representatives of U.S. research laboratories in the field of immunology, including academic institutions as well as pharmaceutical and biotech corporations. Apart from these leaders' cutting-edge scientific knowledge, their up-to-date insights in recent developments of the industry in the U.S. were also illuminating with respect to potential customers of GenPat77.

Michael Terhoeven was very satisfied with the outcomes of the journey. On the plane back to Berlin, he and Utku developed a list of segments, research fields and patents to be targeted in the visited institutions during the upcoming year. He had the feeling that Utku's closely-knit network to leading research facilities would offer him a few more opportunities to travel to Massachusetts and other parts of the world.

Investing in other laboratories' patents was one thing. Selling GenPat77's products-to-come another. Even though the company's first generation product was still to enter the first phase of clinical testing, the management team needed to map out the strategy on how to market the results of the second phase fairly soon. Due to their well-equipped cash positions, large pharmaceuticals appeared to be most promising strategic partners and customers. They might be interesting partners for the future sale of licenses; however, further strategic alternatives were taken into account, this included explicitly all forms of co-operation. In particular, being merged with a larger pharmaceutical player was a potential scenario which also fit "big pharma's" approach to external know-how acquisition. Therefore meeting with the strategic decision makers of international pharmaceutical corporations was another key element in GenPat77's business development plan.

For phase I in the clinical trials, Dr. Utku and her project manager had already identified a number of capable contract research organisations (CRO's). Also, carefully preparing the second stage of the clinical trials was critical in order to ensure that first-class physicians executing these tests would already incorporate their knowledge in the pre-clinical stages. Here, top medical institutions both in Berlin, such as Buch Hospital and Charité, and the world, for instance the Harvard Medical School in Massachusetts, offer a wide field of activity. Members of the Scientific Advisory Board are in most cases affiliated to one of the institutions mentioned here and could therefore well serve as contacts initiating a cooperative agreement.

Investor Relations

Carrying out the first and second stage of clinical testing requires extensive amounts of cash. A back-of-the-envelope estimation results in a one-digit multiple of the money raised in the second financing round.

Triggered by the global economic downturn, Venture Capitalists were significantly less willing to invest. When the management team started reaching out for new financing opportunities, they encountered a tight community of venture capitalists, reflecting a shift of bargaining power to their ends. Capital increases were kept on small scale and often staggered. Elaborate clauses with regard to the determination of milestones, preferred liquidation options and protection from equity dilution had become integral part of contractual components dictated by VC's. Since the last financing round, access to capital appeared to have become even more difficult.

Additionally, former round investors became concerned about how to recoup their investments. With capital markets suffering from a major breakdown, initial public offerings did currently not appear to be the most lucrative exit option, perhaps not even a feasible one. At the same time, pharmaceutical corporations smell opportunities to acquire the most promising among the biotech candidates. Consequently, most small biopharmaceutical companies have become increasingly flexible, including a trade sale as exit option. Also, prices have kept declining at a significant rate. Since GenPat77's size was rather at the lower boundary of what was considered as critical mass in the industry, a merger with another biopharmaceutical company is increasingly favoured by GenPat77's management (see figure 9 for a list of the industry's financing sources).

The Next Meeting of The Supervisory Board

Soon, Michael Terhoeven would have to present the results of his journey to the US in front of GenPat77's supervisory board. Meetings of the board are scheduled in regular intervals and are conceived to inform the board members of the latest business developments, the progress in reaching milestones, financial status, etc.

At the next meeting, Michael Terhoeven planned not only to report the most recent results and agreements but also to sketch out GenPat77's future. There would have to be a decision on GenPat77's strategy. If the plan was to reach a value-creating stage, a third financing round would become necessary. Otherwise, the company had to find an attractive strategic partner. During his trip through the United States, he had met both potential licensing partners as well as candidates for a strategic alliance or even a merger. However, he was not quite sure yet about which option to advise to the members of the supervisory board.

A third financing round would ensure an efficient in-house development of the product to end of phase II which in turn represented a substantial value added and a significant increase in the estimated licensing revenues to be generated from it.

Yet, considerable risks had to be assessed. Pre-clinical trials and phase I and II testing are not as costly as the subsequent tests but feature a higher probability of failure. The

board members might consider these risks as too important to be taken on alone. They might prefer the significantly lower but as well more secure return of a trade sale.

Sure, Nalân Utku, Fritz Kopitzki and Michael Terhoeven would present the status quo of the company, but was that enough? They felt that the team had to dig deeper into the ground. They would have to review the business model that GenPat77 had followed so far, an analysis of their strengths and driving success factors in the past, at the present and in the future. Ultimately, the members of the supervisory board had to be persuaded that the goal of reaching phase II of development could realistically be reached, as the management firmly believed.

Appendix

Figure 1: US industry statistics

Year	2001	2000	1999	1998	1997	1996	1995	1994	1993	1992
Sales*	20.0	19.3	16.1	14.5	13.0	10.8	9.3	7.7	7.0	5.9
Revenues*	27.6	26.7	22.3	20.2	17.4	14.6	12.7	11.2	10.0	8.1
R&D Expense*	15.6	14.2	10.7	10.6	9.0	7.9	7.7	7.0	5.7	4.9
No. of Public Companies	342	339	300	316	317	294	230	265	235	225
No. of Companies	1,457	1,379	1,273	1,311	1,274	1,287	1,308	1,311	1,272	1,231
Employees	179,000	174,000	162,000	155,000	141,000	118,000	108,000	103,000	97,000	79,000

* USD billions
Source: Ernst &Young LLP, annual biotechnolgy reports, 1993-2002
Financial data based primarily on fiscal-year fiancial statements of publicly traded companies

Figure 2: Market capitalization 1994-2002 (in bn USD)

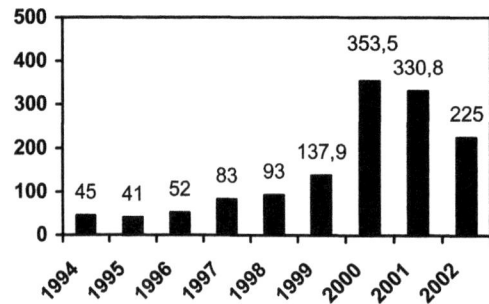

Source: Ernst & Young LLP and BioWorld

Figure 3: Biotech-companies act on different levels of the industry-specific value chain

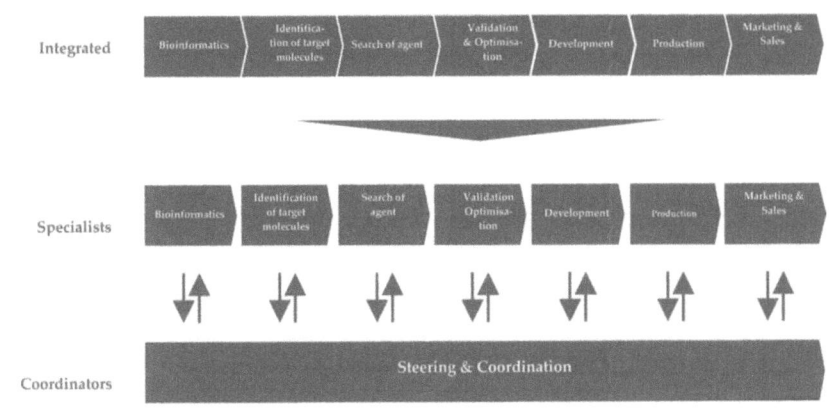

Figure 4: Business model affects timing of cash-flows

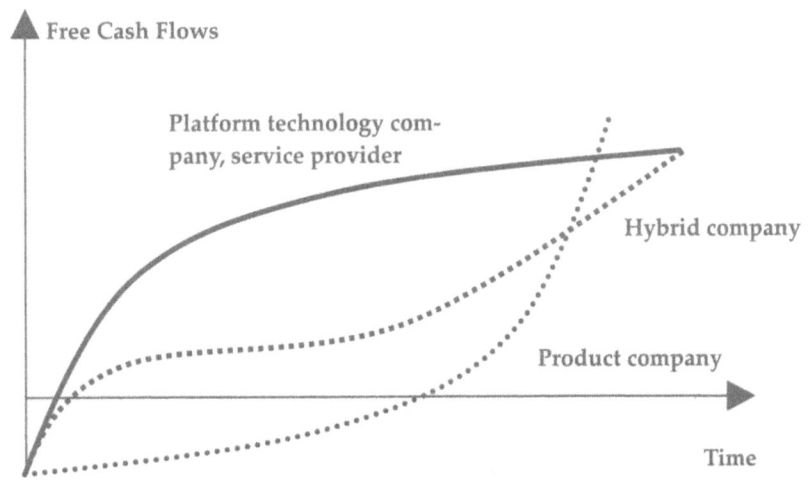

Source: Bain: Trends in der Biotechnologie, 2001

GenPat77 Pharmacogenetics AG

Figure 5: Biopharmaceutical products have to go through a tough regulatory process

	Pre-clinical		FDA****	Clinical			FDA	Market
Status	Identification	Animal-model	IND*	Phase I	Phase II	Phase III	NDA**/ BLA***	Phase IV
Goal	Identification, introductory tests		Approval for human trials	Security	Effectiveness	Superiority, long-term effects	Approval	Long-term studies
Duration	6-7 years		30 days	1-3 years	2 years	3-4 years	1-4 years	Continuous
No. of product candidates	100.000		100 handed in for IND	85 reach phase I	70 reach phase II	33 reach phase III	25-30 handed in	20 reach market
Prob. of approval	0,02%		20%	23%	28%	60%	70-80%	

Time Horizon

Cost of development process per product: approx. USD 500 million

* IND: Investigational New Drug ** NDA: New Drug Application *** BLA: Biologic Licensing Approval **** FDA: Food and Drug Administration

Figure 6: U.S. total financing, 1997-2001 (in billion US$)

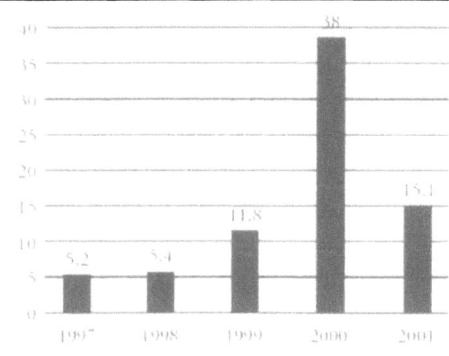

Source: BioWorld

Figure 7: GenPat77's targeted indications can be divided into three areas

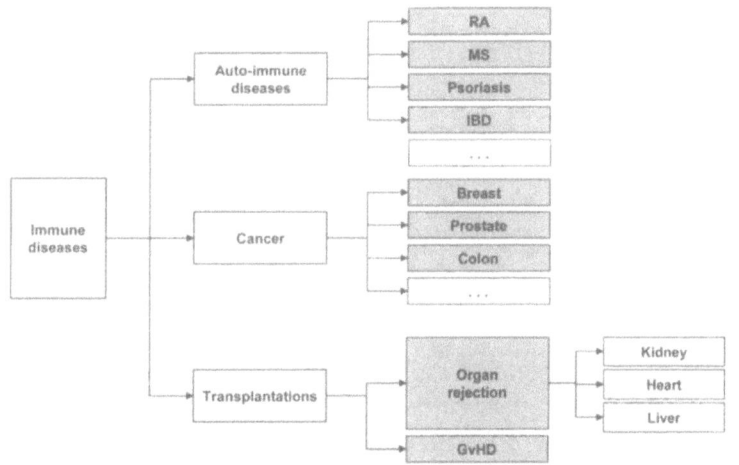

Figure 8: GenPat77 currently has 11 products in the pre-clinical phase

Figure 9:Biotech Industry Financing

Source	Amount (total)	Amount (in percent)
IPOs	292.2	2%
Follow-ons	3,510.8	23%
Public/Other	7,227.0	48%
Venture funding	3,763.3	25%
Milestones and Equity Buys from Partners	300.7	2%

Anna Bassler, Martin Heibel and Simone Sipply

Getgo

1 Introduction 129
2 History 129
3 The Ticketing Industry 130
4 Getgo's Business 133
5 Financing The Venture 136
6 Operational Challenges 137
7 Marketing 138
8 Establishing Strategic Alliances 140
9 Getgo – A CTS company? 140
Appendix 141

"From our competitors' point of view, it should have been impossible for us to exist."

(Daniel Grözinger – founder of getgo)

1 Introduction

Daniel Grözinger, one of the four founders and CEOs of getgo, the leading German online ticket provider, was looking out of the window of his frugal office located in Bahrenfeld, Hamburg. It was September 2002 and still hot outside; the sun had been shining all day long. Going out with some friends and enjoying this late summer evening would have been great, but Grözinger had decided to come to the office to think about what had happened the last days. CTS Eventim, the leading German ticket system provider, had made an offer to buy getgo. Grözinger was still overwhelmed by this news, which proved to the founders that their business had been a great success. He wanted to reflect upon the events of the last two and a half years and find out where this success had come from, although they had started in a time that had not been rosy for new start-ups.

2 History

Getgo was founded in March 2000, at the time when the Internet hype started to come to its end. Nevertheless the four founders Björn Söder, Burkhard Funk, Christoph Schäfer and Daniel Grözinger had been confident about the success of their business, even without the support of the Internet hype. They had come together from two different backgrounds. Three of them had been working for a leading international consulting firm. One of them, Schäfer, had acquired the fourth entrepreneur, Grözinger, whom he knew from their studies at the same business school.

The idea of starting an online ticket provider had been the result of a systematic search for a suitable start-up business opportunity. When the founders had thought about starting an online ticketing shop in Germany they looked over to the US where 20% of tickets were sold online compared to 1% in Germany. Inspired by the success of ticketmaster.com in the US, they had realized that the German market was still underdeveloped compared to the US, which had made this business model the most attractive one. Being totally convinced by their business idea, the founders were willing to pay the required capital stock for the foundation of the corporation out of their own pock-

ets. Like the business idea, the company name "getgo" was derived in a systematic process. It was protected immediately after the foundation of the company.

Until April 2000 the founders were busy writing a business plan to acquire venture capital. In May 2000 – after receiving first VC funding – they started building up their business in a modest office in Hamburg, which they equipped with second-hand furniture. In September 2000 the getgo-website was launched and the first tickets were sold. In January 2001, in terms of number of tickets sold, getgo was already the market leader in the German online ticketing market. The final breakthrough came in March 2001, when getgo signed an exclusive partnership for the U2 tour in Germany. The deal required getgo to build up a ticket sales interface on the official U2 homepage exclusively accessible for members of the fan club. Thanks to its flexible technology, getgo was the only German player who was able to provide the required online platform.

In mid 2002, getgo had become an established business in the online ticketing market and pursued its growth although the continuing industry downturn caused other Internet start-ups to run into problems. With sales of 6.2 million Euro for the first two quarters of 2002, getgo could achieve the break even in July (for further data on sales and customer development see figure 1).

3 The Ticketing Industry

The ticketing industry not only was comprised of tickets for concerts and soccer games but also cinema, theater or fair tickets. In 2001, the German ticketing market had a size of approximately six billion euros. Since then, sales volume has increased, mainly due to higher ticket prices with an average price of around 40 euro per ticket.

The market was quite complex due to the various types of tickets. However, not all of those were equally relevant for the presales ticketing industry. Tickets for fairs, for example, were usually sold right before the event since most people decided to go spontaneously and tickets usually had a high availability. Cinema tickets theoretically represented a big presales potential but the large cinema chains in Germany refused to accept innovative ticketing concepts, which would have allowed customers to arrive just before the start of the movie. The reason for their reluctance was the fact that cinemas earn a lot more money on drinks and snacks they sell to visitors before the movie than on the movie ticket itself. Therefore they are keen on having people arrive at least half an hour before the movie starts.

Although other categories such as soccer tickets and theater were bought in advance, they were subject to special sales conditions like subscriptions and therefore not inter-

esting for the presales industry. Soccer tickets were traditionally sold by the regional clubs. Some of the tickets were sold directly to the fans, while the rest was sent to the club of the competing team. Hence, the focus of the presales ticketing industry was on concert tickets.

The business of ticket presales was time-lagged, since tickets were sold a few months before the actual event. Additionally, it was a cyclical business. Sales reached a peak in December due to the Christmas business and huge presales for concerts in summer. They experienced a downturn in summer time (for seasonal fluctuation of ticket sales see figure 2).

Ticketing offline

The ticketing industry is characterized by a high degree of fragmentation, not only due to diverse event categories, but also because the multitude of parties involved: event organizers, system providers and points of sale.

Event organizers could be segmented on the basis of the different types of events they organized: culture, classical music, rock/pop, sports and diverse entertainment, such as TV shows and fairs. For the German rock/pop market, the major players were the Deutsche Entertainment AG and CTS Eventim AG, a holding of several smaller event organizers. In addition to that, there were a huge number of small and regional players. In the sports segment the event organizers were the sports clubs themselves. Cultural and classical events were organized by the individual theater or opera house.

The following element in the value chain of ticketing business was constituted by the system providers and the different points of sale. System providers had streamlined the process of selling tickets to the end customer. About ten years before, the event organizers had printed all tickets for a specific event and had distributed them physically to their different points of sale e.g. travel agencies or ticket agencies. This process had been afflicted with huge logistical challenges concerning the allocation of tickets, especially when an agency facing less demand than expected had to transfer tickets to places with higher demand.

With the upcoming system providers these problems had been solved. They developed computer-based ticketing system platforms, to which the participating event organizers and agencies were connected via telephone lines. The event organizers put their tickets in a virtual pool, namely on the system platform, where they were stored. Every participating point of sale had access to this pool and whenever an agency sold a ticket, they could print it out directly and the contingent in the pool was reduced by one. The new system was used for all big events. Smaller and regional event organizers, who at that time sold about one third of all tickets in Germany, still used the old process of physical distribution. At the time getgo was thinking about entering the

market, there were several systems in place, the major ones being CTS with their Euroticket system, Ticket Online, and Starticket, the latter being linked to the travel agency booking system Amadeus. Additionally, several regional ticket systems had established such systems. An event organizer typically operated with one, maximum two, system providers. Therefore the offer of a point of sale depended on the system to which it was linked.

Ticketing Online - The Competitive Fray

The first steps of the ticketing industry towards the Internet were done by the event organizers who started building up online platforms offering the tickets for their events directly to their end customers. Additionally, the big system providers launched Internet sales platforms in order to generate a new sales channel to their business. Examples were CTS and Ticket Online, which had already both been online when getgo entered the market. An interesting project was the platform Qivive, a joint venture between the event organizer Deutsche Entertainment AG and the system provider Starticket, financed with 20 million Euro by Springer Verlag, a German media company. This venture started shortly after getgo had launched their website.

When getgo entered the market, it faced different competitors. On the one hand there were the system providers who had launched their ticket web shops, such as CTS or Ticket Online. CTS not only was a system provider but also an event organizer and therefore a quite powerful player, especially due to their strong position in rock/pop events. CTS' financial power had been strengthened by its IPO in 2000, which had reaped in 58 million Euro in cash. Ticket Online was a pure system provider with an online platform, especially strong in theater and niche sports. On the other hand, there were early-stage joint ventures, such as Qivive and Ticketworld, a strong alliance of event organizers who were selling their tickets directly over the web without using any intermediary ticketing system.

But getgo also had to face a more direct type of competition: Wannago, a Swedish online ticket shop, who entered the German market, and Tomondo, both having a business model similar to getgo's. Wannago was more funded than getgo and had already been in the market when getgo took its first wobbly steps. Tomondo had received high funding from T-Venture, the venture capital branch of Deutsche Telekom, the German ex-monopolist in telecommunications (for an overview of market shares of the competitors in 2002 refer to figure 3).

4 Getgo's Business

The Business Model

Getgo's business model was actually straightforward. Having seen the fragmentation of the market due to the multitude of system providers, the idea of getgo was to centralize the different offerings. The intention was to provide the end customer with one single point of sale where he could access the most complete ticket offer available. Thus, getgo provided a pooling of tickets offered via different systems (See figure 4 for an illustration of the business model).

The web was the perfect means to realize this centralization in a fast, cost effective, and easy way. Wondering if customers would accept buying a quite expensive product such as a concert ticket online, getgo observed that a ticket was actually the perfect product to be sold via the Internet. Physical properties of a ticket were not important to the customer, so he experienced no risk in buying online. All that mattered was to get a seat for a concert, which could become time critical when events were highly popular and tickets were quickly sold out. In fact, the risk lay within the event itself rather than in the ticket, since the customer could not know what the event would be like.

The ticketing market in general was a market of rather low margins, realized as percentages of the ticket price. The event organizer retained 5% to 10% of the ticket price to cover its costs, the system provider could keep approximately 0.80 Euro per ticket, around 2% of the ticket price. Getgo was able to reach the same margin as ordinary ticket agencies or call centers, i.e. approximately 10% of the ticket price.

Besides the ticket sales over the web, getgo's business model included innovative ticketing concepts like "mobile ticketing" and "print at home". Mobile ticketing was the idea to send a barcode on a mobile phone instead of a paper-based ticket by mail. The barcode could then be scanned at the entrance of an event. Print at home was another barcode-based concept that relied on the observation that anybody buying online could print his ticket on his personal printer at home. The printed voucher could then be used instead of a normal ticket. Both mobile ticketing and print at home were not accepted by the market in a way that the founders had expected.

Anna Bassler, Martin Heibel and Simone Sipply

Value Added - The Customer's Perspective

"At the end, customers buy where they find the products they are looking for."

(Daniel Grözinger)

Getgo tried to reduce the remaining risk of purchasing tickets online by providing a large amount of information about artists and events on their homepage to keep the customer informed. If, for example, an artist cancelled his tour or changed dates for specific concerts, the customer could always be sure to find this information on the getgo homepage. Additionally, getgo provided other services like an event calendar and useful links, like a babysitter service. Even special insurance could be purchased, which protected the customer from the risk of not being able to go to the event on the actual day.

Besides the content, the crucial and unique value added provided by getgo was that the customer was able to find tickets from all different event organizers and systems on one single Internet site. The customer did not need to search the Internet anymore in order to find the organization presenting the specific event he was looking for. Even in the offline market, such a complete assortment of tickets could not be found.

Value-Added - The Supplier's Perspective

At first sight, getgo did not have anything to offer to the ticket supplying parties. Why should system companies agree to cooperate especially if they had their own Internet platforms in place? They were more in the line of a competitor than a business partner.

The answer was simple. The companies organizing events distributed the tickets through intermediaries, the system providers. Hence, system providers were dependent on the generation of high volumes, which made them more attractive for organizers. Most system companies were therefore interested in linking getgo's web-based platform to their system in order to generate additional volume to their business.

The Customers

The ticketing market has a very broad customer base, with customers in all age groups. However, the focus of getgo's customers was on rock/pop events, which reflected the main field of interest of the typical Internet user being under the age of 30. Since the age of web-users could be expected to rise in the future, getgo was aware of the fact that it needed to broaden its offer by strengthening other categories such as theater and opera.

In 2002, over 90% of getgo's customers were first-time buyers. The re-buy rate was low due to two factors. Firstly, most customers visited concerts and events only every once in a while, e.g. when their favorite artist was in town. Secondly, the real re-buy rate was actually hard to track since customers returning to the website had often forgotten their passwords and consequently created new logins. Therefore, the real re-buy rate was probably around 20%.

Organization and Internal Communication

The four founders of getgo made up the executive board and had equal voice. Each one was responsible for an individual business field. In the beginning, almost all decisions were made unanimously, but over time, they all perceived less need for common decision-making. Contracts could only be signed with at least two of the four founders signatures. Though not having really been friends before, they developed a trusting relationship, which also implied that everyone relied on the decisions taken by the others.

The management was eager to maintain a culture of open communication through regular meetings and cross-functional work. This culture was nurtured among all employees. With hierarchies being relatively flat, new ideas could easily be brought to the management and were pursued if they were convincing. This gave getgo the opportunity to act fast when promising opportunities were spotted. There was no need for a separate innovation management since the creativity and motivation of the employees often yielded new ideas. Besides the culture, another great motivator was having CTS as an "enemy". With their importance in offline ticketing and their huge financial power, CTS was the biggest player in the overall ticketing market. Despite the strong position of CTS, getgo had succeeded in winning 31% of the online market, where CTS only held 21% of market share (for an overview of market share of the competitors in 2002 refer to figure 3). This situation was perceived at getgo as a fight between David and Goliath and employees worked hard to extend their superior position in the online business.

Just like many other start-ups, getgo employed a large number of interns, which besides being very cost efficient, this arrangement brought in new ideas. Interns were often sitting in an office together with the founders. Working long hours and sometimes going out together at night contributed to the good relation between employees and management. The payment structure was flexible and could be adjusted to the performance of the individual employee. When new employees were recruited, they were always interviewed by one or two of the founders and special attention was paid to the fact that they fit the getgo culture.

Getgo was organized into four functions. The technical function, headed by Funk, managed all activities related to the portal itself as well as the technical connection to the partners. Operations, headed by Grözinger, was understood as a broad concept and also was comprised of the content of the website as well as customer service. This was also the field in which most of the approximately 35 employees were working. Furthermore, there was the marketing function, headed by Schäfer, and the finance and business development section, led by Söder.

5 Financing The Venture

"Getgo was probably the last B2C company in Germany to receive VC funding."

(Björn Söder)

The seed financing, needed for the creation of a corporation, was provided by the founders. After writing the business plan, the four had been looking for VC funding. Although, in April 2001, markets were on a steep downturn, getgo achieved being financed by two venture capitalists.

The two VC firms Econa AG and Equinet Venture Partners AG financed getgo's start-up for 20% of the shares. Being part of the network of the renowned advertising agency Scholz&Friends, Econa contributed to the venture in terms of marketing and brand development advice. Equinet, with its experience from their participation in other ventures like mytoys.de, the leading German online shop for toys, could give advice concerning issues of technological implementation. The investors' influence was perceived as good help, but over time and with growing experience of the getgo managers the value of investor's input depreciated. Overall, getgo was very satisfied with their VC partners: They contributed to the business with their advice, the contract clauses were fair and there was no pressure put on the founders.

Being satisfied with their VCs, there was no question of whether or not the four founders would approach them again for the second financing round at the end of 2001. Due to the bad market conditions, negotiations were harder and the VCs demanded a higher share of equity. Nevertheless, the four founders were able to keep far more than 50% of the business.

Even though getgo generated profits from July 2002 onward, a third round was needed to finance further growth. Increasing sales volume had also increased circulating assets. When for example a large stock of tickets was bought, high liquidity had to be available. While looking for new funds, getgo was approached by two companies. A big German publishing company offered a partial share deal, CTS Eventim offered a complete take-over of getgo.

6 Operational Challenges

"We stepped into the market without having anything. We did ticketing without tickets."

(Christoph Schäfer)

Getgo's business model highly depended on the cooperation with the major system providers. The cooperation with Ticket Online was realized without any problems. Soon, both had established a well functioning technical interface, i.e. a connection between the systems of both companies. Starticket was also willing to cooperate, but the technical implementation was less perfect and a lot of data still had to be entered manually into the getgo system. Getgo also got several important regional system providers on board.

Only one company represented a serious problem, CTS Eventim. They were number one in the system business but despite their latest efforts they had only made it to number two in online sales, right behind getgo. To the contrary of the founders' expectations, they refused any cooperation, relying on their own web-based platform. For this reason, CTS did not provide getgo with an interface, which would have allowed getgo to access the CTS contingent pool and print tickets just like a ticketing agency. This refusal had a serious impact on getgo's business. CTS was the strongest player in the rock/pop segment, and rock/pop ticket sales represented about 80% of the total German online ticketing market, meaning that an online ticket shop not being able to provide a high availability of rock/pop tickets would have to close its doors immediately. Tickets in this category were crucial for the success of the business, assuring high website frequenting.

The theoretically perfect business model of getgo had met its limits - reality. The founders realized that it was actually difficult to be in the ticketing business without being vertically integrated, i.e. without having direct access to tickets.

But the four founders did not want to give up easily. If they could not get the tickets from CTS, they would have to get them from somebody else. One strategy – especially for big events – was to meet directly with event organizers, purchase bags full of physical tickets and sell them later via the getgo website. Another strategy – more frequently used in the day-to-day business – was to cooperate with ticketing agencies connected to the CTS Euroticket system. Whenever getgo got an order for a ticket only available on the CTS system, they transferred it to a ticketing agency and shared the margin. Getgo's intention was to assure a high availability of the tickets on their website, not imperatively a high margin. This process was streamlined later on: whenever an order came in via the getgo homepage, an automatic fax order to their partner ticketing agency was generated. Tickets were then delivered once a day with a courier.

The distribution of tickets that had been ordered online required total quality processes. Sending wrong tickets to customers could cause severe problems since those

incidents were hard to track and customers could hardly be obliged to send the wrong tickets back. As fault tolerances of most machines were quite high, there were only little possibilities for automation in the shipping process.

7 Marketing

"If the product isn't right, even intensive marketing does not lead to success."

(Christoph Schäfer)

Internet-based companies faced different challenges in attracting customers than "offline companies". In the Internet, customers were exposed to an unmanageable amount of information, which made it sometimes hard to find what was actually needed. Furthermore, an Internet company had to "buy" all its customers in the beginning. In contrast to the brick-and-mortar world, no customer would notice the new shop on the web unless being directed there by a banner or some other referral. This had a major impact on getgo's marketing strategy.

Having observed other Internet start-ups' failures because of exaggerated marketing expenses, getgo's strategy was to maintain a strong cost focus in marketing. Schäfer was convinced that offline marketing would not pay off, with an average acquisition cost of at least 50 euro per end-customer, depending on the chosen medium. A customer, he argued, would never have been able to contribute 50 euro to the business. In contrast to most of their competitors, getgo therefore never did offline advertisement.

At that time, there were enough examples of bad marketing management around. In the fall of 2002, getgo's competitor Qivive for example spent an important budget for advertising in the German BILD newspaper, promoting the sale of Kylie Minogue tickets on their website. Getgo instead, knowing that tickets were extremely rare, directly bought a large number of tickets from the event organizer and offered those on their website. Fans soon found out that the best availability could be found at getgo's website, which increased their customer awareness without any money spent on marketing.

Even in online advertising, the classical model of putting banners on other websites was considered as too expensive and thus a new model had to be found. Schäfer therefore decisively relied on the success of a cost-per-order cooperation model. By establishing alliances, he integrated the getgo ticket shop into the affiliate's site. Getgo was able to implement their shop in the "look and feel" of their partners' websites by simply adapting the HTML templates of their software. Getgo only paid fees to their affiliates when a ticket was actually sold on the particular site. With an average fee of 2.5 Euro it could be assured that each transaction was profitable from the beginning. In

early 2002, about 50% of sales were made through affiliate partners, which proved that Schäfer's strategy worked out. The acquisition cost per customer had consequently fallen to 1.25 Euro at that time (for the development of acquisition cost per customer refer to figure 5).

Getgo had bought a proprietary web shop application from TWT Interactive, a web-solution provider that was run by one of Grözinger's friends. The price for this software was 50,000 euro, a remarkable bargain, since comparable solutions could cost up to 750,000 euro. In order to be easy to integrate into partners' websites, this solution had been enhanced internally. When purchasing a ticket through any of the affiliates' websites, the customer realized at the end of the purchasing process that the contracting party was getgo. The next time this customer wanted to purchase a ticket, getgo expected him to visit their site right from the start.

Getting a lot of media attention was another possibility to raise customer awareness at low cost. For this reason, getgo continuously developed innovative ideas to be published in press releases. The babysitter service promoted on the website as well as the ticket insurance were good examples for this. Those ideas were very effective since they demanded low management effort but still represented a nice feature for customers and gave the press something to write about.

The special events category on getgo's site often got remarkable customer attention. There, customers could find tickets for events such as the Oscar ceremony or Formula One races as well as passes to the VIP-lounge of hot concerts. Those tickets were not meant to make profits but rather to be an instrument of virtual marketing. Getgo customers who read about those special tickets in the newsletter often forwarded the information to their friends, which also increased the awareness of getgo's services among potential customers.

During the U2 tour in 2001, the idea of selling travel packages including concert tickets was born. These package deals turned out to be very successful. By bundling tickets with hotel rooms, an extra margin could be earned and fixed ticket prices could be circumvented. When ordinary tickets were sold out, buying the whole bundle could be a customer's only choice to still getting a ticket .

Just like almost every Internet company, getgo made use of the opportunities of one-to-one-marketing, which were technically easy to implement on the Internet. Registered customers were informed on upcoming events via email. Pre-registration for certain categories of information was also possible. However, getgo tried to evaluate the trade off between value added for the client and a growing objection against spam mails by the customers.

Getgo got feedback from its customers every day through emails, which helped maintain a close relationship to the customer. Incoming emails were organized in a database, read and bundled by employees and then distributed to the different departments.

Anna Bassler, Martin Heibel and Simone Sipply

8 Establishing Strategic Alliances

"Today, almost all big German online portals are our affiliates."

(Christoph Schäfer)

Experience at getgo had shown that Internet customers had little loyalty to the supplier, at least in the market of online ticketing. Customers mainly focused on the product, the choice and its availability. They did not care too much about where they bought the ticket and only tended to build up loyalty by making good experiences on a particular site.

At that time, big portals were used to receive high fixed payments from banner advertising. When the online advertising market started its downturn, companies could be persuaded to use the cost per order model more easily, because for most of them, getgo's offer turned out to be unique and value-adding. In fact, being in alliance with getgo was of common interest for both sides. For any portal service on the Internet, it was attractive to add the getgo ticket shop and event calendar, because this enriched their own offer at no initial cost. Especially when events were highly promoted or when tickets were rare, the integrated ticket interface generated traffic and kept customers on the affiliates' websites for a longer time. As a first important partner, getgo could convince VIVA - the biggest German music TV channel - to integrate the getgo shop into its corporate website (for a list of getgo's most important alliances in 2002 refer to figure 6).

9 Getgo - A CTS company?

After having passed through all these events that had come to mind, Grözinger was still walking back and forth in his office and trying to make up his mind about the CTS offer. For the four founders, it was evident that they would not accept the offer made by the publishing company, since the CTS offer was a lot more attractive: a complete trade sale and the possibility to become managers of the new media division of CTS incorporating getgo and CTS' own online ticket shop. Additionally, he saw the synergy potential. Getgo had a real value for CTS, because it could help them improve their own online activities, which up to now had not been successful at all.

But he was wondering what would happen to getgo once integrated into CTS. Would CTS be able to implement the getgo venture into their running business successfully, although they had not succeeded with their own online shop? He knew that selling to CTS meant destroying the original business model, because CTS would not be willing

to offer tickets for events on their website which were actually sold by other system providers. Additionally, the other system providers would not want to sell their tickets via the CTS website, this way generating traffic and also sales for their competitor CTS.

But what would happen to them as managers? Would they have any possibility to influence the further development of getgo? Would they be able to transfer to CTS what had made getgo such a big success? But he stumbled in this thoughts: what exactly had been the success factors of getgo? Why did so many others like CTS or Qivive fail, even though they had had better starting conditions? To especially evaluate this question he thought it would be best to sit down and elaborate those factors that had been crucial for the success of getgo.

Appendix

Figure 1: Sales and customer development

	Q4 2000	Q1 2001	Q2 2001	Q3 2001	Q4 2001	Q1 2002	Q2 2002	Q3 2002
Sales (Mio. €)	0.7	2.1	2.6	2.3	2.9	3.0	3.2	3.7
Page Impressions (Mio.)	2.2	6.1	6.9	7.7	11.2	12.3	13.5	14.9
Visits (Mio.)	0.6	1.9	2.3	2.3	3.4	3.9	5.7	6.8
Newsletter	5,000	20,000	38,000	52,000	75,000	98,000	112,000	130,000
Registered customers	8,000	65,000	88,000	103,000	135,000	182,000	202,000	250,000
Events	10,000	10,000	18,000	18,000	18,000	18,000	18,000	18,000
Employees	34	35	37	35	30	30	30	32
Orders	7,800	21,000	21,900	23,600	31,100	32,000	32,800	35,000

Figure 2: Seasonal fluctuations of ticket sales

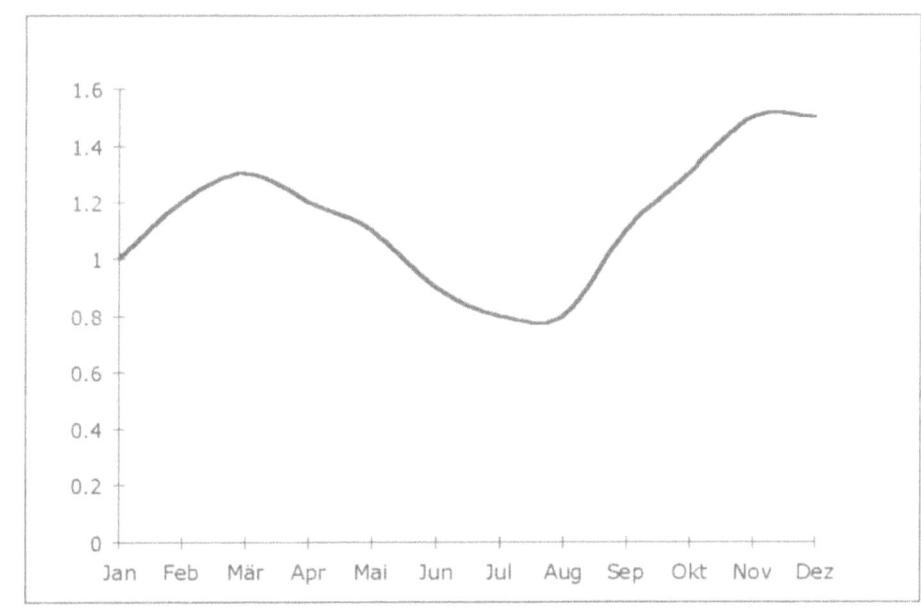

Figure 3: Market share of competitors in online ticketing in 2002

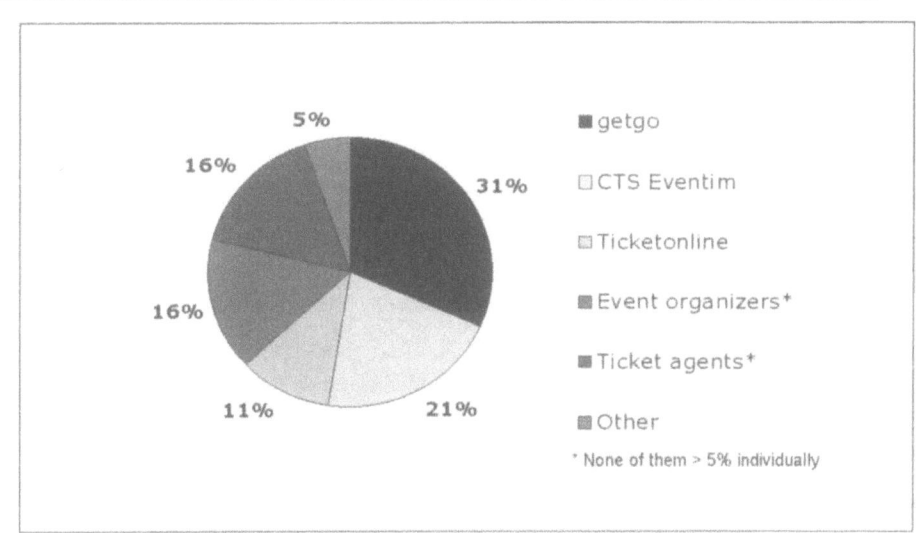

Figure 4: Getgo's business model

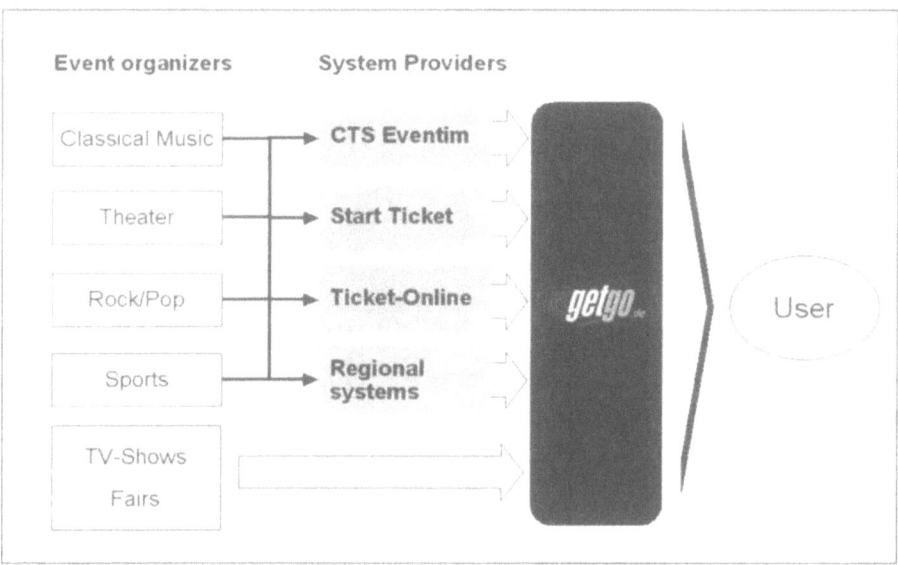

Figure 5: Development of acquisition cost per customer

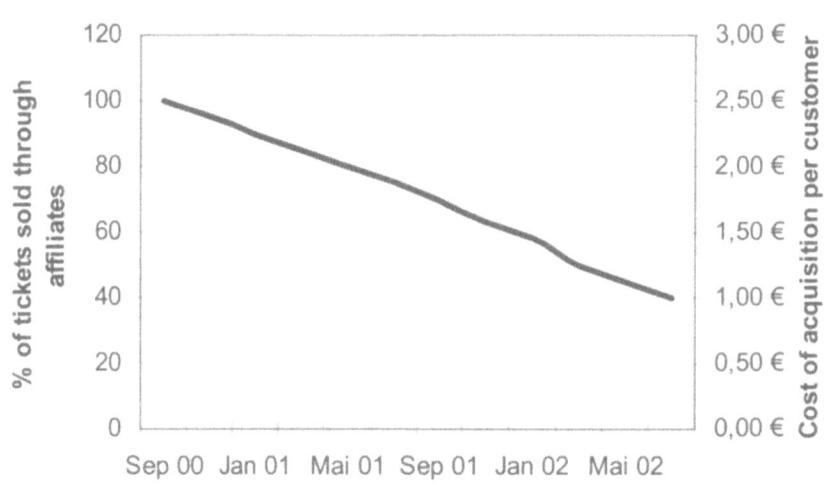

Figure 6: Major getgo partners in 2002

- **Music:**
    - Viva
    - Virtual Volume
    - BeSonic
    - Intro
- **M-Commerce**
    - Handy.de
    - Genion
    - Jamba
    - Destefora Mobile
- **Shops**
    - T-Online
    - Letsbuyit
    - Ciao
    - Dooyoo
    - MSN
- **Calendar**
    - Kulturekalender
    - Nexgo
    - Wunder Media
    - KulturNews
- **Radio/TV**
    - Radio NRJ
    - Radio Nora
    - Delta Radio
    - Radio Schleswig-Holstein
    - NTV
- **Other**
    - Tui
    - Primus Online
    - Abacho
    - Popkomm

Florian Beba, Sebastian Kösters and Tore Meyer

Guenstiger.de

1	Introduction	147
2	Market & Industry	147
3	Company Overview	149
4	Products & Services	151
5	Company Characteristics	154
	Appendix	158

1 Introduction

In October 2002, Philipp Hartmann, co-founder of the small Internet-company Guenstiger.de, looked at the latest company results. He was close to leaning back in his chair and to calling it a day. In the course of the last 3 1/2 years his website had grown from a small Internet start-up to the market-leader of price comparison sites in Germany, and generated considerable profits. His goal to add more transparency to the market was accomplished. Almost half of the German customers trying to find the best price for a certain product turned to his site. The development of a new holding structure was in progress, under which several new price comparison platforms such as Preissuchmaschine.de or erotica.de could address growth opportunities and new technologies in the near future.

Nevertheless, he was worried. Would he be able to carry forward the lessons learned; to make the new projects just as successful as the first one? He realized that in order to address this problem, he first had to identify the key success factors of Guenstiger.de and in a second step analyze how to apply them to future E-commerce start-ups.

2 Market & Industry

Comparison Shopping

E-commerce enlarges the possibility of search and comparison for shopping. The capability of searching for goods on hundreds of websites in seconds puts unprecedented pressure on online retailers to beat their competitors' prices.

Comparison shopping sites provide consumers with a tool, not only to search for products, but also to compare them in terms of characteristics and price.

The core of most sites like this today is a database, a so-called index, which retrieves the relevant data automatically from different sources on the web, or alternatively is updated manually. In this process, the question of product comparability arises. Price comparison sites mostly compare products from the same brand with the exact same characteristics (except the price) to circumvent this problem.

Florian Beba, Sebastian Kösters and Tore Meyer

Industry Structure Price Comparison

Over the last years a large number of companies, such as Preisauskunft.de and Price-contrast.com, went out of business. Torsten Schnoor, co-founder of Guenstiger.de, estimates that from 15 companies alive in 1999 only one third is still online. Most of these companies were VC-financed trying to achieve high brand-awareness through extensive Marketing expenditures. Due to a slow-down of the new economy and falling advertising revenues in the online market, future cash flows turned out to be overestimated. Especially international entrants were forced to recover their high investments by charging service fees from dealers, which turned out not to be accepted by users.

Today only four companies are left in the German market, not counting the entry of international competitors like the French Kelkoo. Guenstiger.de's direct competitors, Evendi.de, Idealo.de and Preistrend.de have been established in the market for at least 2 years, but have much smaller numbers of users and page-impressions. Guenstiger.de accounts for about 45 % of all price-queries while its closest competitor averages only about 15%, making Guenstiger.de the undefeated market leader in terms of users, visits and revenue. For cost saving reasons, competitors shrunk to a minimum size, mostly consisting of only a handful of employees, and heavily depending on automated data-retrieval and administration.

Through Philipp Hartmann's work experience and knowledge of the mobile market, Guenstiger.de remains the only company having transferred its business-model to the wireless application market, with a WAP and SMS service.

Market for Price Comparison

The target customer segment for online price comparison consists of price sensitive online shoppers, mainly interested in modern, technical products, e.g. computing or telecommunication products and consumer electronics. With over 30 million Internet-users in Germany and around one third of them being online-shoppers[1], the Guenstiger.de's relevant market potential amounts to approximately 10 million users, not counting users from the mobile service branch. The growth potential of this market can be considered as closely related to the number of online-shoppers.

With standardized products, most online shoppers do not care about the identity of the vendor as long as the price is right. Especially in times of economic downturns they are willing to use price comparisons, if the information can be retrieved in a fast and convenient way, while being accurate and valuable. The difficult economic situa-

---

[1] Source: NFO-Infratest - Internetnutzer-Monitor Euro.net

tion in the years 2001 and 2002 therefore helped Guenstiger.de and its competitors to increase its customer base, as more people actively searched for cheap prices.

3 Company Overview

The Early Days

In early 1999, Torsten Schnoor and Philipp Hartmann, both frequent Internet shoppers, started wondering how to find the best price for a product among the many offers on the Internet. They felt the necessity of completing the online shopping market, which had so far been characterized by severe asymmetric information problems. They decided to seize the opportunities of the Internet by providing independent and reliable price comparisons to all market participants. It became clear that a formal intermediary was needed to provide this service and in March 1999, still as a side job of its founders, Guenstiger.de went online.

In the beginning, it was top priority to have a working system, even if it did not include all possible functions right from the start. Adaptations and changes were implemented almost instantly, without much lead-time. Even though all prices were researched and verified manually, it was possible to start business with only a few (part-time) employees. About 90% of all search queries are for only 100 products and by concentrating on these popular items the founders were able to research all necessary prices by themselves.

The critical mass of users was reached after a co-operation with T-Mobile in the WAP service business. Although the mobile segment itself did not profit overly from this co-operation, the spillover effects of joint advertisement efforts on the Internet site's traffic doubled the number of users.

It soon became clear that Guenstiger.de could no longer be managed as a side job, as user demand rose constantly. As it was the continuation of a hobby on a different scale, Guenstiger.de chose the legal form of a GbR[2] and accepted no outside capital, in order to stay independent and be able to implement new ideas rapidly. There was no business plan, since the primary purpose had been to provide a necessary service, not to create a valuable company.

Torsten Schnoor: "We believed in the necessity of our product for the market and its superiority over competitors due to our independence. Consequently we decided

---

[2] GbR: „Gesellschaft bürgerlichen Rechts", German for „Partnership under the Civil Code"

against large-scale marketing efforts, thinking that by keeping our product superior it would advertise itself to potential customers. Plus, to be frank, we just did not have the money."

One year after going online, Guenstiger.de reached the financial break-even point and was able to finance its operations out of its own cash flow.

Stages of Development

Ad-sales on the Internet site were the only source of revenue for Guenstiger.de until the beginning of 2000. When prices for ad-space deteriorated new opportunities had to be seized. Based on the search engine, it was possible to record queries to generate anonymous data on customer behavior, which was useful to derive preferences and trends. This information was then sold to companies and wholesalers. Guenstiger.de decided to extend alternative streams of revenues by relying more heavily on data mining, as well integrating new products, like fee-based mobile comparison-shopping and price comparisons for financial services.

By summer 2001, the general economic environment turned from a state of rapid growth to almost recession, making customers increasingly price-aware. Demand for independent information on best prices rose rapidly. During this time, Guenstiger.de enjoyed a further period of high growth depicted in figure 1. Today Guenstiger.de is a GmbH[3].

Business Model Today

In October 2002, Guenstiger.de's business model of price comparison service still mainly relied on the same two revenue streams. On the one hand the user traffic on the Internet site enabled Guenstiger.de to sell ad space on the site to other companies. This stream of revenue is directly dependent on the number of users, meaning visitors to the Internet page generate approximately 40% of total revenues. On the other hand information on user queries is sold, generating about 60% of total revenues. Thus, direct customers of Guenstiger.de are advertising companies and organizations interested in anonymous user data. The actual users of the service of price comparison only generate revenues when using the fee-based SMS-service. Revenues generated in this line of business are marginal to date. Guenstiger.de acts as an intermediary and does not sell products directly to users.

The business model is based on four USPs (Unique Selling Propositions):

---

[3] GmbH: Limited Legal Company

1. *Independence* - meaning Guenstiger.de receives no provision from dealers for referred customers, and the process of ad sales is clearly separated from price information research.
2. *One-price strategy* - For every product only the best price is revealed to the user. This gives clarity and increases competition among dealers.
3. *User-friendliness* - The process of price comparison is designed as simply as possible. Users are encouraged to suggest improvements of the process and e-mail inquiries are answered within 24 hours.
4. *Price advantage* - resulting in an average advantage of 17%. In other words, customers save 17% when finding a merchant through the Guenstiger.de platform

A further point of interest is Guenstiger.de's complete concentration on online services. There are no comparisons for "offline" prices (although further new businesses of the founders offer for example comparisons of financial services) and no phone support for users. This is being complemented by mobile price comparisons via WAP and SMS.

4   Products & Services

Price Comparison

Guenstiger.de's core service for their users – price comparison – was initially launched as a personal website for the founders' friends and the idea that maybe other people might be interested in that kind of service. In order to minimize investment and ensure the quality of the data, research was done manually. Despite the rising trend of automated web search[4] used by other Price Comparison Services, Guenstiger.de stayed loyal to that principle.

Content Generation

Today a team of nine employees is responsible for researching the web for prices and updating the database. Research is triggered either from within the team or by suggestions from users about interesting products and prices. Users making suggestions are

---

[4] Automated web search uses bots (computer programs) to automatically search the web for relevant content. In the case of "Price comparison", websites of online dealers are searched for relevant products and prices are automatically stored in a database.

mainly dealers wanting to have their products listed but also people in search of products. After the verification of suggestions, users are notified of the listing of their suggestion or the reason why it has not been added to the database. Users also passively trigger research since search queries for non-available products are recorded, evaluated and, if suitable, are researched by the team to match demand and supply.

Guenstiger.de focuses on popular high-value, items in the categories: "Telephone", "Audio", "TV/Video/Photo", "Computers" and "Home Appliances", complemented with "Specials" heavily queried by users (even if they do not fit in the regular high value scheme). About 10,000 products are covered in the database and according to Philipp Hartmann it is imperative to cover the up-to-date trend products demanded by the market to satisfy users. The database is only used for Guenstiger.de and is not syndicated to third parties. To leverage users attracted by Guenstiger.de who can not find the desired products, HSID Verlagsgesellschaft mbH refers them to preissuchmaschine.de, their recently launched price search that uses automated web search to create the broadest product range available at German price comparisons.

To ensure quality, every dealer, product and price is verified and checked before being entered into the database. Checks are mainly done by web research and calling dealers. They range from verifying prices and shipment conditions, checking availability and ensuring nationwide shipment (corresponding to Guenstiger.de's nationwide service) but sometimes also include sample orders to guarantee compliance of standards. In order to present reliable information to the user, all data is updated frequently and, with the exception of the recently added area of geld.Guenstiger.de[5], is generated in-house.

To maximize the value that users can derive from Guenstiger.de's database, it can be accessed via Internet and WAP as well as SMS messages. The website shown in figure 2 is designed to provide users with simple access to basic functions, like a quick product search and links to the most popular categories, if users are not searching a specific model. When entering a category, users are presented with a list of ten products and their respective prices and the possibility to view all products of a company according to the category. The search-engine for products is optimized with regard to speed to reduce waiting time for users.

When selecting a product, users are presented a short description, a picture of the item (if available), one price and the contact data and shipment conditions of the dealer making the offer. The "One-price strategy" further reduces complexity for the user and, since prices are verified and nationwide shipping is guaranteed, other dealers and prices are not necessary. To maximize value for the user, this requires always the

---

[5] In the new area Geld.Guenstiger.de users can search for best terms and conditions for financial services, like loans, brokerage, building society savings, accounts and mortgages. The content presented is completely syndicated from forium GmbH, a company specialized on financial price comparison.

cheapest offer to be displayed. Guenstiger.de's price research is completely independent from any dealers or companies and no influence on the selection of the top offer is possible. The only criterion for selection is price which according to Philipp Hartmann is highly valued by the user and ensures Guenstiger.de top rankings in tests of price comparisons (for example the test of Stiftung Warentest in figure 3). Additional features and functions in relation to the product are available on the product page. The product information including some technical data is complemented by test results of the product (if available), user opinions and recommendations that are either displayed or referenced. If the user is not willing to buy for the current price, the "price alarm"-feature gives him the possibility to enter the price he is willing to pay. If this price is being offered by any dealer, the user will be notified via email. A direct link to the corresponding category is provided; the user can enter alternative sources and prices for the product, he can recommend the product to friends and he can also give feed-back with regard to the product and the dealer he bought/tried to buy the product from.

The WAP-Site offers basically the same service but is adjusted to the limited graphical possibilities of WAP and – in line with the generally low acceptance of WAP – is barely used.

Mobile price comparison is more accepted via the SMS access. The user can send an SMS with a product description to Guenstiger.de and Guenstiger.de responds by either sending a list to further refine the search or with price and dealer information similar to the webpage. This service momentarily costs 0.49 € per SMS and is the only way Guenstiger.de generates revenues directly from the user. To enhance the convenience of this service, it is also possible to use the barcode to exactly specify the product. Ideas had been around to create a regional price comparison (based on mobile access) for metropolitan areas and their regional dealers, but complexity of ensuring the quality of dealer information and limited demand halted further development of this project.

Ad space

In spite of the downturn of the online advertising market, ad space still generates about 40% of the revenues of Guenstiger.de. As a graphical format the company kept to simple standard banners to minimize objection by the user. To increase the value for advertising companies the ads are content related. Depending on the product searched, the ads will relate to the category the product and are dynamically adjusted while the user searches the site.

Florian Beba, Sebastian Kösters and Tore Meyer

Market Research

Market research was initially not even considered as a product but now is the second main pillar of Guenstiger.de's revenues and is intended to be further exploited. While ensuring the privacy of the individual user, behavior and preferences of users, in general, such as the products searched and prices demanded, are then analyzed and information about the market is derived. The marketing of research data is done without co-operating with special market-research companies but rather via direct contact to manufacturers, followed by wholesalers. So far, data is neither further customized nor processed with sophisticated marketing tools. In line with other areas, products are kept simple and the value is mainly derived from the high number of users, as the quality of market research statistically increases with the size of the sample. With increasing demand for trend research, new revenue potential for Guenstiger.de's abstract user data is created as seen through shifts in interest prior to sales. Companies like Sony already spend around 30% of their two digit million Euro trend research budgets on online data.

5 Company Characteristics

Guenstiger.de's sales amount to approximately € 1 million, with a margin of 30-40%. The volume of sales generated by users referred via Guenstiger.de with third-party dealers amounts to approx. € 200 million. With a market share of 45% Guenstiger.de is the market leader in Germany in terms of users, revenues and profits.

Financing

From the beginning, Guenstiger.de has been and still is being financed without any outside capital, whether debt or equity. Philipp Hartmann says:

"We intended to reduce business risk, as we had the legal form of a GbR and would be personally liable in the case of bankruptcy. At the same time, we wanted to retain the highest possible degree of independence, in order to decide and implement changes as fast as possible."

The cost of founding the company amounted to approx. € 7.700 and was regained after only a few months of operation. After one year, Guenstiger.de was able to finance their operations internally from cash-flow.

Organization & Human Resources

Even though personnel costs are the largest cost factor, the degree of corporate organization is rather low, thanks to a lean structure and somewhat flat hierarchy. Three levels can be distinguished. Firstly the founders, also being the current executive directors, who decide on business strategy, develop new products and manage public relations, as well as relations to customers. The founders are Torsten Schnoor, a former real estate agent and talkative networker, with many contacts in TV, radio and print media and Philipp Hartmann, who studied business economics for a few semesters and worked as a sales manager for E-Plus and as an account manager for B2B clients at Viag Interkom, both large German mobile service providers. Torsten Schnoor states: "We – as founders - see ourselves as rather risk-averse and economical. We are both interested in computers and technology in general. As a principle, we are never satisfied with our work and constantly seek to improve it."

On the second level are the six full-time employees, doing price research, team co-ordination and data base supervision. They also function as product managers, staying in contact with merchants and seeking the best prices. They need to be able to identify themselves with the product, be intrinsically motivated and be able and willing to offer constructive criticism where necessary.

Finally, there are eight part-time employees, all of them students for reasons of lower cost and higher flexibility concerning working times. They do the database research, for which no special qualification is necessary. Team meetings for all employees are held once a week.

Guenstiger.de is the largest company in this market and according to the founders, expanding made some hierarchy and organization necessary in order to relieve founders of some duties while giving second-level employees the freedom and authority needed. However the still very unnoticeable hierarchy and lean structure enables flexibility and quick decision-making and fast realization of new ideas needed to adjust to the changing market environment.

Technology

The use of technology is limited, but highly customized to meet the requirements of manual database input and data mining. Over time it was developed according to changing requirements and new features are added gradually. There is no systematic process for technology improvement but feedback is given directly from the employees using the software. Both, the software and the database were developed internally and by outside developers, mostly friends of the founders.

Florian Beba, Sebastian Kösters and Tore Meyer

The same was true for the Web Site itself, which was developed by a friend of the founders at extremely low costs. This was in part possible due to the simplistic design, which was necessary to guarantee a high level of clarity to the user and the possibility to update gradually. While downtime of the webpage was no problem during the early days, the increasing number of users now makes it necessary to plan changes of the live system carefully.

Innovation & New Product Development

There is no specific process or procedure for new product developments. The founders analyze opportunities for business enlargement on a non-regular basis, considering input from employees as well as users. After reaching the decision to implement certain changes, the "time-to-market," meaning the time span between the decision and the final steps of implementation, is extremely short.

While feedback from users is welcome and is checked for value-enhancement potentials, it turned out that few revolutionary ideas came from customers. They usually make minor suggestions with regard to the price comparison process or the form of information display.

Business Practices

When initially thinking about success factors, the founders identified various business practices they thought were important for business success and to differentiate Guenstiger.de from competitors.

First, Guenstiger.de never profited from "smart capital", from business angels or Venture Capitalists and did not seek any other kind of networking advantage to get started in the industry, even though both were offered from different organizations and individuals. The idea behind this was the desire to create a unique product, designed to fit the requirements of the market and the users, rather than the focus on the creation of a profitable and long-lasting company.

Secondly, Guenstiger.de recognized the importance of co-operations with large and financially liquid old-economy firms, like the T-Mobile co-operation mentioned before. While keeping most of their independence, Guenstiger.de could profit from large-scale marketing investments made by the partner.

"The end justifies the means," is also a practice used repeatedly to convince potential partners and customers of the quality of the company. This includes exaggerations of current features and numbers– only to a degree that these features could be added

quickly if necessary, of course – as well as shedding fear of contacting high-level people in large corporations if necessary.

Contrary to most business in virtually all industries, Guenstiger.de did not consider competition or the impact of their competitor's decisions on their business, for the same reason for which no outside capital was accepted. The goal was the development of a high-quality product to satisfy the needs of the users, which was possible without external benchmarking, but by analyzingown behavior. Nonetheless, Guenstiger.de constantly benchmarks internally, always trying to enhance the level of service.

Marketing (Price Comparison)

The founders believe in customer retention through a valuable product / service, rather than the constant acquisition and re-acquisition of customers.

For this reason, the marketing budget for Guenstiger.de to date has been less than € 500, excluding campaigns financed by partners. That does not mean that Guenstiger.de did not advertise itself in several different ways, but rather that it was done without spending money. Effective management of public relations was all they needed. Guenstiger.de has a database of 150 journalists in TV, radio and print media. Via personal contacts and after initial success, they managed to convince the media of the high quality of the product. Guenstiger.de was thus reported to readers and spectators as a new innovation in the e-commerce intermediary industry and benefits were explained in articles rather than through advertising. On the other hand, Guenstiger.de profited greatly from strategic co-operations with partners such as T-Mobile, in whose brochures and commercials Guenstiger.de was advertised at no cost to the latter.

Appendix

Figure 1: Development of traffic statistics for the website Guenstiger.de

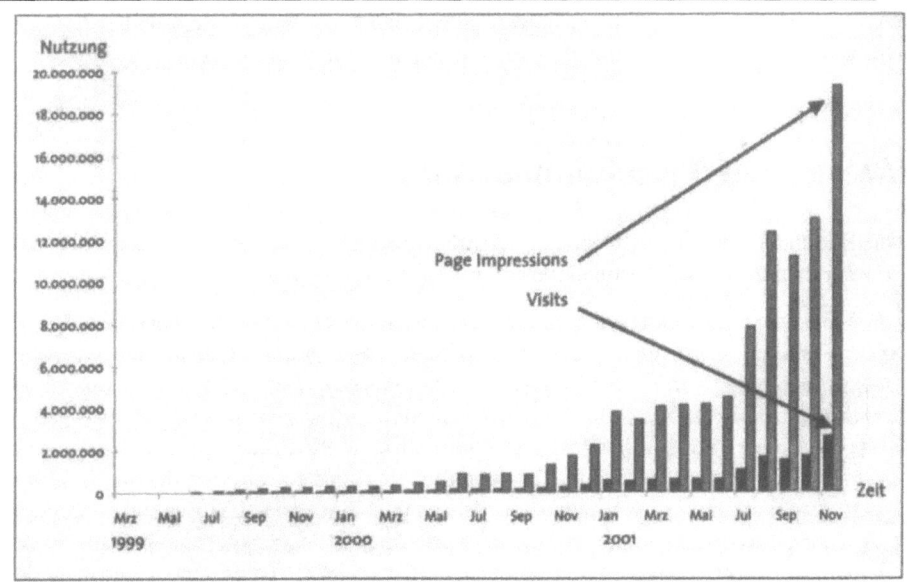

Figure 2: Main page of Guenstiger.de

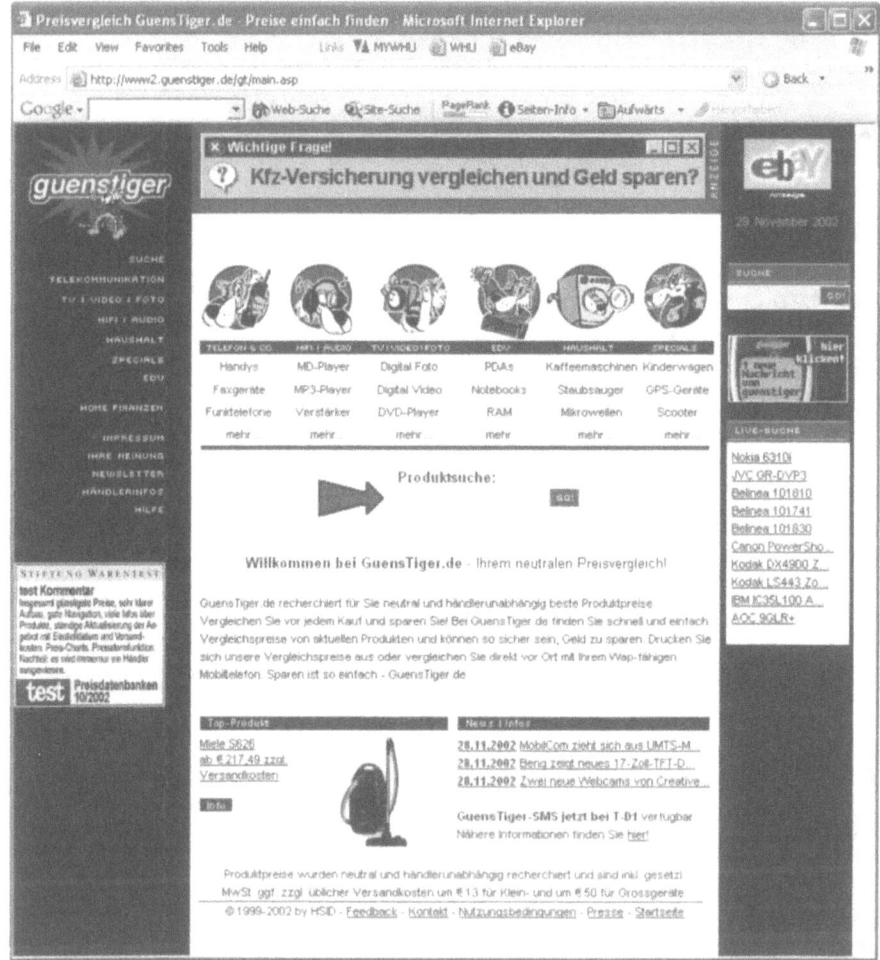

Figure 3: Analysis of German price comparison websites by Stiftung Warentest

STIFTUNG WARENTEST test KOMPASS						Preisvergleich im Internet test-Ausgabe 9/2000	
Anbieter	Preisersparnis (Durchschnitt)	Versandkosten	Angebot (gefunde Produkte)	Produktinfo	Handhabung		Urteil
Angebot-info.de	Relativ hoch (13.3%)	Keine Angabe	Meist mehrere Angebote pro Produkt (23 von 24)	Kaum	Etwas umständlich, Kennzeichnung best. Produkte (Neuheit, Testsieger). Suche weitgehend über Kategorien (keine freie Suche)		Empfehlenswert
DealTime	Schlechtestes Ergebnis im Test (9.3%)	Keine Angabe	Im Aufbau, mehrere Angebote pro Produkt (17 von 24)	Keine	Umständlich, verwirrende Aufteilung der Kategorien, Suchmaschine arbeitet nur innerhalb einer gewählten Kategorie		Eingeschränkt empfehlenswert
guenstiger	Relativ hoch (15.6%)	Keine Angabe	Sehr gute Angebote, nennt nur den günstigsten Anbieter (20 von 24)	Ja	Einfache, flexible Suche		Empfehlenswert
McWin	Relativ viele günstige Preise (16.8%)	Versandkosten angegeben	Sehr schmales Angebot, nennt nur den besten Preis (11 von 24)	In neuem Fenster (zeit-aufwendig)	Umständlich, Suche nur über Herstellermarken		Eingeschränkt empfehlenswert
preisauskunft.de	Unter-durchschnittlich, Ergebnisse sehr schwankend, kaum Top-Preise (10.4%)	Keine Angabe	Breites Produktangebot, meist nur wenige Angebote pro Produkt (18 von 24)	Gering	25 Kategorien, gute Suchmaschine		Eingeschränkt empfehlenswert
PriceContrast	Durchschnittlich (12.7%)	Versandkosten u. Lieferbedingungen angegeben	Bis zu drei Angebote pro Produkt (19 von 24)	Umfangreich	Nennt Handlernamen erst nach verbindlicher Bestellung, sehr gute Suchmaschine, zum Kauf Registrieren notwendig		Eingeschränkt empfehlenswert
vivendo	Unter-durchschnittlich (einzelne Highlights) (10.5%)	Keine Angabe	Sehr viele Produkte im Vergleich, wenige Angebote pro Produkt (24 von 24)	Keine	Einfach, Suche in Kategorien, nach Produktgruppen oder Produkten		Eingeschränkt empfehlenswert
Auf Computer und Telekommunikation spezialisierte Anbieter							
PT PreisTrend	Relativ hoch	Detaillierte Handlerangaben	Mehrere Angebote pro Produkt	Keine	Einfach und schnell, gute Suchmaschine		Empfehlenswert
eVendi	Durchschnittlich	Detaillierte Handlerangaben	Meist mehrere Angebote pro Produkt	Keine	Einfach und schnell, Suche über Kategorien		Eingeschränkt empfehlenswert

Stefanie Keuler, Fabian Neuen and Julia Reichert

Jamba! AG

1 The Company 163
2 Market and Competition.. 165
3 Business Development 168
4 Internal Processes and Facets 172

1 The Company

On Monday, the 7th of June 2003, 6:30pm, the area around the Schlesisches Tor train station in Berlin is still lively. Despite the late hour, there is still a crowd in the area, sitting outside pubs chatting and drinking beer. The Spree river flows gently and the atmosphere becomes more calm, young couples from all nations sit by the water, next to old industrial buildings, watching ships passing by. A mix of chaos, different cultures and summery idyll, and in the middle of all this, in one of these industrial-buildings, neon lights are still switched on and activities are hectically taking place.

Walking up the grey and derelict stairs, entering into a large loft, another world opens up when entering into the open space office with basic drawing desks and computers on it, young people in jeans and t-shirt breathlessly running around. Excitement and stress alike is in the air, you can feel the motivated spirit of getting things done – welcome to the Jamba! AG headquarters – one of the last "resorts" that manages to keep up a long lost era: The hot phase of Germany's New Economy. With the original idea of being a WAP-portal, ready established for the expected UMTS boom, Jamba! is today one of Germany's leading provider for mobile games, ring tones, logos and other entertainment services related to the mobile industry.

Not only the environment, but also the team has not changed much since the times of the DotCom-bubble. Like their idols from Silicon Valley such as Jerry Yang from Yahoo, the Samwer brothers, young "heroes from the Internet fairy tale", as German weekly newspaper "Die Zeit" named them, survived the internet bubble and are now successfully running and expanding their new business Jamba! AG. The "boy group" Oliver, Alexander and Marc from Cologne that had become famous for the spectacular founding and selling of their first company Alando in 1999, does not seem to have changed. Everything appears still very exciting, nice and colourful in their IKEA-furnished office and it is difficult to imagine that they are actually tough bosses and business men towards employees and partners.

6:45pm, thirty year old Oliver Samwer is standing in front of his desk, holding a mobile phone in his right hand. He is discussing frantically with a content partner and finally hangs up the phone. He pauses for a minute, wrinkles appear on his forehead, and he is thinking about a solution for the new Ilove-website, the company's latest internet service that will go online in less than a month.

At first sight, Oliver with his boyish "nice guy" looks might still pass as an enthusiastic undergraduate student. Only the words and expressions he uses do not really seem to match this picture, and his hair, covered by first slight tints of grey, make him look a bit more like his real age. Oliver, like his younger brother Alexander, 28, and his older brother Marc, 33, can boast an impressive curriculum.

Alexander finished high school with the best diploma in his state, North Rhine-Westfalia, and thereafter studied politics and economics at Oxford University. Marc studied law in Berlin, Cologne and Geneva and completed his studies as one of the best of his year. Oliver studied business administration and management at the Otto Beisheim Graduate School of Management (WHU) in Koblenz.

Oliver and his brothers have been exposed to an entrepreneurial environment all their lives as both their father and their uncle are entrepreneurs. Their early interest in entrepreneurship and their dream of establishing and managing their own company was highly supported by their parents, who gave them all the encouragement and help that was necessary: "They told us that we are unbeatable in a team and that they are always there for us", Marc recalls. During his studies at WHU, Oliver experienced entrepreneurship first hand as his university nurtured many entrepreneurs at the time of his studies: Nearly 25% of the graduates opened their own business. This environment matched very well with Oliver's prior positive contacts with entrepreneurship. Subsequently, Oliver founded his first company for felt slippers during an exchange semester in Chile. Fascinated by the upcoming start up boom in the US, Oliver decided to write his diploma thesis in Silicon Valley doing a success factor analysis of more than 100 of America's most successful start ups.

During his thesis writing with his friend Max Finger, also a WHU student, Oliver learned about the IPO of Ebay, the famous US-based online auction platform. He was fascinated by the success of this company and convinced his brothers to travel to Silicon Valley to assess the business model of this company, which they did in late December 1998. Even today, Oliver's eyes glow when thinking of this second trip to Silicon Valley. Everything went very fast and was incredibly hectic. Knowing that the German internet scene was about two years behind that of the US, they spotted the unique opportunity of developing a sustainable business. Two weeks after coming back from their trip they had gathered the required venture capital and founded Alando, a perfect copy of Ebay.

Only a hundred days after the launch of their copycat-website Alando, they went for a trade sale in August 1999. They sold their company to the US auction house Ebay for approximately 43m Euros in mid-2000. Having worked for one year in managerial positions at Ebay, the three brothers felt an "internal urge" to be entrepreneurs again. Even though the start up boom in Germany had already passed, they left Ebay to start a new venture. Again, similar to what they had done one and a half years earlier, Oliver and his brothers went travelling, this time to Japan, always in search of new business opportunities.

After a few months of hectic planning, they founded Jamba!, an internet-based portal for mobile applications. Using their network and especially their good relations to Dr. Cleven, Chairman of the advisory board of Metro AG at that time, they found strong old-economy retail partners to assist their venture. Debitel, MediaSaturn and Electronic Partners provided the initial capital of 30m Euros.

The passion and entrepreneurial spirit of the Samwers is still there today and is in the air, infecting all other employees today, and is certainly one of the success factors for Jamba!. The Samwer brothers had an exceptional educational background that served as an excellent basis for starting up their own business Jamba! as they were everything but inexperienced concerning entrepreneurship. The entrepreneurial history of the Samwers helped them to avoid typical start up-mistakes and allowed them to be faster and more visionary than competitors when founding Jamba!.

Jamba!'s management has always been highly committed to what they were doing. This included their lifestyle during their studies, their first business and also their first two years with Jamba!, which required high personal sacrifices from all of them. The founders of Jamba! have been convinced of their ideas at all time, fanatical about them, and, most importantly, they have always managed to convey these ideas in a passionate way to the growing number of Jamba! employees. Oliver knows: "If you want people to construct a sailing boat, do not tell them how to construct it, but fascinate them with the dream of sailing."

Another factor that contributed to Jamba!'s early success is the composition of the founder team. Oliver started Jamba! together with his brothers, two people he can wholly trust, and his close friend Max Finger, who belonged already to the Alando founder team. The team certainly constitutes a success factor, even though the founders may not be very complementary with respect to their educational background. They know each others strengths and weaknesses, and due to the similarity of their skills, they are able to perform the same task, e.g. negotiating with investors or partners. Extremely open communication allows them to use all their potential within the management team. The brothers' determination to build up something new was responsible for Jamba!'s creation, and the vision of building a business that will earn sustainable profit rather than short-term money ensures its long-term success. "If we look back today, we sold Alando too early", Oliver mentions. He also feels that they "have never really experienced the end of the New Economy", because Jamba! is operating in one of the most dynamic and rapidly changing markets.

2 Market and Competition

Jamba! is positioned as an entertainment provider in the mobile communication market. The company delivers information in a mobile phone compatible format to end users, but also value added services, such as premium SMS services, games and logos. To do so, Jamba! has to interact with several other industry players, such as network constructors, mobile phone manufacturers, network operators, service providers, and other content providers.

Stefanie Keuler, Fabian Neuen and Julia Reichert

Network constructors build radio towers and radio stations and thus provide the fundamental basis of mobile communication: The hard- and software needed to operate a mobile network. Main players include Lucent Technologies, Siemens, Ericsson and Nokia. Mobile phone manufacturers like Nokia, Motorola, Samsung or Siemens assemble mobile phones and thereby determine decisively the technological standard of mobile communication available in a certain region. Network operators like T-Mobile, Vodafone, and eplus buy technology and hardware from network constructors and mobile phone producers, and then connect different customers with each other. They do this by selling mobile phones to the end users and closing mobile phone contracts. The latter is also done by Virtual Mobile Network Operators like Debitel or Mobilcom. However, these do not operate their own mobile network, but buy the required amount of network volume and bandwidth from network operators.

Content providers offer self-produced or bought content to mobile phone users. This content ranges from information-driven content like stock market news, weather forecasts or traffic reports to entertainment driven content like logos, games or ring tones. Some content providers clearly focus on the information side (e.g. Financial Times Online), whereas others like Jamba! mainly provide entertainment services.

2.1 Market Development and Growth

According to a market survey by Axel Springer Verlag, the telecommunications market achieved a moderate growth of 0,9% to 63,8bn Euros in 2002. A significant contribution to this growth was achieved in the segment of telecommunications services, which grew by 5,1% to 53bn Euros. Mobile communication services grew especially rapidly. For the year 2003, the telecommunications sector is predicted to grow by about 3%.

Mobile communication services are expected to be the main drivers of market development in the future. About 70% of the German population possesses a mobile phone. Furthermore, a trend towards more technical features and supplementary equipment can be observed, nearly five million Germans are using the GPRS standard. The main hope for future market growth lies in new wireless services. Market specialists predict that multimedia messaging service (MMS), mobile email, instant messaging and mobile internet portals should further stimulate demand.

2.2 Main Competitors

Within Germany, there are only few companies that offer a similar product range as Jamba!. Handy.de, Wapme Systems and Zed can be regarded as the main competitors in the German market.

Handy.de offers similar products and services as Jamba! such as SMS based services, logos, ring tones, Java games and a WAP portal. Apart from that, the company also operates an online-shop, which comprises more than 15,000 articles of about 50 producers. Since the launch of the web page in April 2000, the recognition of Handy.de has increased significantly. About 750,000 possible clients visit the homepage per week. Handy.de has more than 3.5m registered users. The Hamburg based company employs about 60 people and has been a subsidiary of the large media corporation Bertelsmann since February 2002. The company markets its products mainly via the internet. Advertising banners on frequently used web pages like Google and free of charge logos or ring tones serve to draw the attention on Handy.de. As the company's products differ, so do the costumer groups. In order to account for these differences, the company presentation and image created is rather neutral and not focused too much on one target group.

Wapme Systems AG, founded in 1996, was one of the first companies to offer mobile internet services. Its services include SMS brokerage, premium SMS, MMS, WAP and software development. In addition to that it engages in software and hardware trade via its web page. Following its going public in July 2000 at the Neuer Markt segment at Frankfurt's stock exchange, the share price of the company has nearly steadily declined from an issue price of about 20 Euros to a low of 0.58 Euros. Only since spring 2003 has the share price been rising to a current level of 2.50 Euros. The initial issuing price reflects the enthusiasm for WAP services in the year 2000, the subsequent decline is explained by the disappointment of shareholders about the fact that the company could not live up to these expectations.

In the second half of 2002 the management of Wapme Systems decided to undertake a significant restructuring of the company with the aim of increasing profitability. As a consequence, the number of employees was reduced by half by the end of June 2002, one year later. On the revenue side, the company extended its activities in the most profitable business field of SMS based services and reduced its activities in the field of software development. In the first half of 2003, Wapme Systems generated revenues of 52m Euros, which is mainly driven by its online trading business. The main part of the EBITA, however, results from the value added services that are offered. Wapme Systems is based in Düsseldorf and has subsidiaries in Romania and the USA. In the future, Wapme Systems plans to concentrate on the most profitable business unit, value added services, narrow down the less profitable activities in software development and geographically expand its activities in North America.

Stefanie Keuler, Fabian Neuen and Julia Reichert

Zed is a Finnish company with subsidiaries in six countries: Germany, Finland, UK, Italy, Malaysia and the Philippines. The main shareholder of Zed is the telecommunications company TeliaSonera. Yahoo has a 15% stake in the company. Zed mainly offers SMS based products, like logos, pictures, ring tones and chat. It does not offer WAP based services or an online shop. The main target group is the entertainment seeking younger generation. Therefore, the appearance of the company and the image created is young, cool, and colourful. Ring tones, logos, and similar products are marketed according to the target groups needs via short and often repeated TV spots played on music television channels like Viva or MTV. In addition to TV spots, zed uses internet banners to attract potential customers. The company already has more than 5m users in Germany. In the near future, Zed Germany plans the extension of its Java games section and the introduction of MMS products.

Jamba!, in contrast to most of its competitors, mainly focuses on the entertainment market and is only engaged in information services via a limited number of SMS services, e.g. for news, sports and weather. This turned out to be a major success factor, as the entertainment business was accepted by the customers more than any other business and has currently about 5.2m registered clients. Another major success factor, with respect to the market, was the flexibility with which the management reacted to market changes. This proved to be critical, especially when operating in a fast changing and highly uncertain market like the telecommunications market.

6:50pm: Dirk Hoffmann, Jamba!'s CFO arrives with the latest edition of the daily business newspaper "Handelsblatt". He interrupts Oliver in his thoughts. "UMTS is not expected to break through before the second half of 2004" is written on the title page. Oliver feels affirmed: "Luckily, we didn't wait for the arrival of UMTS – as opposed to our competitors".

3 Business Development

3.1 Start Up Phase

When the three brothers and their friend Max Finger founded Jamba! in August 2000, their main idea was to create a WAP portal, in other words to become the home on every mobile phone. This idea had come up some time before, when the Samwers were travelling through Japan in order to get inspired by the telecommunications and entertainment driven country. The experience in that country, where DoCoMo's I-mode had already been spread widely, and the quite optimistic market forecasts for the German telecommunications market, made them believe that a WAP portal could become a successful business model quickly.

As in the case of Alando, they realized both the opportunity and the necessity of acting fast. The business plan was written within no time: From November 2000 on, the modern mobile surfer should have a vast number of possibilities of using WAP. It was the founders' declared goal that every mobile phone sold in Germany should have the Jamba! WAP portal pre-installed offering news ticker, stock exchange news, travel, and entertainment information, all individualized to the respective user's needs. Realizing the opportunities that would arise in the case of the spreading of GPRS and later UMTS, the founders deeply believed in their business model and the mobile economy.

The Samwers managed to get renowned co-operation partners and investors on board: MediaSaturn and Electronic Partner are both large chains of electronic stores in Germany. Debitel with 6.5m customers in 2000, is the largest independent telecommunications service provider in Europe. These co-operations made Jamba! much better equipped than potential competitors.

At the beginning of their operations in the summer 2000, the main task for the management and the first twenty employees was to get the business started, establish further co-operations with main partners and start selling their services. Consequently, all employees, no matter whether they were content managers, programmers or had a finance background had to work on productive, market related issues until 6pm. Tasks not directly related to market issues including press interviews and recruiting activities had to take place after 6pm, after the more important activities had been completed. With everybody working so hands-on, they achieved goals much faster than competitors did and therefore got a better feeling for the market which proved to be a main success factor in the following years.

During the first two years, there was not enough need to justify high costs for support functions like controlling, human resources or detailed market research that are not directly profit-creating. These business areas were necessary to some extent, but did not occupy a whole position. "Everything at the right time!" has been one of the basic principles at Jamba! right from the start that helped them to be flexible, move forward quickly, and stay efficient. During the start up period, there was no strict division of labor either. Nobody carried the CFO title, simply as there was no such role. Again, everything at its time was the key at Jamba!. The founders were flexible with regards to their work, and having similar skills and abilities means they could undertake the same tasks when necessary. To make this system work it was important to ensure trust and a constant flow of information within the core management team.

3.2 Expansion Phase

Nearly one year had passed by, but in the summer of 2001 the WAP market was still not taking off in Germany. The independent demand of consumers for WAP services

was not as strong as expected. The main bottle neck were mobile phone producers like Nokia and Siemens who failed to come up with mobile phones capable of GPRS and UMTS. It proved to be a miscalculation that mobile phones shown at fairs in early 2000 would be sold on the market only a few months later. At that time, experts estimated that the market for WAP services would not start developing before mid-2002.

Psychologically, this was a critical phase for the founders of Jamba!. Slowly, doubt started spreading around among Jamba!'s employees. The founders were sure that there was a market potential for WAP services and presumed that one day this market would develop. However, they were asking themselves over and over again, how long it would take until that day would come. How much longer would they have to wait for mobile phone producers to bring the necessary hardware equipment to the market? How long would it take before consumers adopted WAP services?

In these times, Jamba!'s actions were different from those of its competitors. Driven by their sense for opportunities as well as their extreme belief in getting things done and moving their business forward, the Jamba! founders did not simply want to wait. Instead, they realized that the ring tone business was developing much better than anybody had expected. Jamba! had started the ring tone business right from the beginning, but had expected it to be only a minor part of the whole business. In the meantime, it had become obvious that ring tones, which were inexpensive in development and production, were a successful cash machine.

In line with their principle of being proactive, the Samwers did not hesitate. Quickly, a marketing strategy was developed to extend activities in this business field significantly. Ring tones were marketed aggressively: They were sold on CDs in department stores or in form of so called Jamba! boxes at gas stations and supermarkets.

In terms of advertising, Jamba! joined its partners' activities in order to co-advertise its brand and services. Every month 20m flyers were distributed through the magazine of MediaMarkt, 12m flyers via Saturn and another 5m flyers through Electronic Partner in which Jamba! was marketed as the favourite WAP portal and ring tone supplier. In order to push the ring tone business even further, Jamba! aimed at charging the lowest price in the market to maximize its market share. As a result, their customer base doubled within a few months.

3.3 Further Growth and Diversification Phase

2002 was an important milestone in Jamba!'s history. The company had reached German-wide recognition and built up significant brand awareness. Based on that recognition and on a growing customer base of about 3m customers in 2002, Jamba! was able to accelerate growth. Additionally, Jamba!'s team understood how to use the technological advances in the telecommunication market in their favor: Mobile phones

with colored displays and Java functionality quickly gained market share. Jamba! continued to extend its product range and further marketed its polyphonic ring tones and its logos.

Jamba! turned digitalized current music chart hits into ring tones on a weekly basis in order to satisfy the increasingly demanding customers. Also, Jamba!'s highly skilled graphic designers and programmers continuously designed new logos and composed new sounds – a first step towards wireless entertainment. Further services such as mobile phone games were increasingly pushed into the market and met high acceptance among the mobile phone entertainment users.

In order to reach the maximum number of clients, Jamba! expanded its distribution channels by offering downloads not only via the webpage but also via mobile phone. Payment methods for these services included value-added phone numbers (0190-numbers at premium cost), prepaid cards, text messages and direct cash withdrawal from the bank account.

In March 2002, Jamba! introduced its first monthly subscription packages for ring tones, logos, and mobile games and thereby ensured a continuous revenue stream. For a certain discount the mobile phone user enters the obligation to purchase at least five of Jamba!'s services. Content billing takes place in the form of a partnership with the users' respective service provider. Here, once again Jamba!'s management used their networking skills to form co-operations with all service providers operating in Germany. The price of subscriptions are charged as a fixed amount on the regular telephone bill. This content billing via regular telephone bill turned out to be so successful that in a later stage it was also offered for single downloads.

Advertising was conducted in a more aggressive way than before. Jamba!, for the first time, invested considerable amounts of money into its own advertising campaigns, such as TV spots on music television channels such as MTV, Viva and Onyx. Furthermore, their print campaigns in youth magazines were intensified. To satisfy the Samwers' emphasis quest for proftable operations, detailed analyses were conducted after the first campaigns. These compared actual sales data a few days after the marketing efforts with their projected figures. There was no doubt that these substantial expenses would have been cut if they had failed to produce the desired outcome: Showing positive contributions to Jamba!'s bottom line. Since this was the case, the campaigns were continued. The Samwer's realized that it became increasingly important for their company to underpin management decisions with market data. Thus, a data researcher was hired to conduct market research based on website statistics, call center information, and general market data.

In addition to the original business area, Jamba! has offered a new product and service range since August 2002. In collaboration with Winterthur and Axa, Jamba! started selling comprehensive insurance packages for mobile phones, but soon expanded to various electric and electronic products, such as television sets or digital cameras. In

the start up phase of that business division, it was, once again, MediaSaturn who supported the launch of these services.

Jamba!'s revenue stream was again broadened which proved to be important for Jamba!'s further development by strengthening the brand in the offline world. Its offline presence was supported by its partners MediaSaturn and Electronic Partner, but also various gas stations, fast food restaurants and department stores.

The success factor of "everything at the right time" once again paid off. In this third phase, Jamba!'s management used all resources to further expand the business. By searching for new opportunities and evaluating then systematically, they secured an ongoing growth of the company. Due to their good intuitions, they expanded their current product and service range and entered into profitable new business areas. Actively pushing marketing activities on a broader basis avoided a decline in revenues which occurs to many young companies when they grow out of the "baby stage".

4 Internal Processes and Facets

4.1 Controlling

The role and the importance of controlling has changed significantly over time. As there was no role for a CFO in the beginning, Dirk Hoffmann, formerly employed at the consulting company Booz Allen, who joined the company shortly after it had been founded was first assigned to other jobs, especially new business development. All accounting work was done in the evenings. This ensured that "productive time" with (potential) clients and partners was not wasted on back-office work, that does not directly generate additional revenues.

With Jamba! continuously growing and gaining a more solid financial basis, the necessity for a controlling department arose. There again, as in all business areas, the basic principle of 'doing everything at the right time', stemming from the management's deeply inherited cost consciousness, became visible: Expected benefits of a quantitative controlling function finally justified its costs.

Currently, about five people are working in the accounting and controlling department, supporting Dirk. His main working area today lies in checking the effect of all kind of business decisions on the company's quantitative performance using financial data, as well as call center and website statistics. With increased performance of the controlling department and due to his very analytical background, Dirk has turned into the numerical consciousness of the more creatively thinking founders. Oliver admits that "Dirk has turned into a grey eminence in the background", but he thinks

of it as a key success factor. He believes that Dirk secures rational decision making and that he helps to balance the innovation-driven ideas of the entrepreneurs with solid cost-benefit analyses. As Dirk has been involved in all contract developments since the very beginning, he knows exactly how the business model works and uses this extensive knowledge to firmly evaluate new business ideas and deviations from the current system.

At 7:00pm, Marc enters the founders' office. "Oliver, the candidate for the game programmer position is waiting in the meeting room. I have another phone call with MediaMarkt concerning our new campaign. Do you mind interviewing him?" - „No Problem". Just as Marc and Alex, Oliver knows exactly what Jamba! expects from employees and what character traits and skills they have to possess in order to contribute to Jamba!'s success.

4.2 Human Resources

Oliver believes that a good business is not only driven by a gifted management, but also by a competent, diligent, and hard-working team. Thus, careful staff recruitment was a major issue for the success of the company. Currently, Jamba! employs about 60 IT specialists, 40 content managers, 20 employees in a new business division and about 15 persons in the insurance business – and is still looking for additional staff.

For its operations, Jamba! continuously needs a certain number of well educated IT-staff. For other job positions, such as content provider, the kind of education is less crucial than the actual skills. Nevertheless, in the beginning, at least two managers interview the applicants and decide on a unanimous basis whether to offer them a job or not. Selection criteria include having specific knowledge and, equally important, social competence and flexibility. These criteria are valid for all employees, no matter whether they are regular staff, interns or part of the core management team.

The legally available concept of a 6 months probation time is fully used at Jamba!, and it is a hard knockout criterion for many people. Management is ready to be tough and take all necessary actions, such as not employing people after their probation time. Only those employees are offered a permanent position, where management feels that they belong to the company, understand the corporate culture, and possess an entrepreneurial spirit. This intentional sieve process is necessary and helps Jamba! to stay as flexible and entrepreneurial as it has been from the beginning. Working hours were quite long in the company's first stage, but have been reduced to about 40h to 45h per week on average after the first two years for staff and management.

At Jamba!, there is no such thing as a continuous career development – Jamba! is still too small for predefined career paths, internal coaching systems or career monitoring by HR employees. Nonetheless, management tracks employees' performance. This will

eventually result in better job positions or monetary incentives, no matter in which position one has started to work at Jamba!.

The Samwers have started to selectively establish a second management level. Dirk Hoffmann, Jamba!'s CFO, who already joined Jamba! shortly after foundation in 2000 and Markus Berger-de León, COO, who joined the company in 2002 belonged to the first members of the "core team". Frank Biedka started as CTO in December 2000. Furthermore, additional junior management staff was directly recruited from various business schools: Jens Begemann is now Chief Content Officer, Martin Ott is responsible for Jamba!'s marketing activities, Christian Vollmann takes care of the soon to be launched online dating business www.ilove.de and Sebastian Rieschel is running the insurance division. Hiring new junior management staff became even more pressing when Max Finger left the company at the beginning of 2002, in accordance with his friends, in order to take over his parents' company. Compared to other companies in the mobile industry, Jamba! employs a large number of very well educated young professionals.

It was crucial for Jamba!'s further growth to develop a core team that supports the founders in further expanding and developing the business. As Oliver puts it: "I trust my core team to move our current business forward, selling even more entertainment products, so I can concentrate on identifying the next generation of entertainment trends." The Samwers knew precisely, what employees the company needed and when to fill each position. Having a team they can trust also results in enriching ideas, and a stimulating working atmosphere. This has two major consequences: Valuable inputs and perspectives are generated for Jamba! and people enjoy the responsibility and the way they are contributing to the company's success.

In retrospect, a mistake, that slowed down Jamba!'s development was to wait just a bit too long before delegating more responsibilities. The founders had never experienced that business size and stage of corporate maturity before. Only slowly, they realized the importance of balancing control and delegation. Since then, the Samwer brothers have been concentrating their efforts on what they think they know best: New business development and working on the conceptual rather than the operating level. They have delegated more responsibilities for the daily business to their core team. Close interaction between the founders and the core team still exists to the same extent, while the flow of communication with the rest of the company slightly shifted towards the respective business area directors.

While for regular staff, payment terms are comparable to the ones of large companies, (e.g. Deutsche Telekom), management's compensation packages are very lucrative. Some managers have left renowned companies, such as McKinsey or Booz Allen in order to work for Jamba!. Jamba! succeeds to attract and retain highly qualified managers by offering attractive compensation packages, even though no shares in the company are offered. Equally important is the transparent, dynamic working culture which enables employees to gain responsibility quickly.

Jamba!'s founders recognised the fact that people are a decisive success factor in their business. They managed to find the right way of being cost-consciousness but also knowing when someone is worth attracting. "I have been here only since two months, but apparently, the brothers like what I do. Now I am already responsible for the contracts for TV commercials with MTV", Martin Ott claims and thus confirms that the fast gain of responsibility and the entrepreneurial working style at Jamba! is real. Nevertheless, the founders still retain the final decision making responsibility, especially for deals and projects of greater importance and investor relations.

While Oliver is conducting the interview in the conference room, there is still immense action in the office, since the launch of the new web-based services Ilove and MyFriends is only one month away and there are still many things to be prepared. Even now, at 7:15pm, a time when many offices are already closed, there is no question about going home for the respective employees working on the launch project. Both, employees and management leave when the work is done. They all understand the necessity of being more flexible and faster than other big players in the mobile industry, giving Jamba! a vital competitive advantage. „It is important to understand and like our corporate culture, since we will only have mutual benefit if you fit with us", Oliver is explaining to the candidate during the interview.

4.3 Corporate Culture and Leadership

Corporate culture at Jamba! is characterized by the New Economy working style, which implies casual clothing, extensive but relatively flexible working hours and a relaxed atmosphere, which is supported by the modern open space office with large windows, friendly colours and a great location, next to the river Spree. Everyone at Jamba!, including management, is still walking around in sneakers, jeans, and t-shirt, preferably with a Jamba! logo printed on it. The founders and the entire management differentiate themselves from many other start up-managers. In public, they always appear modest, very approachable and extremely pleasant – and not arrogant or egocentric. They are like the nice, smart guys from next door.

However, unlike many Berlin-based start up companies, they did not participate in organizing large Caipirinha-parties on a weekly basis in 2000 and 2001 for their staff. This was not the way they wanted to present themselves and it was considered a waste of money rather than effective employee motivation. It is more important for the three brothers to create the feeling of a corporate family which makes employees feel that they all belong to Jamba!. This was considered a long term motivational factor, which seems to pay off. Many new economy companies failed to create a working atmosphere that supported the development of a sustainable business after the initial start up phase. The Samwer brothers understand the importance of living and executing a

corporate culture with realistic and simple principles. A clear understanding of those principles by every employee is absolutely essential for Jamba!'s long-term success.

A symbol for the high level of integration of all employees into the company's operations is the corporate kitchen. Virtually, the entire staff meets in there, gets food or drinks provided by the firm and exchanges ideas and opinions. The management knows that the kitchen enhances an open communication flow and supports the already open culture in the office. Shortened paths of information and increased employee motivation, as well as less lost working time for outside breakfast, lunch or dinner are valuable side aspects for the company that are still valid today. Due to the corporate kitchen and the open office, communication is uncomplicated, teams are able to get together quickly and a huge brainpower-pool for upcoming challenges is nurtured.

Hierarchies at Jamba! are flat and responsibilities are clearly assigned for each project. One of the basic characteristics of Jamba!'s corporate culture is the extreme sense of urgency that was built up and that implies the constant pressure for action and improvement, but also for a zero defect mentality. The latter refers to the quality of work employees have to deliver. Management expects all documents, presentations, and files to be delivered of the highest quality and ready to be handed over to third parties.

The sense of urgency is considered as so important because the brothers believe that it gives Jamba! a competitive advantage to be faster and better than competitors. Their motto is to "change the world today rather than tomorrow". Thus, the words "execute, execute, execute!" were literally in everyone's mind. This principle is not just inherited by every single employee because he experiences the pressure of working fast and precisely on a daily basis, but primarily because the founders and the core team are living according to the same principle. They represent a credible role model and motivator for their staff.

"Every day I walk several kilometres", Oliver states, showing the importance of a close bond between the founders and the employees. The brothers' leadership style is characterised by an approachable attitude. A culture, that should help increase the employees' motivation and their feeling of always being supported and their work being taken seriously. To support this action, the founders know, despite the company's size, all 135 employees by their names. The brothers believe that, especially at this quite early point of time, their direct leadership style is a major success factor. Not every employee matched into this environment which also implied steady control, but those who could stand the pressure of having to deliver the highest quality results and being constantly monitored, are enthusiastic about working for Jamba!. It is these people who would then stay longer than the six months probation time.

A second basic characteristic shaping Jamba!'s corporate culture is the fact that everyone is expected to help and support projects, whenever the need arises. As a start up faced with the challenges of having too little manpower, it was obvious that everyone

had to offer support when asked for. This attitude led to spontaneous get-togethers and a very hands-on working style: When projects received a 'go', they immediately started operating. The same was true for important daily issues: Instead of organizing "monday meetings", spontaneous updates were regularly held at the respective individuals' desks.

Finally, cost consciousness is the third characteristic within Jamba!'s corporate culture. Employees are expected in all situations to fullfil their tasks at minimum costs. This results for example in flights in economy class. Christian Vollmann smiles and says: "In order to save travelling expenses, we often sleep at our friends' places or otherwise rent cheap hotel rooms when travelling for Jamba!." The cost awareness is also permanently visible through simplistic, modern IKEA furniture in the office.

Regardless of age and position, everyone at Jamba! has to follow these simple, but essential rules framing the company's culture. Oliver Samwer knows that these rules are only accepted because the founders 'walk the talk' and show everyone that they also stick to them. Keeping up and living these principles is a major success factor for Jamba! since credibility is an extremely important factor when leading people. Although Jamba! has grown to 135 employees, the corporate culture has remained the same. It is still based on friendship, trust, and a familiar start-up atmosphere, but also high demands, constant time pressure, and total passion about the company. Thanks to their distinct culture, clear principles on all employee levels and the right role model behavior of the founders' enables Jamba! to move faster than competition and to survive times of difficulties even with a larger employee base.

Oliver Samwer considers himself and his brothers as some "sort of control freaks", which is expressed, amongst other initiatives, by management walking around. Since its founding, Jamba! always had a distinct leadership style, pushing all employees to be productive in their work, mainly by marketing the Jamba! brand and services efficiently or by closing new partnerships and exploiting further revenue sources in the financial area. In the start up stage, employee performance was measured on a daily basis. During meetings in the evening, each employee had to present to the team, what he had done and achieved within the last 24 hours. Jamba!'s management understood the importance of practising a controlled and open communication and information flow.

With the increasing size of the business, this review system was changed. Nevertheless, even today, directors of each business area within Jamba! now monitor their team's work and effort closely. Marc Samwer justifies the control mechanisms in the following way: "Being an entrepreneur consumes a lot of energy. It really hurts seeing people just wasting energy by doing a bad job!" Thus, praise was always immediately given for a good job, but managers also approached employees directly if they did not fulfil a task well. "Although this can be demotivating sometimes, I must admit, that their criticism is always justified and constructive!", an employee says.

The Samwer brothers cultivated a patriarchical leadership style but at the same time encouraged an unhierarchical, transparent, and open communication flow. Oliver claims that "sharing information when interacting with the team members is also an important part of the way we conduct our business". He knows that, besides tight control over the main business activities, sharing brings a high added value via both new business ideas and increased employee motivation. For the brothers, interaction plays a key role in the way of doing business, not only with their staff, but also with their business partners where they seek for a continuous relationship improvement.

4.4 Partners

When starting Jamba!, the brothers were already known in the start-up scene. During their time with Alando, they had established excellent networks in the business, media, and financial world. The brothers managed to maintain these relationships, which ensured them to have favorable access to both various material resources and emotional support. Their ability to negotiate with partners, suppliers and investors alike, turned into a major success factor for Jamba!. Oliver and his brothers understood the importance of good connections to other people. "Do favors for others and favors will be done for you" is one of the principles that has helped the brothers grow their business successfully until today. Using their excellent networking abilities in favor of Jamba! ensured the company to receive exceptionally high support in the mobile industry.

One of Jamba!'s success factors in the early phase was certainly that they did not only have people investing into their business, but also giving important advice and opening many doors. In a time, where the DotCom bubble was about to burst and venture capitalists were reluctant to support young start ups, they felt the advantage they had due to their first start-up experience with Alando.

The most prominent supporter of Jamba! has been Dr. Cleven, until recently board member of Metro Group, Europe's leading retailer. When the brothers told Dr. Cleven about their new business ideas and finally presented their business plan, he recognized the opportunity and was ready to use his connections in order to establish the right contact to future investors. Dr. Cleven acted as "door-opener" and successfully established the ground for several partnerships between Jamba! and old economy investors. Since its foundation in August 2000, Jamba! managed to attract several strategic partners and investors from the old economy with the help of Dr. Cleven.

But Dr. Cleven's role comprises more than that of an influential contact person: He was Oliver's, Alexander's, and Marc's mentor offering a lot of immaterial support. He supported them in business and management situations that they had not experienced in their 100-day business at Alando before and helped them to successfully

overstep the threshold from a start-up to a young, growing company, a point where many start ups failed. "Dr. Cleven helped us to improve our meetings with the supervisory board, he was completely egoless and was always acting in the best interest of the company. He played a key role as chairman of the supervisory board at Jamba! where he managed to balance the strategic investors' interests."

"We do not want to operate business on a small scale but rather capture a large part of the market", explains Peter Wagner, CEO of Debitel, a major telecommunications service provider in Germany. Debitel believed in the Samwers' business ideas and their ability to set standards. Hence, Wagner was ready to invest heavily and use Debitel's extensive German customer base of 6.5m as a starting point for Jamba!'s successful market entry in the mobile industry. One main attraction point for the investors was that only about 5% of users change the presetting of their mobile when going online. Thus, the use of Jamba!'s services by WAP-users was pretty easy to encourage by marketing and pre-setting actions.

To increase people's awareness of Jamba!, the management teamed up with large electronic retailers. MediaSaturn, Germany's largest electronic equipment retailer, took a share of 15% in the company, just as Debitel. The reasoning behind their heavy investment was the business idea combined with the right people executing it. "Jamba! has the right strategy and the right management team" praised Leopold Stiefel, CEO of MediaSaturn. Electronic Partner, another large electronic equipment provider took a stake of 10% in Jamba!.

With these strategic partners the founder team ensured both their financing by acquiring initial investments of Euros 30m and the marketing of their company and its services. Again, their ability to network and negotiate saved Jamba! large sums that other start-ups were investing in advertising. Jamba! received a high publicity via co-advertising with their strong partners. By 2003, all German mobile phone operators were co-operating with Jamba!, including T-Mobile, Vodafone, eplus and O2. Furthermore, many new partnercontracts, especially in the retail and content business were signed.

8:00pm at the office entrance: Oliver accompanies the interview candidate to the door. While walking back to his office, he notices: "Even our chairman, Dr. Cleven, could not teach us on how to run our business with low operating costs".

4.5 Finance

Cost consciousness is executed everywhere at Jamba! and helps to avoid financial difficulties, compared to other start-ups that burned tremendous amounts of cash each week and therefore did not survive the first phase of growth. Since the founders were recognized throughout the entire German-speaking finance community, including

business angels, venture capitalists, investment banks, and their most valuable contact Mr. Cleven, Jamba! had an unusually good head start. Although the equity share market was in decline in summer 2000, Jamba! received about 30m Euros within a short period of time to establish their business in Berlin Kreuzberg. The founders invested part of their private capital as well, highlighting their entrepreneurial commitment. The founder team kept about 30% of the company. Oliver Samwer remembered, that "for the original business plan, we would have needed all that money, but then everything changed!". Jamba! would only have needed about 4m Euros during all these three years".

Three years after starting Jamba!, the Samwers have proved that they are not only able to found companies, but also to ensure sustainable success. In retrospect, Oliver even regrets that he and his brothers have misjudged the initial market situation. "Jamba! would also have been a success without that comfortable cash reserve. From our personal view, it would have been more motivating to hold more shares in the company".

The Jamba! team has not only been cost-conscious at all times, but also profit-oriented. Every single activity had to lead to measurable results. "Many new, great ideas are coming up each week in our company. If after a preliminary check these ideas still sound monetarily interesting and receive two thumbs up by Dirk Hoffmann, small project teams are assigned to them", business development manager Tabi Bude explains. "This team has then to show that it is able to launch the idea with a minimum of resources." Thereby, most ideas are gathered top down, but it is even more welcome to propose new business ideas bottom up.

This principle of taking opportunities, that proved to be beneficial, is one of Jamba!'s success factors. Since the company's start, all activities that generated cash were massively expanded. A good example is the fast growing high margin ring tone and logo business which developed into a major revenue source, although it had been planned as a marginal business in the beginning. On the other hand, manpower in the WAP business had to be reduced significantly in 2001, as WAP had not turned out to be the much-desired "killer application".

There have always been rumours about Jamba! concluding an IPO, but until mid-2003 market conditions have not favored this action, and the management did not see the added value and necessity in raising additional funds for the price of being public. Nevertheless, Jamba! would be ready for an IPO. Internal processes have become more and more standardized and the juridical form of an incorporation exists since Jamba!'s inception in 2000.

4.6 Current Situation and Outlook

Today, Jamba! is in a relatively comfortable position: The most recognized telecommunications service providers in Germany hold equity stakes. More than 5.2m users have downloaded a ring tone or a logo from the Jamba! website. Jamba!'s advertising spots are present on various music television chains, such as Viva, MTV and their affiliates. Furthermore, Jamba! still benefits from its enormous marketing exposure thanks to its strategic partners, like MediaSaturn or Electronic Partner, and is highly present with its on- and offline marketing mix. Print advertising is done in youth magazines, like Bravo, Young Miss, and Mädchen. Online campaigns are booked as run-over-network campaigns, "as they are less expensive", Christian Vollmann adds.

While Jamba! enjoyed large media presence for their new product launches, corporate news is hardly communicated. From the founders' perspective, the discreetness about company information is considered as a success factor. However, 2003 will bring numerous important milestones for the company. "We now know the internet and the German multimedia market very well" states Oliver: The founders learned from the market and it appears to be a question of time until international expansion will be continued. Apart from moves into the Netherlands and Switzerland in its early stage in 2001, Jamba! currently focuses more on the German market.

Today, there is an increasing number of indications that Jamba! might soon go international and either grow internally or externally abroad. It is thinkable, that Jamba! will enter the American market by an acquisition. Additionally, the Asian market has a high priority for Jamba!'s management. Due to market entry regulation, a joint-venture into Asia's booming telecommunications market would be the most likely entry strategy. However, Jamba! will ensure, that an engagement abroad would be worth the efforts put into it, which was not the case for Switzerland and the Netherlands where growth rates are low. In Germany, the company has ambitious goals for 2003. "In fact, we are convinced that Jamba! could become another 'United Internet'", Oliver Samwer draws out his vision. Thereby he refers to the publicly listed German company United Internet AG, which successfully offers various internet-based services.

9:45pm in the Ilove-corner of the office: While it is getting dark outside, Christian Vollmann, the responsible manager for the new business division of dating services, broods over a development issue for the future website of Ilove. Oliver Samwer comes to his desk and both young men discuss the challenges for Ilove and MyFriends, that are waiting ahead. Oliver points out that these two new services will be a highly important step towards the new corporate vision of being a holding company for mobile and web-based applications.

Only one month ago, the idea for Ilove and MyFriends was born. In fact, Jamba! is imitating a successful German and American internet business model comparable to Friendster.com or Match.com. Friendster is a friends network application, where those

registered have the possibility to get in touch with friends of their own friends. Match is an online dating channel. Shortly after this business opportunity for the German market had been recognized, the first programmers and web-designers were assigned to prepare the respective websites. After three busy days, the first results were available for further discussion. Layout was set, but technical implementation still requires to enable a tracking systems which should eventually allow effective online marketing.

Concerning the dating division's future, Oliver Samwer believes that in the medium run, Ilove and MyFriends will turn into a profit center, via advertising, value added services, cross-selling and – some months after the launch – membership fees. "People will always pay for dating and friendship-networks", Oliver is convinced. He expects to have about 250,000 registered members at the end of 2003. Interestingly, Christian and Oliver do not intend to launch the new services under the Jamba! brand, as this is the case for the insurance division. "This would rather dilute the brand, that's why we intend to launch them separately", they explain. "We do not want to become another Yahoo!, where you get lost on the portal page." However, the two are aware of the fact that at least for the dating platform, they would be not be a pioneer in this market – an untypical situation compared to Jamba!'s original business idea.

However, Jamba!'s basic principles and corporate rules remain and the most important one at the moment is the focus on profitability. "All of our businesses should be profit centers", Oliver emphasizes. The hiring of more than 20 people within the last two months shows that major investments in future business activities are wanted. After the consolidation of Jamba!'s original businesses, excitement for the new division is enormous.

Again, the Samwer brothers show their employees, how they believe in them and trust them entirely. This would be Oliver's third major venture and most likely prove one of his theories: "There always was this saying that an excellent team with an average business idea would be better than an average team with an excellent business idea. Within the last months however, we realized, that the idea is as important as the team. Having realized this helped us in delegating more operative work and concentrate on finding more business ideas in order to secure future growth." According to industry experts, Jamba!'s vision to transform into a holding company for mobile entertainment applications looks very promising. First services are launched, targets are set high and Jamba! already has reached the break-even point. Having taken a closer look at the company, one can be confident to hear again from Jamba! and their exceptional founding and management team in the near future.

Matthias Ehrgott, Peter Herrmannsberger and Felix Reimann

OnVista AG

1 OnVista - Company Overview 185
2 Business Environment 189
3 Founders 190
4 Business Idea 191
5 Motivations 192
6 Perspectives on Success 192
7 Corporate Strategy 194
8 Clients 196
9 Financing 196
10 Human Resources Policy 198
11 Outlook 198

1 OnVista - Company Overview

1.1 OnVista AG

OnVista AG, with its wholly-owned subsidiaries OnVista Technologies GmbH and OnVista Media GmbH, operates in two distinct markets for financial information provisioning. Since its foundation in 1998, the young company has experienced considerable growth to reach revenues of EUR 13.45 million (under US GAAP) and a headcount of 133 employees in late 2002. Today, OnVista ranks amongst the top European providers of financial information. With 33.6 million monthly page impressions in 2002, the company's Internet platform www.onvista.de is the leading bank-independent finance portal in Germany (see figure 1).

Figure 1: Monthly Page Impressions of Major Finance Portals

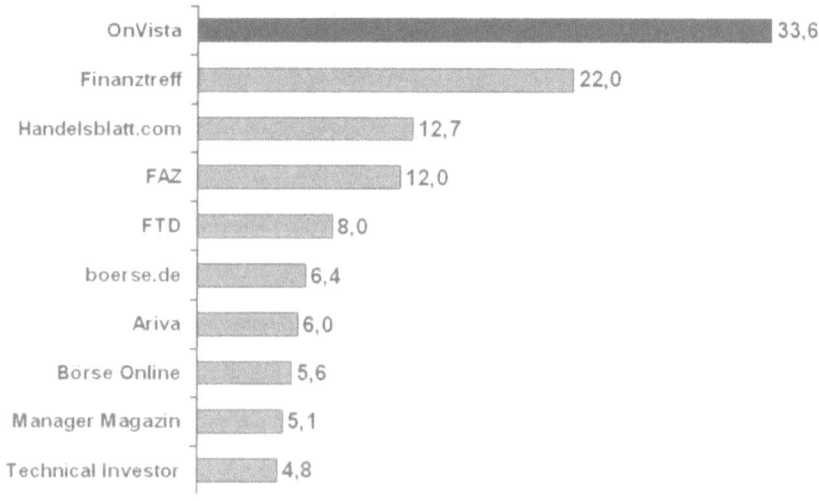

Source: Company materials

Matthias Ehrgott, Peter Herrmannsberger and Felix Reimann

This enviable development has been a result of both stringent and effective management decisions and numerous success factors rooting in the firm's business environment.

The case study at hand is to discuss the essential drivers behind OnVista's remarkable evolution. Against the background of this objective, it provides an outline of the company's history and current organisation as well as insights into the diverse building blocks of OnVista's business. Many of the aspects touched upon are based on information reported by Fritz Oidtmann, spokesman of the Board of OnVista AG, during an interview at the company's corporate headquarters on October 24, 2003.

OnVista AG is headquartered in Cologne, Germany. It has two subsidiaries, OnVista Technologies GmbH and OnVista Media GmbH which operate in two distinct business segments: OnVista Technologies is a system provider in the area of financial market information. OnVista Media operates a bank-independent finance portal primarily consulted by German users. As such, OnVista's client base consists of financial service providers and media companies as well as advertising clients and private and institutional investors.

Michael W. Schwetje and Stephan Schubert, both former students of the Otto Beisheim Graduate School of Management (WHU) in Vallendar, Germany, and Fritz Oidtmann, a Partner at McKinsey & Company at the time, founded the company in May 1998 as OnVista.de Finanzanalyse GmbH & Co. KG. Business started four months later when www.onvista.de went online. Three months after its transformation into OnVista AG in November 1999, the company became listed on the stock market. Break-even was reached in June 2000, a quarter of a year ahead of schedule (see figure 2).

Figure 2: Development of OnVista - Overview

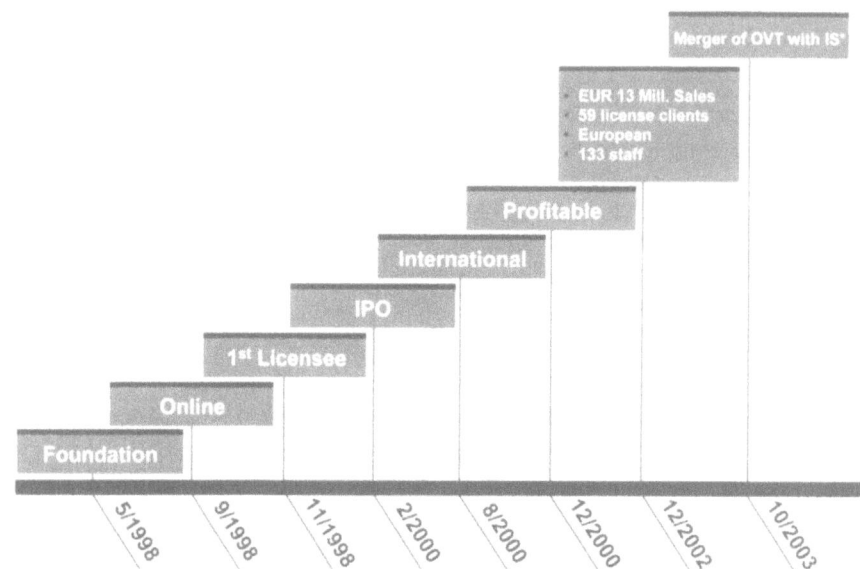

*) IS = Innovative Software AG

Source: Company materials

1.2 OnVista Technologies GmbH

OnVista Technologies sells licenses for integrating OnVista's unified IT platform, the Market Data Gateway, with its clients' proprietary Intra- and Internet sites. Further services offered include the complete provision of IT systems, the supply of financial market data and the operation of front-end applications. This includes diverse bank-internal and mobile features. The information supplied is acquired from various raw-data providers and, subsequently, processed further by OnVista. This processing includes the calculation of supplementary ratios, the condensation of detailed information and the adaptation of the same to different customer needs and perspectives.

Licensees benefit from a considerable reduction in complexity with respect to their own IT infrastructure. This entails greater flexibility concerning updating and / or changing the data layout while at the same time resulting in cost savings with regard

to the acquisition, integration and actual provisioning of data. Licence fees, generally stemming from longer-term agreements, are paid on a monthly basis (see figure 3).

Figure 3: OnVista Technologies GmbH - Business Model

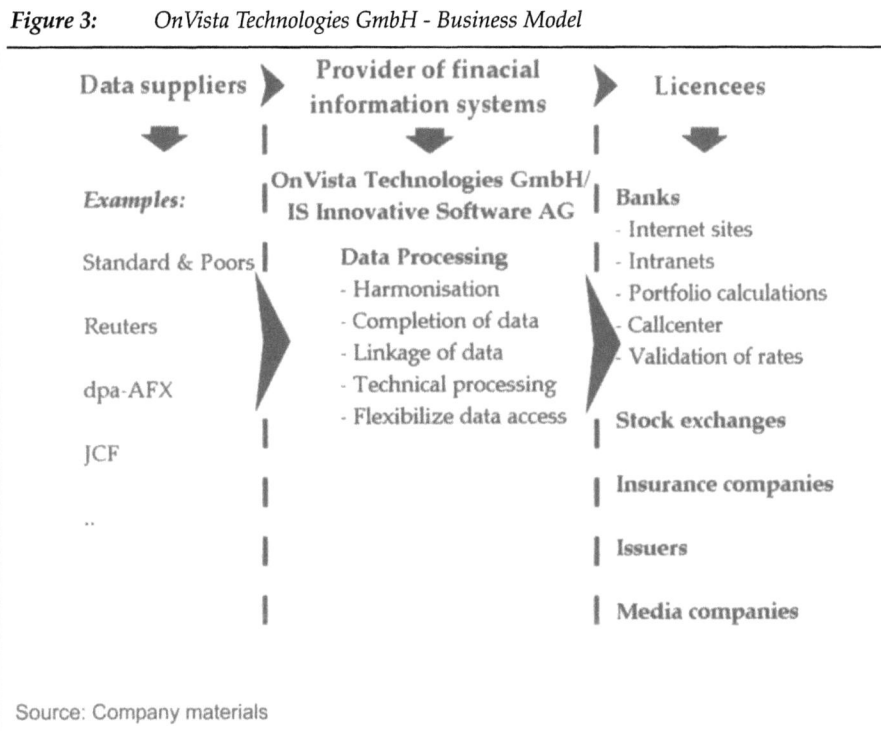

Source: Company materials

In the last quarter of 2003, OnVista Technologies was about to realize a merger with IS Innovative Software AG to form Europe's leading provider of Internet-based financial data information systems, IS.Teledata AG. OnVista AG will hold a 31.5% stake in the new corporation making it the single largest shareholder in the venture.

1.3 OnVista Media GmbH

Being a licensee of OnVista Technologies, OnVista Media GmbH operates and markets the finance portal www.onvista.de. The website offers comprehensive information on financial markets and occupies the premiere position in the German marketplace. In addition to capital market-related data services, OnVista Media has continuously ex-

panded its offerings to the supply of information in neighbouring areas such as life insurance quotes, building savings agreements and offers in the retail banking segment.

Most of the company's revenues are generated through advertising and content collaborations. However, OnVista Media does not only provide advertising space but also offers its customers advice on planning and placing their respective online campaigns.

2 Business Environment

Up to 1998, hardly any company had covered the financial data supply segment for private investors. Thus, competition was very limited at the time: Teletext and print-media represented the sole sources for warrant quotes. Professionals could alternatively rely on information provided by high-end terminals installed on the spot, such as the Reuters system. These services, however, were high-priced (and still are to date despite a significant decrease in fees over the past years). Costs associated with this sort of terminals largely depend on the functionality required, but, nonetheless, amount to approximately USD 1,000 per month as a minimum. In any case, they considerably exceed the budget justifiable for a small investor's trading volume. Moreover, these terminals were complex to use, requiring specific training.

At the time of OnVista's foundation, the German stock market experienced an unprecedented upswing driven by the rise of the Internet as a new sector in the world economy. As the number of people investing in stocks and warrants multiplied, so did the need for financial information. This evolution was all the more powerful as this period marked the first emergence of a "culture of investing" in Germany. OnVista benefited both from this surge in demand as well as from the growing acceptance of the Internet as a medium for information delivery. Simultaneously, new competitors with similar business models arrived but could not make up OnVista's head start.

After the burst of the Internet bubble in 2000, demand for financial information declined sharply while it stagnated for advertisement space in online media. This situation only improved when the stock market started to stabilise towards the end of 2002.

Matthias Ehrgott, Peter Herrmannsberger and Felix Reimann

3 Founders

"When you go on a boat trip, you need someone who sails and another one who cooks. He that sails must be good at sailing, he that cooks must be good at cooking - not everybody needs to be able to do everything, but the right person must act in the right place at the right time." Fritz Oidtmann, 2003.

The OnVista founding team features a wide variety of competencies, professional experience and backgrounds. Fritz Oidtmann, 42, is the spokesman of the Board and is responsible for strategic business development, public relations as well as internal communication. Additionally, Oidtmann heads the Human Resources and Legal Affairs departments.

Before starting OnVista, Fritz Oidtmann had spent twelve years at the international management consultancy McKinsey & Company where, most recently, he worked as a Partner and head of the German retail sector team at the Cologne office. As opposed to his colleagues Schubert and Schwetje, Oidtmann initially kept his job during the early phase of OnVista's foundation. He only joined the start-up full-time in July 1999, as the young company needed additional senior management capacity for its further development.

As a founder and member of the board of OnVista, Stephan Schubert, 34, is responsible for managing the company's IT infrastructure. In this role, Schubert is in charge of the Technologies business segment encompassing data acquisition, product development, sales, and project realisation. Prior to creating OnVista in co-operation with Michael W. Schwetje and Fritz Oidtmann, Stephan Schubert had joined McKinsey & Company after graduating from WHU in 1995. At McKinsey's offices in Munich and Cologne, Schubert was responsible for the development of new business segments as well as for increasing sales in existing markets. Besides these responsibilities, he was in charge of IT projects focused on database solutions and linear optimisation.

Michael W. Schwetje, 35, bears responsibility for the operation, continuous development and marketing of the company's media services, including the www.onvista.de platform. Moreover, Schwetje supervises the Accounting, Controlling and Investor Relations units. Prior to the formation of OnVista, Michael W. Schwetje had worked in the Investment Banking division of Commerzbank and had later been in charge of international corporate finance activities at the Freudenberg Group of Companies.

Knowing each other from university and from work, Schwetje, Schubert and Oidtmann have placed, from the very beginning of their venture, high trust in each other. This trust is in regard to their respective capabilities and their reliability. Fritz Oidtmann expressed the importance of mutual trust in a concise way: "Trust in capabilities does not mean that everybody knows everything, but that everybody must have capabilities which are employed in the right place, at the right time. Trust in

character means that one can rely on his partners not to defect or cheat on each other." Moreover, their long familiarity has entailed a collaboration characterised by open communication and honesty between each other.

4 Business Idea

Having graduated from WHU, Michael W. Schwetje and Stephan Schubert continuously came up with different business ideas. Careful assessment revealed several concepts which seemed feasible as well as sufficiently lucrative for a market launch. In order to gain a clearer picture and receive a sound evaluation of the miscellaneous business models, they consulted Fritz Oidtmann whom Stephan Schubert knew from his McKinsey background. Oidtmann possessed long-grown professional experience and was considered competent and trustworthy to give reliable advice. In the subsequent discussion all proposed concepts were scrutinized as to whether they bore sufficient potential to create customer value to a satisfyingly high number of clients. Thus, many of the suggestions brought forth, such as the sale of ties via the Internet, were discarded until finally, only one evaluated idea seemed promising: the creation of an online information portal providing real-time quotes for investors in warrants.

The idea was that warrants were an investment vehicle which had gained enormous popularity, especially with private investors over the previous years. Buying these derivative instruments means acquiring the right to buy or sell an underlying asset at a specified point in the future at a price fixed today. Individuals can instantaneously gain exposure to different asset classes by using warrants while benefiting from a leverage effect inherent in this investment vehicle. Warrants are generally several times more volatile in their price movements than the underlying assets. This makes reliable real-time information a pre-requisite for profitable trading in these instruments. However, at the time, the only sources of price quotes for warrants were newspapers and other print media (in which the information was obviously outdated) as well as teletext (slow and inconveniently accessible information on television).

The suggested business model was to remedy this problem by creating an Internet portal which would provide the necessary real-time quotes along with supplementary information such as pre-calculated financial ratios via an intuitive interface to its subscribed users. The concept was supposed to create value for a sufficient number of users having the necessary resources as well as a large enough turnover to invest in premium information for their trading activities. However, there was still a long way to go for the idea to be implemented in the form of OnVista's foundation.

Matthias Ehrgott, Peter Herrmannsberger and Felix Reimann

5 Motivations

In founding OnVista, Schwetje, Schubert and Oidtmann traded their promising careers in well-established enterprises for an uncertain future in a start-up company with an unproven business model. While each of the three had personal reasons for this decision, they all shared one common motivation: they were fascinated by the perspective of being an entrepreneur, building a business that no one had tried before and making it strong enough to stand the test of time. Two of the founders were also driven by the prospect of personal wealth, one of them by the opportunity of improving his standing in the community.

While it was their common objective to reduce their personal workload once OnVista would be established, none of the three had plans to sell the company rapidly. They were aware of the innovativeness of the business model and were determined to develop it into a sustainable company.

6 Perspectives on Success

In retrospect, all three founders feel that the development of OnVista as a company has been a true success story. However, based on their individual motivations and characters, they consider differing aspects in the development of the company as the true milestones for success:

Michael W. Schwetje, being a finance person both from background and character, draws his personal satisfaction mainly from the positive and swift development of the company's financial performance (see figure 4).

Figure 4: OnVista AG - Revenues (1999 - 2001)

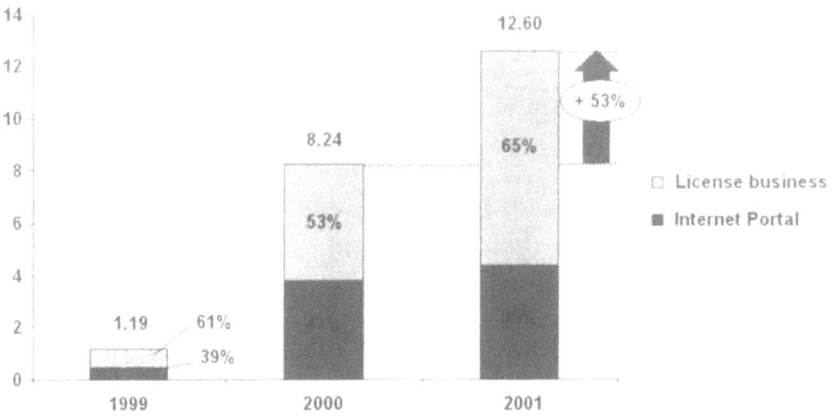

Source: Company materials

From his viewpoint, OnVista's landmark achievements were the ability to create its first cash flows already in 1998, to go public successfully in 2000 (much earlier than the founders had expected) and to reach profitability in the same year.

Fritz Oidtmann, on the other hand, places stronger emphasis on the operational development of the start-up. Milestones which he highlights were getting the system online and seeing it at work, as well as the first customer subscribing to OnVista's service one day after going live. The fact that OnVista has been able to build up a significant workforce and not only provide the founders' living but also that of other people is of high importance to Fritz Oidtmann. This is especially true as the company has been able to constantly attract and retain highly qualified personnel (see figure 5).

| Figure 5: | Development of Staff Size |

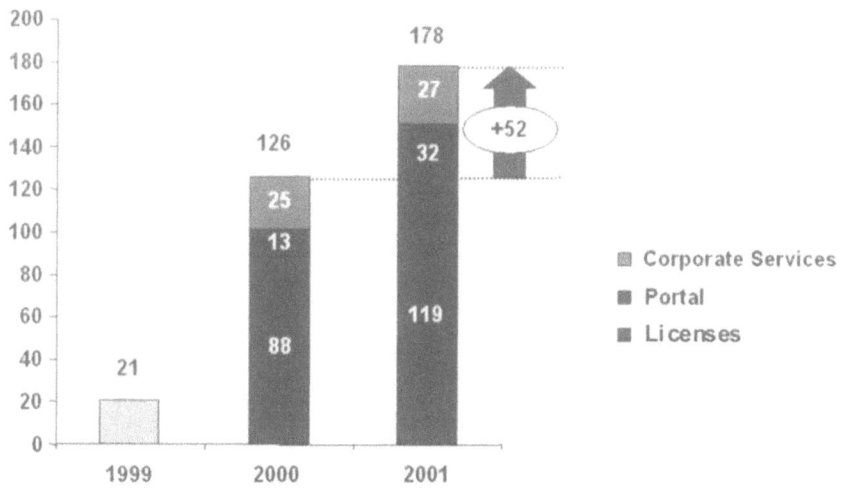

* Incl. 11 employees of Trade & Get AG

Source: Company materials

The most notable achievement in his view, however, is the fact that OnVista has succeeded in acquiring some of the most reputable companies in the finance industry as its customers.

Stephan Schubert's view on success is a mixture of his colleagues' perspectives, attributing equal weight to financial performance and operational progress.

7 Corporate Strategy

"If you make more wrong than right decisions, you are dead. If you only make right decisions, you do not take enough opportunities." Fritz Oidtmann, 2003.

The decision to realise an online information portal induced rapid planning of the project. As initial funding (mainly stemming from private assets) was limited, time-to-market as well as time-to-break even were to be kept as short as possible. Moreover, the necessity to pay the founders (OnVista has been the only source of income for Schwetje and Schubert right from the beginning) forced a swift and effective set-up of the business. However, very early on, the original business model underwent numerous adaptations and redefinitions:

The initial business plan implied that the majority of revenues were to be created by subscribers of the portal who would pay fees in order to get access to the information offered. These revenues were to be complemented by the sale of advertisement space on www.onvista.de. Yet, already towards the end of 1998, it turned out that the number of customers willing to pay for a subscription remained lower than expected. In turn, the relatively low traffic on the Internet portal (only subscribers could access the website) strongly limited revenues generated through advertising. At this point, OnVista radically changed its business model granting free access to all web-services, thus increasing online traffic and realising higher prices for advertising space.

During fall 1998, OnVista was repeatedly approached by institutions with the request to integrate the OnVista technology of processing and presenting financial data into their own corporate Internet and Intranet platforms. Without fully understanding the technical nor the financial implications, the management team agreed to the proposal, which meant the starting-point of OnVista's licensing business, later transferred into OnVista Technologies GmbH.

As soon as these two pillars of revenue (the portal and the market data gateway) proved adequate to offer a long-term perspective for the company, Schubert, Schwetje and Oidtmann began a sustained process of both product and process innovation with the first aspect constituting the primary focus. Particularly the licensing business required an expansion into the supply of quotes and information on additional financial products such as equities and bonds. In the wake of the burst of the Internet bubble, especially the enhancement of the bond-section needed to be forcefully pushed forward. Furthermore, innovative products were introduced via www.onvista.de. A recent and prominent example of this strategy are ClickOptions marketed for Société Générale. ClickOptions are essentially warrants with knock-out barriers (when these are hit, the option ceases to exist), that are easier to handle for investors. OnVista designed and provided a customised sub-section of www.onvista.de for this new product. Thus, the company increased the value added for its client, in this case Société Générale, reaped more advertising revenues and, at the same time, enabled the establishment of beneficial long-term relationships with financial and related institutions. These partnerships constituted a major innovative addition to the company's business. Asked how it is possible for a comparatively small firm to create this kind of network with far larger players, Fritz Oidtmann provided a brief but concise answer: "You just have to be good yourself and people will approach you."

Despite the high relevance of the decisions depicted above, the OnVista management team never relied on an explicit strategic planning process. In the early stages after the foundation of the company, the rapidly growing market allowed OnVista to expand merely by taking emerging opportunities. Instead of formalized planning, Schubert, Schwetje and Oidtmann opted for carefully listening to market trends: Many of OnVista's product innovations are based on customer or user ideas collected through frequent surveys and voluntary feedback. By developing these ideas further, OnVista succeeded in not only following but also setting trends.

8 Clients

Considering the role that OnVista's clients played in the development of the company, "customers" and "users" are to be differentiated. The portal www.onvista.de creates its revenues through advertising, therefore its customers are marketing departments of financial institutions as well as B2C firms such as insurance brokers. While financial service providers account for the majority of sales, customers from other industries like car manufacturers are increasingly attracted to OnVista's users, i.e. individual investors accessing the portal free of charge. Research has revealed interesting features about them: They are mostly male, affluent, well-educated and share rather homogeneous interests in electronics, finance, cars and sports. These characteristics are reinforced by strong growth in the segment entitled by banks as the "mass-affluent" investors (USD 50,000 -USD 500,000 net investible assets) to which many of OnVista's users belong.

On the contrary, the licensing division works with IT, sales, and marketing departments of financial and related institutions. In this field, OnVista's systems are used not only for Internet, but also for Intranet applications which are increasingly destined to substitute the far more expensive Reuters terminals. This development was intensified over the past three years by the economic downturn creating significant cost pressure, especially on financial service providers.

9 Financing

Since the company's creation, Schwetje, Schubert and Oidtmann have consequently pursued a conservative financing strategy. In fact, the three founders created OnVista using private savings. No substantial loans or venture capital was used. The predomi-

nant reason for not trying to speed up OnVista's expansion was that the entrepreneurs wanted to safeguard a maximum of flexibility and liberty in building their business.

On the cost side, the OnVista founders always kept a close eye on expenses and only allowed money to be spent if there was a clear potential to increase profits. The founders proved highly efficient in controlling the virtually unlimited creativity of OnVista's employees who oftentimes were so motivated to enhance the firm's service offerings that they almost lost sight of profitability. Thanks to this entrepreneurial parsimony, OnVista has never incurred any serious financing worries.

Moreover, there were sufficient investors, especially customers, willing to take a stake in the company. Such offers, however, were refused as the entrepreneurs feared losing their independence and, consequently, being limited in pursuing business opportunities with other clients.

A change in the financing structure therefore only occurred in November 1999. At this point in time, OnVista was transformed into a stock corporation (German "Aktiengesellschaft"), a step which facilitated getting new investors on board. In the course of this procedure, the Burda Beteiligungs-Holding GmbH took a 10% stake in the start-up. This meant a considerable inflow of cash allowing the company to continue its growth backed by a solid financial position. In addition to the financial benefits, the involvement of Burda also entailed a significantly positive effect on OnVista's reputation. Many customers perceived the engagement of the well-reputed investor as a hallmark for the young start-up company. Thanks to this newfound reputation and with the prospect to take the company public in the near future, financing no longer was an issue for the three entrepreneurs.

In preparation of the IPO, negotiations with banks were predominantly focussed on mainly one topic - the speed at which the public offering could be completed. This proved an extremely smart move since, in this way, the IPO could take place as soon as February 2000. Despite the fact that a significant amount of uncertainty accompanied the whole process, the IPO turned into a great success itself. The issue price was fixed at the upper end of the book-building range at EUR 22 per share and, still, the offering was 80 times over-subscribed. On the first day of trading, the closing price of OnVista's stock was EUR 50.60. When the share price reached its peak, the start-up was valued at more than EUR 400 million. Ever since the IPO, the company has been "sitting on a pile of cash", as Fritz Oidtmann described it. Furthermore, the IPO greatly aided the company in other respects, as well. It did not only help OnVista grow but it was also a clear proof of its business model. This signal was perceived as a validation of the company's respectability by both internal and external parties including employees, customers, and competitors. In addition, OnVista's presence in the press skyrocketed in the wake of the public offering and matched that of companies with a multiple of its revenues. Therefore, the well-timed IPO had an extraordinary impact on the firm's reputation.

Matthias Ehrgott, Peter Herrmannsberger and Felix Reimann

10 Human Resources Policy

Recruiting has at all times held a prime role at OnVista. All recruiting activities had long been conducted personally by the three founders, who, in turn, sacrificed a considerable amount of management capacity. Only in 2000, Schwetje, Oidtmann and Schubert hired a head of HR.

Standards regarding candidates' profiles have remained demanding even in times of tense labour markets: employees have been required to show substantial qualifications as well as a high degree of flexibility and motivation to achieve above average performance. The management team has felt that any hire not fitting the corporate culture would harm the work climate in the entire organisation. As a consequence, some of the company's departments remained severely understaffed for an extended period of time. The sales department, for example, was run with a staff of only two people for a long time.

Also, extrinsic incentives have been kept in short supply. OnVista has abstained from offering additional benefits like free meals, company cars and fancy offices. Being role models for their employees, this policy was also applied to the members of the board. In order to inspire entrepreneurial parsimony throughout the company, management treated themselves no different from their employees. This included seemingly unimportant issues such as using exactly the same office chairs.

11 Outlook

Having effectively operated in a dynamic market environment and having overcome various obstacles with great success, the founders are left with the question of how the company will be able to face the challenges of the future. More importantly, will the drivers behind OnVista's past success be able to ensure a prosperous development in the future or will additional or different factors play a more significant role? Could there be shifts in the relative importance of these drivers which are to be considered? Answering these questions, the extremely dynamic market environment OnVista operates in needs to be carefully taken into account. One thing is clear, however: at least the founders themselves must have an idea about what the future may hold and what it will take to react adequately to those future requirements.

Jens Bender, Sophie Nietfeld and Philipp Reinke

Qiagen N.V.

1 Introduction 201
2 Qiagen's Strategy 203
3 Organisation 205
4 The Product Portfolio 206
5 Sales and Marketing 209
6 Product Development and Pricing 210
7 Patents 211
8 Human Resources 211
9 Co-operations and Acquisitions 213
10 Outlook 215

1 Introduction

In 1996 Dr. Metin Colpan had prepared a very detailed business plan, when he got into the cab together with Moshe Alafi, who had been a very well known investor in the biotechnology world for more than 15 years. Quite in a hurry, Moshe did not show any interest in the sheets full of numbers and product descriptions, but just asked Metin to tell him about his plans within ten minutes and how he could possibly contribute to them.

Metin was not really used to this kind of business, so while he seemed to be a bit surprised, the last twelve years of his business career beginning in 1984 rushed through his head.

Everything started with Metin's doctorate degree which he obtained in 1983 from the Darmstadt University of Technology from where he moved to the University of Düsseldorf to join the institute for biophysics as a research assistant. He only spent a couple of months there, creating a spin-off in 1984 called "Diagen Institute for Molecularbiologic Diagnostics GmbH". Metin wanted to offer a toolkit to researchers, which would allow them to easily purify nucleic acids. The first toolkit he actually sold was brought to the market in 1986.

Metin's idea was based upon his personal experience with the often very tedious procedure in genomic research. Preceding the steps of analysis and identification of genomes, the purification of DNA is a very crucial but time demanding procedure. Since every day of additional research is costly (both actual costs and opportunity costs of not being faster than the competition), the idea to make purification easier seemed to be quite attractive. Besides the cost argument, Metin's method allowed researchers to retain a higher proportion of their initial genomic sample, because previous methods involved the use of multiple tools for purification, each of them retaining a small fraction of the initial sample. The risk of loosing the whole sample was therefore rather high. These drawbacks of commonly applied research methods were significantly reduced by the technology Metin had invented.

This technology was perfectly suited for the North American market, a market said to be more dynamic and flexible with regards to innovation and research. However, for establishing a considerable marketing and sales force, Metin estimated a total investment of about US$ 6 mn.

Faced with this story, Moshe Alafi sat quiet, turned his head and said: "Well, if you can provide US$ 3 mn by other investors, I'll be willing to provide you with another US$ 3 mn upfront." To confirm this, he took out a little note, repeated his statement and handed it over to Metin. With this prominent support, Metin was sure to find some other investors willing to provide him with the remaining US$ 3 mn. And in fact, he

did. One of them was Prof. Riesner, who is still a member of the company's supervisory board.

After having collected all the funds he needed, the company's name was changed to Qiagen, which was easier to introduce as a brand to the American market than Diagen would have been. So, in 1996, Qiagen N.V. was incorporated. The company's legal headquarters were moved to the Netherlands mainly due to two reasons. Primarily, the Dutch law entailed a more effective protection of listed companies against hostile takeovers, which was, considering Qiagen's small size but promising business model, a risk not to be underestimated. The second reason was that all of Qiagen's employees were to receive a partly performance-based salary by providing them with stock options. Under Dutch law, this was possible without having any diluting effect.

The funds provided were mainly used for the establishment of a well-functioning distribution system in the U.S. The R&D expenditures for the existing product portfolio had already been made at that stage.

At this point in time, Peer Schatz came into the company. He had a business administration degree with a major in finance and had gained some experience in the pharmaceutical industry before. It was his eagerness that drove the company to go public at the Nasdaq. He reasoned that the American attitude towards innovation was not only favouring the acceptance of products but also the provision of funds. In the case of a further expansion of the business this could eventually become a crucial factor. The IPO had, of course, also a supporting influence on the American sales and marketing activities.

One year later, when the company's sales had reached US$ 74.3 mn, the "Neuer Markt", a stock exchange segment for technology stocks, was established in Germany. Qiagen used this opportunity to get listed on the German market from then on.

To foster external growth, Qiagen bought the Swiss Rosys AG in 1998 which is today Qiagen Instruments. It started a joint venture, PreAnalytiX, another systems provider for purification, together with Becton, Dickinson & Co. In 2000, Operon Inc. was acquired, a technology leader in high-throughput production of synthetic nucleic acids. Incorporating Operon Inc. as Qiagen Operon, Qiagen entered the genomics market. This strategic move was followed by an expansion of Qiagen's business to the Japanese market, which was attained by the acquisition of the Japanese Sawady Group. Acquisitions of the U.S. Xeragon Inc. and the Norwegian Genovision AS followed in 2002. At that point in time, sales had reached a level of US$ 298.6 mn.

Since its IPO in 1996, Qiagen was able to increase sales at a high compound annual growth rate of 33% while profits rose even stronger over the same time horizon.

When comparing Qiagen to the overall biotechnology sector, the most important point to be considered is the role of R&D. Qiagen spent up to 24% of its annual revenues for sales and marketing, and about 9% for R&D. Comparing this to an industry average, a

clear "underinvestment" into R&D may be assumed. But as Qiagen has a rather simple product, its main focus always was an efficient sales & marketing department.

2 Qiagen's Strategy

Until the end of 2003, Qiagen followed its original strategy consistently. This fact is demonstrated by one slide that remained unchanged in company presentations since the IPO of Qiagen in 1996: It is titled "Qiagen strategy". The strategy of Qiagen was to (1) expand its leadership in the research market and to leverage such leadership to diversify the company's opportunities for future growth into an array of developing commercial markets. Additionally, Qiagen wanted to (2) maintain and further expand technology leadership by investing significant resources in research and development and through strategic acquisitions. The company tried to (3) provide a comprehensive portfolio of products for specific nucleic acid handling, separation and purification applications as well as to (4) increase the utility of its consumable products in certain market segments by providing automation product lines. Finally, Qiagen strived to (5) emphasize customer contacts and service.

These aims are also put down in Qiagen's mission statement:

"Our mission is to provide an outstanding contribution to our customers' success by innovating and supplying our products and services in all areas where they require this expertise.

Our products and technologies enable our customers to achieve breakthroughs in research and new standards in healthcare which both contribute to improving lives.

By focusing on increasing our customers' success, the exceptional talent and commitment of our employees bring excellence to all segments of the value chain and outstanding success to Qiagen."

The strategic and tactical decisions were not influenced extensively by the shareholders of the company (for example, Moshe Alafi was regularly informed about the state of the company but did not intervene). All strategic decisions were discussed with the members of the supervisory board, but ultimately left to the top management.

To reach these goals, Qiagen focused its activities on its core product, consumables. While products in the beginning were mainly applied to the purification of blood, the emphasis has changed and products are now primarily used for the purification of tissue. Furthermore, Qiagen discontinued its activities in veterinary and agricultural research. Finally, the focus to retain purified DNA changed to purified RNA. All other

products offered by Qiagen are related to the core activities of the company – representing flanking substances and services to round up the product portfolio.

Qiagen's market research revealed that the company is well positioned with respect to other companies in the biotech market. Suppliers deliver standard receptacles and packaging material while Qiagen itself produced the chemical substance for the purification process as well as the instruments for purification. Products are delivered to the Qiagen sales force and distributors worldwide and are then sold to the customers by the key accounts of the sales force. Potential new entrants and substituting products were not in sight at the end of 2002.

With its new technology, Qiagen was able to speed up the purification process in the laboratories significantly. While the traditional way of purifying involved several steps to receive the purified molecules, modern technology replaced these steps and therefore saved valuable research time. Considering that research time is especially valuable as patents only guarantee a distinct timeframe for the development of new products to the patent holder, this new process of purification is of great value to the research companies.

Qiagen holds a market share of around 90% among the companies offering substances for purification and therefore is the clear market leader. The largest of the companies which serve the remaining 10% of the purification market holds a 4% market share and therefore is about 25 times smaller than Qiagen!

Qiagen's success can – to a large extent – be attributed to the stringent strategy of the company. At an early stage (before the IPO) Qiagen started to focus its business on the purification segment. The company discontinued activities that did not contribute to the core market of purification of molecules. That decision, as well as the technological leadership, positioned Qiagen as one of the first movers in this market, enabling the company's reputation as expert in the field of purification.

Additionally, Qiagen did not only focus on a market niche, but also kept the value chain activities simple. All activities were closely related to Qiagen's core competencies in the field of development of services. The packaging material as well as all other input factors were sourced from suppliers while Qiagen focused on the development of the substance and its distribution by its own highly-qualified sales force.

The timing and especially the location of Qiagen's IPO in 1996, made it possible to gather sufficient financial resources for expansion and investments. It also positioned the company as a major player in the innovative, fast growing and open-minded North American market.

With these factors being in place, Qiagen was able to conquer a dominant position in the purification market segment. A 90% market share clearly portrays the company's market leadership which is secured by high market entry barriers. Qiagen has become

the brand for purification and its patents make it easier for the company to defend that position.

3 Organisation

With the acquisitions in the past years, Qiagen grew to a global company with subsidiaries in several countries around the world. Where the company did not have its own sales force, it took advantage of distributors. These contribute about 6% to the total sales of Qiagen, from more than 30 countries. The company has its global headquarters in Venlo, Netherlands, while the European headquarters are located in Hilden near Düsseldorf, Germany. The production facility in Hilden serves all markets except North America. Since the end of 2002, the North American headquarters have been located in Germantown, Maryland, USA. Products for the North American market are produced here, in an own production site amounting to 54% of annual sales. Other production sites are located in Switzerland, Japan and Norway. The remaining 10 subsidiaries mainly focus on marketing and sales activities.

A matrix-like organizational structure has been installed which leaves enough room for communication between the business units of different countries. On top of regular contact between employees of different branches via telephone, email and videoconference, meetings of the general managers are held regularly (e.g. International Sales Meeting, International R&D Meeting). The start-up spirit of the fast growing company can still be observed, even though the company is not small anymore. Corporate culture is characterized by an open-door policy, reaching up to the senior management level. Employees with innovative ideas and comments are inspired to communicate their thoughts.

The North American and European subsidiaries are integrated using SAP as a business information system. Additionally, Qiagen integrated systems with third party contract manufacturers via SAP and implemented a module to improve field service operations for the instruments products. Additionally, a global intranet provides employees with standard documents. Every employee is able to post news that might regard or interest others.

While employees in the sales division are responsible for key-accounts personally, employees in the R&D division decide jointly and develop new products in teams.

The structure in the top management provide Dr. Colpan and Schatz with large decisional freedom during the start-up and growth phase of Qiagen. Qiagen is organized in a matrix structure. The subsidiaries have their specific fields of competence and remain the exclusive producers of the respective products. The separation and inde-

pendence of the units – most of them joined Qiagen through acquisitions – is one important factor for the quality of the products and the specific expertise within the subsidiaries. Each company focuses on its core competence.

Qiagen's decision to market its products on a global scale with its own sales force and external distributors supported the rise of Qiagen's strong reputation in the field of purification.

The production facilities of the core product for purification are separated in terms of the markets they serve. The North American production facility in Germantown is responsible for the North American market, while the facility in Hilden, Germany, serves the rest of the markets. One the one hand, this set-up reduces the effect of exchange rate fluctuations on Qiagen's results. On the other hand, Qiagen is able to react faster to changes in demand in the respective market and is closer to its customers in North America.

One very important factor contributing to Qiagen's success is the company's corporate culture. Qiagen was able to create an atmosphere that inspires its employees. Not only the social facilities but also the events and the meetings that promote personal interaction have an effect on this culture. The open-door policy stimulates employees to bring up new ideas and fosters contacts and knowledge exchange between employees about any company matters.

4 The Product Portfolio

Qiagen's products are used for genetic research and serve as a tool for the purification of nucleic acids, i.e. DNA and RNA. These can be found in the core of cells in different forms, such as blood, tissue or bacteria. However, in order for researchers to work with nucleic acid material for analytic purposes, they need to extract them from the respective biological sample. The extraction process consist of filtering the material in a way that remove all disturbances such as proteins or harmful substances. Figure 1 depicts the research process and the relevance of nucleic acids for later analysis purposes.

Figure 1: The research process

The purification of DNA and RNA is just one out of a series of activities in the research process. There are various applications that genetic information is used for: clinical, academic or industrial research, molecular diagnostics or gene therapy. Therefore, even with purification just being one small step, it has an enormous impact on the quality of the outcome.

Applying the traditional method for the purification of nucleic acids, a researcher or laboratory assistant needs to add off-the-shelf chemicals, such as phenol and ethanol, to a given biological sample, pouring the mixture from one test tube into another, repeating the proceeding several times. This purification method is not only time-consuming but also risky in different ways: on the one hand, there is a constant danger of contaminating the sample in case the test tubes are not perfectly clean. On the other hand the sample becomes smaller and smaller with every step of the process as a small portion of the sample remains in every tube.

With Qiagen's kits, the purification has become significantly faster and less risky. A kit consists of a plastic container and a white substance which represents the heart of Qiagen's products. The substance contains so-called bearing molecules with a surface structure that absorbs nothing but the pure DNA. To purify the nucleic acids, the respective sample is filled into the container together with the white substance. The DNA is absorbed by the bearing molecules while the rest of the cell is filtered away. With the help of a salt solution, the pure DNA can now be washed out. The container with the remaining liquid inside can then be disposed. This procedure is fast and guarantees a clean sample without any toxic substances remaining. At a price of around three to four dollar per application, this method is however more expensive than the traditional one, as the substance developed by Qiagen is significantly more complex than the off-the-shelf ones.

Thanks to several acquisitions, Qiagen's product portfolio comprises more than this purification kit: Apart from the proprietarily developed consumables, Qiagen also offers instruments for automated purification as well as synthetic DNA. The first were crucial for customers active in molecular diagnostics because in this area, hundreds of genetic samples need to be handled each day. The purification process therefore has to be done automatically by a robot. The latter are mainly used in clinical research and

serve as a basis for comparing patients' purified DNA with an "ideal" synthetic sample.

Because researchers wish to extract pure DNA or RNA from ever new sorts of biological samples and due to a variety of applications the nucleic acids are intended to be used for, Qiagen offers more than 320 products based on around 20 different technologies. However, in spite of this variety, consumables still represent the majority of sales accounting for roughly three quarters of revenues, while all other products together make up for the rest. As to gross profit margins, consumable products generate about 70% to 75%, other products about 55% to 60%.

It becomes obvious that the core product, consumable kits for the purification of nucleic acids, represent a major success factor. This is due to several reasons. First of all, it serves a multitude of targets. Moreover, it is used in a step of the research process that is not specifically dependent on the research objective nor the application the sample is intended to be used for; it rather represents a commodity in the process of purification that is crucial to every genetic research conducted.

In spite of their rather basic function, Qiagen's purification kits represent the decisive factor for the success of the respective research in two dimensions: first, they prevent that the sample is lost during the purification process. It has been shown that with the traditional method, there was significant danger of loss which in many cases implies the end of a study altogether as oftentimes, a sample is available only to a very limited amount. The cited example of a biochip gives an idea of the monetary consequences of an unsuccessful purification.

The second aspect, however, is much more important: Using Qiagen's purification kits, researchers can save an extensive amount of time. This includes working hours of laboratory assistants resulting in lower development costs, but, most important of all, research time. This implies that products can be brought to market faster and that patents can be applied before competing researchers are able to do so. In industrial research, for example in the pharmaceutical industry, every single day of earlier protection of a technology or market introduction of a preparation equals thousands of dollars in additional revenues.

In the light of such security and savings that Qiagen's purification kits offer to research projects, the fact that these kits are more expensive than the substances needed for traditional purification method becomes unimportant, especially when the price difference equals no more than US$ 0,25 or so.

A second success factor regarding products is what can be called the logic of the portfolio: Apart from the core product, all additional products and services help to generate more sales of the purification kit in different ways. Instruments for automated purification are essential in the molecular diagnostics research. Without robots using Qiagen's kit for the purification, this target group could not be reached as automated processes are essential here. This means that instruments are not only the key to this

segment, but also that every instrument sold will result in sales of thousands of purification kits afterwards. Synthetic DNA has a similar effect. In order to compare the synthetic DNA sample to that of a patient, the latter needs to be cleaned beforehand, i.e. every set of synthetic DNA sold implies the sale of a purification kit.

The complementary property of the additional products is especially beneficial to Qiagen as the purification kits generate the highest gross profit margin throughout the portfolio.

Lastly, the broadness of the portfolio can be seen as success factor. By adapting to changes in biological samples and applications that researchers are interested in, Qiagen enables them to stay loyal to their products. Researchers can stick to using Qiagen purification kits no matter what project they are currently working on. Also, Qiagen is able to address researchers active in completely different fields with the same basic product adapted to their needs.

5 Sales and Marketing

Spending 24% of total revenues on sales and marketing, Qiagen is maintaining an extensive sales force with more than 400 employees. It was organised regionally. However, 6% of sales are generated by external distributors offering laboratory supplies; they are used in regions where Qiagen is not yet present with their own sales force. While distributors simply sell Qiagen products among other supplies without further services, each Qiagen sales person serves as a key account manager for various customers offering the complete product portfolio. The customers are differentiated by their institutional background, i.e. universities, research institutes, for example the Max Planck Institute, as well as commercial customers such as companies from the pharmaceutical and biotech industry.

The sales people remain in constant contact with their customers, not only taking orders, but also offering advice in product or research related questions. They develop a close relationship to all their customers which enables them to stay informed about their customer's projects' progress and learn about their new application needs and future project plans. Oftentimes, sales people are recommended by their clients to contact other researchers who are not yet using Qiagen's products

The sales force is also in charge of approaching new potential customers. Problems here mostly do not arise due to the unwillingness of researchers to use Qiagen products, but rather because of the implications of a shift in purification method: Every experiment conducted so far in the context of a current project as well as all research findings built upon earlier experiments need to be validated and therefore repeated

using any new purification method. As genetic research projects usually cover a span of three to seven years, the number of these experiments to conduct all over again can be very high. In addition, it requires patience to convince researchers to switch their working habits and research tools. Therefore it usually takes many visits by the sales person to persuade the customer.

It becomes clear that the sales force is an important instrument in order to gain new customers and stay able to serve the current and upcoming needs of the existing ones. That Qiagen customers are satisfied is proven by the frequent recommendations the sales force is supplied with. Furthermore, the diversification of Qiagen's customers provides the company with a stable base for continued growth. Qiagen is making intelligent use of inter-institutional relations.

6 Product Development and Pricing

Qiagen invests nine percent of revenues in research and development activities. The sum was fixed by a budget comprising a five-year-plan.

As a source for new product ideas, Qiagen heavily relies on input from outside of the company. In this regard, especially the academic customers are of utmost interest, as they suggest new applications and fields of research. Consequently, Qiagen invests in interesting research projects by supplying the material needed for purification purposes or even financial support. All of this information usually stems from sales people reporting their observations.

Additionally, Qiagen is running a Business Development department taking care of incoming suggestions by doctorate degree students and others. Moreover, the team is in charge of screening the market for new product ideas and for potential acquisition targets. Also, the open-door policy provided a solid base for the development of ideas.

For all of these means to gather information and inspiration, there is no standardised tool or process in place. The same holds true for internal knowledge – rather than relying on a knowledge management tool or policy, Qiagen's researchers and developers work as teams in changing compositions in order to avoid group specific knowledge and to enable knowledge sharing. Similarly, there is no target for product development, but still, the number of new products launched in one year is measured and communicated to the employees.

Pricing decisions are made on the basis of results from market research in focus groups where the customers' willingness to pay is determined.

The true importance of the sales force is revealed by looking at their role in product development. In fact, they represent the most important source for product innovation ideas. Taking into account that Qiagen spends a quarter of revenues on sales and marketing but only nine percent on research and development, it becomes clear that internal research is not a major matter of concern. The customer contact through the sales force and their intimate knowledge of current and future projects is therefore crucial for Qiagen's ability to introduce purification products that are adapted perfectly to the needs of their different targets. That Qiagen has been successful in that regard has been proven impressively by their ongoing growth in terms of revenues. But to retain this level of growth in the long run, a more systematic tool for knowledge management will have to be introduced.

7   Patents

In order to protect its products from imitation, Qiagen has registered around 400 patents, simultaneously applying for another 200. Many of these applications represent the development of already existing products under patent protection. As a result, Qiagen holds a number of so-called umbrella patents which allow for a renewal of old patents that would otherwise expire. Once it develops a technology, Qiagen may then benefit from a prolonged product life cycle, of about 10 years or more. Its innovative products have won Qiagen, amongst others, the Frost and Sullivan Award 2003.

The number of patents currently held and applied for, as well as the fact that the company's innovative power has been recognized with awards several times, prove that the reliance on external product ideas does not weaken Qiagen's potential for revolutionary products. The combination of new ideas with already existing products, i.e. the development of new products on the basis of existing technologies enables Qiagen to protect its patents for a prolonged period of time and therefore create strong market entry barriers.

8   Human Resources

The number of Qiagen's employees has – similar to revenues – increased continuously and substantially since the foundation of the company. While the workforce was 1,315 the end of 2000, Qiagen employed 1,557 the end of 2001. By the end of 2002, Qiagen employed 1,651 employees globally. Most of them worked at the German site (811),

followed by the employees in the United States (510). These sites represent the most important locations and markets for Qiagen. Most employees work in production and logistics (484) followed by sales (most of them work in the United States, Qiagen's most important market) and R&D (which mainly takes place in Germany). To a large extent the administrational work takes place in Germany, while only four people are employed for administrational purposes in the holding in Venlo, the Netherlands.

The educational and practical background of employees as well as the recruiting efforts to attract new ones vary from one department to the other. New employees in the research and development departments are oftentimes Ph.D. students with a biological or chemical background recruited directly from universities. Recruiting activities, especially for R&D, are not necessary. Qiagen is well known from research projects at universities, so that applications arrived automatically. Additionally, the company has become established to such an extent that potential new employees do not have to fear a bankruptcy in due time. New employees in the sales division oftentimes come from competitors as well as other employers in the biological sector.

Qiagen's products are not only complex regarding their ingredients and substances, but also the specific application is hard to understand for non-natural science graduates. Therefore sales representatives – who are in close contact with their key accounts at academic research organizations (e.g. universities), research institutes and industrial research (e.g. pharmaceuticals) – normally have a biological or chemical doctorate degree. On the one hand, this enables the sales force to act as experts and consultants in the field of purification and to repair damages at the customer's place. On the other hand the close contact to customers and the academic background enable them to gain valuable insights into new developments by exchanging knowledge with researchers at universities.

To assure that employees in the research and development department keep their edge, they receive extensive vocational training by returning to universities and participating in research projects. Feedback for employees and their respective superiors is given top down and bottom up. This means that employees are not only assessed by their superiors, but also the other way around. Superiors work out goals for the upcoming period and determine improvement potential jointly with the employees. Apart from the monitoring system, employee satisfaction is checked in yearly polls. The fluctuation rate at Qiagen is close to zero. The generally pleasant atmosphere within the company resulted in the fact that none of the employees are represented by a labor union or is subject to a collective bargaining agreement. Social facilities like a company-owned fitness center, company parties, a kindergarten as well as laundry facilities contribute to the good relationship between Qiagen and its employees.

All employees take part in a share option program which was initiated in 1996 together with the IPO. The number of share options for the respective employee is dependent on his/her position. While employees in the R&D department are not paid by individual results, because they work in teams, employees in the sales division are

incentivized by variable compensation. Managerial employees receive boni as part of their compensation.

Metin Colpan, the company's founder and the inventor of Qiagen's technology, was certainly an important person especially in the early phase of the company's existence. With his technological advice and know-how he contributed to Qiagen's position as a technological leader among the companies for purification of molecules. Additionally, he had many contacts to researchers and professors at German universities and was able to convince other researchers of the advantages of Qiagen's product.

Peer Schatz, with his managerial background and financial expertise, played a major role during the company's growth phase. Peer Schatz initiated the company's IPO in 1996 and acted as the representative of the company to investors.

Dr. Metin Colpan and Peer Schatz have shown the technological as well as managerial skills to lead a biotech company through the start-up and growth phase. After Dr. Colpan stepped back in fall 2003, he acted as a technological advisor to the management and therefore remained very important to the company. As described, the top management represents a key success factor during the start-up and the strong growth phase.

Additionally, the quality of Qiagen's employees represents an important success factor. Especially the sales force expertise is of crucial importance. Employees know exactly how Qiagen's products work and even more importantly, they are able to talk to researchers about new fields of application. Qiagen safeguards this know-how by progressively employing more of its own sales people, that all have an extensive academic background. Additionally, training assures that employees remain state-of-the art in their field of expertise. Employees at the production site and in other departments are also recruited from sources that guarantee expertise. Employees are compensated with share options and therefore have an interest to work in the interest of Qiagen.

9 Co-operations and Acquisitions

Qiagen has established numerous partnerships with institutes. These partnership agreements are mainly limited to joint research and development with no financial interaction between the parties involved. Additionally, the firm co-operates with other companies from the biotechnological sector. Oftentimes these co-operations also trigger financial implications in the long run, such as an agreement with Roche to use Qiagen's product as part of an item distributed by Roche itself. Additionally, Qiagen participated in the consolidation process that was a general phenomenon in the bio-

technological industry in the late 1990s and early 2000s. The following companies were established or integrated as new members within the Qiagen group:

Figure 2: Expansion of Qiagen

Company (Year)	Target Country	New name	Business
Rosys AG (1998)	Switzerland	Qiagen Instruments	Instruments for purification of acids
PreAnalytiX (1999)	Switzerland	JV with Beckton, Dickinson and Co.	Develops unique preanalytical solutions
Operon Inc. (2000)	USA	Qiagen Operon	Manufacturer and marketer of synthetic nucleic acids, DNA microarrays and synthetic genes
Sawady Group of companies (2001)	Japan	Qiagen Sciences	One of largest supplier of synthetic nucleic acids in Japan
Xeragon, Inc. (2002)	USA		Synthetic nucleic acids
GenoVision AS (2002)	Norway	Qiagen AS	Automated solutions for the purification of nucleic acids based on Genovision's proprietary magnetic particle technologies

Although Qiagen did not rely on a standardized integration process – due to cultural differences of the acquired and newly established companies – there still were some actions being taken in all of the cases. The management of the target company was included in the integration process from the beginning on, while leading employees from Qiagen took over managerial positions. The Qiagen culture was transferred to the new subsidiaries as quickly as possible. This included not only the corporate identity of Qiagen – most companies also changed their names to Qiagen – but also the facilities. The company got access to the firm intranet as well as a connection to internal resources. The standards that were already applied at the other sites of the company like social facilities were also introduced at the acquired companies. The former management was transferred to new positions at another Qiagen company. In the yearly polls that were also carried out in the newly integrated companies, the employees felt like being part of the company and were content.

Apart from the "standard" co-operations, Qiagen also gave donations as part of partnerships or just as voluntary contributions (as for example for the identification of the victims of September 11th and the research for detection of the SARS virus). These donations helped to communicate the broad range of application of Qiagen's products.

Partnerships with universities represent a very important source for possible future applications of Qiagen's products and also promote the product to customers. To be at the source of research makes it easier to see how the market will develop and to react to market trends within a reasonable time frame. With its donations to universities, Qiagen supports institutions that do research that is of potential interest to the company (e.g. research for products that would also involve purification processes). Additionally, these partnerships promote the contact to future potential employees as well as potential future clients (when the researchers start working in pharmaceutical companies).

With constant expansion since its IPO, Qiagen was able to profitably increase in size and to simultaneously gain a stronger reputation. With the acquisition of the instruments division, Qiagen enabled the acceleration of the purification process through automation for its customers. The other acquisitions added more complementary products to Qiagen's portfolio and therefore additional fields of application. However, the important requirement for all the new subsidiaries was that all companies fitted very well in Qiagen's portfolio and under the Qiagen brand. Additionally, acquisitions were used to enter markets that would have been difficult to serve (e.g. Japan) or where existing brands were too strong to compete against (e.g. Xeragon, Inc.).

The early integration of the old management during the take-over process was very helpful to integrate the new subsidiaries successfully. Additionally, the corporate culture supported the acceptance of the new mother company by employees of acquired companies.

10 Outlook

The company's culture was characterized by being very down to earth and realistic in all respects from the beginning. This was obvious when looking, for example, at how Qiagen dealt with the awards they had won. Instead of showing them off and using the awards for marketing purposes, such achievements were kept internally.

A big challenge Qiagen faced in 2003 was its own strong growth in terms of sales, employees and geographical scope. New management structures had to be instituted to support this change. The replacement of CEO Dr. Metin Colpan with Peer Schatz, the former CFO, was symptomatic. Peer had always represented Qiagen to the outside

while Metin had stayed focused on the technological and scientific orientation of the company.

Along with this change of the top position in the company there was a restructuring in form of the creation of an executive board representing all major functions existing within the company. But beyond the changing fields of research, Qiagen had to stay involved in the consistent realignment and development of its product base and the opening up of new markets. The current product program with DNA, RNA and proteins covering all important components in cellular research, provides a solid base for a strong and stable development. In the upcoming future, the focus will be on a reduction of administrative costs, in order to attribute more funds to units like research & development and sales & marketing. Additionally, the level of growth Qiagen is still facing will force the company to a continuous realignment of its set-up.

Malte Bornemann, Björn Hagemann and Udo Kießlich

SAP AG

1 Introduction 219
2 The Company 219
3 The Market 220
4 Corporate History 226
5 The Proposal 238

1 Introduction

A moderate breeze was blowing from the south while Jim Hagemann Snabe was sailing with a longboat just a couple of miles away from Sønderburg, a lovely port along the Danish Baltic Sea coast.

After having finished one of the regular SAP strategy meetings in Walldorf, Germany, he had come all the way up from the corporate headquarters to enjoy the last warm September weekend by sailing through the Baltic Sea. The meeting had gathered all the senior management levels and, of course, Jim had been actively involved as Senior Vice President and COO of SAP's Business Solution Group Financial & Public Services.

This time, the event had focused mainly on the long-term corporate strategy of SAP. At the end of the meeting the CEO, Henning Kagermann, had encouraged all the participants to contribute to the process of outlining the strategy for the upcoming years by making proposals to the board. Considering the issues of increasing industry consolidation, the looming battle for the SME segment against new rivals like Microsoft and the constant struggle to offer superior software solutions, the task did not seem to be an easy one.

Jim lay back in his boat and used the loneliness to remind himself what had made SAP strong in the past and had brought the company where it was. Maybe there was indeed a recipe for success which he could leverage to develop some proposals for the board. Suddenly the wind wangled and came straight from ahead. Taken by surprise, Jim smiled and thought that the corporate history of SAP also had not been a steady sailing cruise over the last 30 years…

2 The Company

In September 2003, SAP was the world-leading provider of business software solutions. In the years before, SAP had expanded its solutions from Enterprise Resource Planning (ERP) to Customer Relationship Management (CRM), Supply Chain Management (SCM), and Product Lifecycle Management (PLM) as well as portals and business intelligence. This expansion took into account the technological advances of the late 1990s and led to a significantly increased product portfolio. In fall 2003, the product portfolio entailed everything from standard business software products to consulting and training activities.

SAP had enjoyed a success story since it was found in 1972 by the five former German IBM employees Hasso Plattner, Dietmar Hopp, Klaus Tschira, Hans-Werner Hector

and Claus Wellenreuther. The name SAP stands for Systeme, Anwendungen und Produkte (German for: Systems, Applications & Products). The five founders were convinced that there was a market for software products which helped companies to optimize their administrative processes and thereby save time and resources. The growth of their company has been impressive (see table 1). In September 2003, SAP's success was reflected in more than 60,000 installations at more than 19,300 companies in over 120 countries. In 2002, SAP's total revenues had reached EUR 7,413 million. They were achieved by about 29,000 employees all over the world.

Table 1:   Key Financials SAP 1988-2002

(in EUR millions)	1988	1989	1990	1991	1992	1993	1994	1995	1996	1997	1998	1999	2000	2001	2002
Product revenues	59.1	118.1	154.5	216.2	243.9	350.6	667.0	988.7	1,345.0	2,039.9	2,719.8	3,094.5	4,129.1	4,701.8	4,713.6
Service revenues	28.9	64.9	93.6	132.7	172.1	197.9	252.5	370.2	532.5	936.2	1,533.6	1,941.4	2,045.8	2,549.1	2,618.1
Other revenues	3.8	4.6	7.1	12.7	9.0	14.8	16.8	19.7	25.7	45.7	62.2	74.3	90.0	90.0	81.1
Total revenues	91.9	187.6	255.2	361.5	425.0	563.3	936.2	1,387.6	1,903.1	3,021.8	4,315.6	5,110.2	6,264.6	7,340.8	7,412.8
Earnings before tax	29.2	55.9	56.5	92.3	88.5	131.3	240.9	344.6	494.5	796.4	932.0	980.3	1,012.9	1,068.8	1,107.7
Holding earnings	12.7	34.9	42.0	63.0	65.1	74.8	143.8	207.0	290.2	446.7	526.9	601.0	615.7	581.1	508.6
Employees	688	1,367	2,138	2,685	3,137	3,648	5,229	6,857	9,202	12,856	19,308	21,488	24,177	28,410	28,797

Source: 1988-2002 SAP Investor Relation

3   The Market

Due to its status as the largest application software vendor in the world, SAP competes in multiple segments of application software including CRM, SCM, PLM, and ERP.

Herewith, the company faces competition from both suite providers, like PeopleSoft and Oracle, and "best-of-breed" vendors, such as Siebel Systems, which focus on one software segment. Estimates by AMR Research show that the total addressable market size will rise to USD 77.3 billion in 2006 from USD 38.8 billion in 2001.

3.1 Market Segments and Competitors

Enterprise Resource Planning (ERP) software consists of many segments, which may be called the "backbone" of a company: human resources (HR), general accounting, inventory management, and additional industry-specific business processes. The main advantage of ERP comes from its unified nature, which leads to fewer errors, improved speed and efficiency, and more complete access to information across the whole organization. SAP's first products were largely ERP solutions. SAP's R/3 enterprise solution consists of ERP with extensions like SCM and PLM able to be added on. When disaggregating the top application software vendors' license revenues, SAP was market leader in ERP in 2002 and in 2000 with Oracle in the second position (see figure 1).

Customer relationship management (CRM) software collects and organizes customer data that come from the various distribution channels (e.g., call centers, point-of-sale operations). Hereby, it provides a comprehensive view of customer behavior in order to help a firm to allocate resources more effectively and derive more revenue from customer relationships. CRM was another important segment for SAP. Here it has reached second position behind Siebel Systems, which is a company focused on CRM software and considered to be the leader in terms of functionality and vertical expertise. According to the Gartner Group, Siebel is supposed to remain market leader until 2004, but SAP, Oracle and PeopleSoft appear to be serious challengers for the leader and will pose imminent threat to Siebel. The four players split the market more or less between themselves.

Supply chain management (SCM) software deals with the integration of flows between buyers and suppliers along a company's value-chain by automating its planning, coordination and refinement. Here, SAP has been the market leader since 2001 with an increasing gap to its competitors. However, this market is much more atomized than the others and encompasses a high number of players with smaller market share.

Figure 1:   Software Vendor Global Market Share in Enterprise Applications

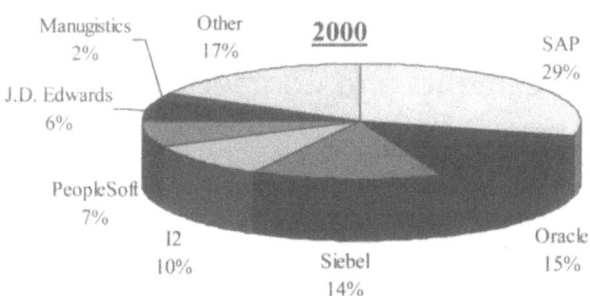

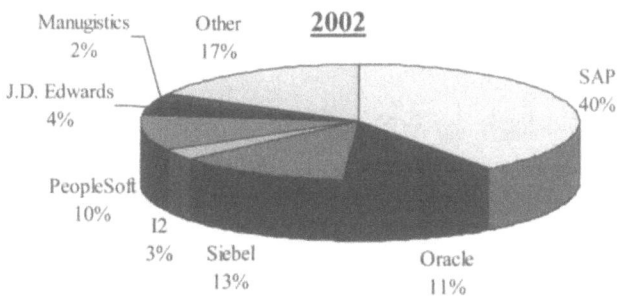

Source: Deutsche Bank Research

SAP does not have a comparativley strong position in product lifecycle management (PLM). The company has a market share of about 10%. Its main competitors include EDS, Parametric Technology and Dassault Systèmes.

3.2   Trends - Technology and Market

The rise of new segments showes that enterprise software does not only try to cater the internal needs of a single company, but that the software is more and more supposed to capture a firm's links to its customers and suppliers. Next to core ERP solutions like

finance and human resources, new functionalities such as SCM and CRM has been added. Within a company's borders, areas like PLM have grown in importance. Portal technology serves as a connection for all the applications plugged into a common user interface and enabled the use of such systems tailored to specific needs of various user groups. The arise of the Internet has made enterprise software vendors adopt open standards and switch to component-based architecture, which increased flexibility and allowed easier integration with third party software. All this has led to the fact that the targeted customer base have grown from a few handful of users within a firm to up to 100% of a firm's employees.

With an increase in general penetration, industry-specific solutions have become more and more important. They do not only offer the opportunity to add additional functionalities for existing customers, but also helps to enter industries that a few years ago were not viewed as target customers. From a traditional customer base in the manufacturing industries, SAP, like other companies, expanded to sectors such as financial services, transportation, and public services.

Finally, the software providers are increasingly addressing the mid-market segment. Especially the expanded use of component structure and the Internet have provided the necessary tools to address mid-market needs. While in the late 1990s smaller local vendors played a dominating role in this segment, the turbulences of the years after the burst of the Internet bubble had forced many of them out of business. Especially in the very low end of the market, competition has intensified, in particular between those smaller local players and Microsoft after the latter's acquisitions of Great Plains in 2001 and Navision in 2002. The two companies created the core of a new Microsoft Business Solutions unit that aim to deliver enterprise software to small and mid-market businesses. Despite its acquisitions of Great Plains and Navision, Microsoft still has a long way to go to accumulate expertise in the business software and develop a functionality set that would convince larger customers to switch to Microsoft. However, as the established vendors are also trying to capture smaller and smaller clients, a conflict between the software giants Microsoft and SAP does not seem so far away (see figure 2 and 3).

Figure 2: SAP Competitive Landscape

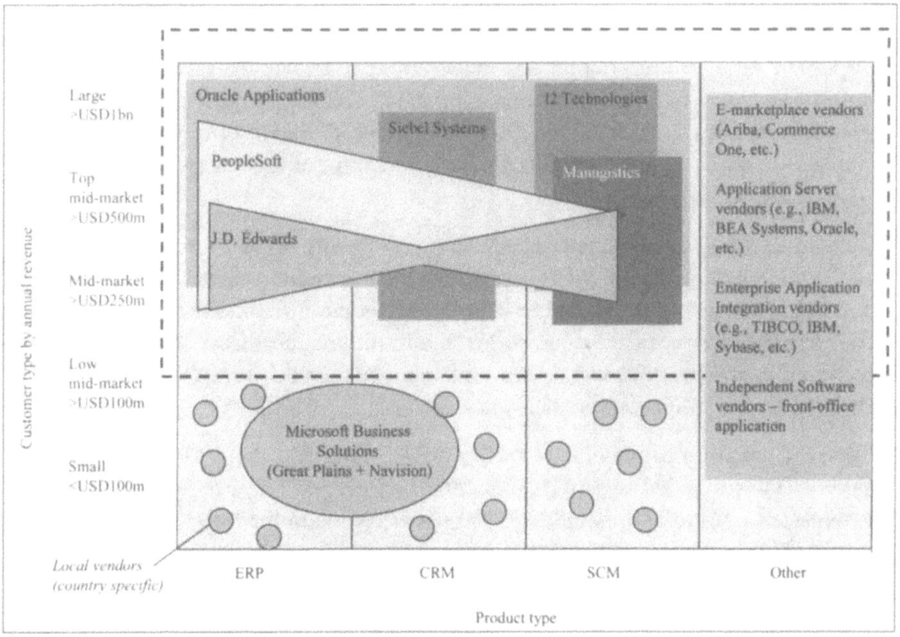

Source: SAP, Company Reports, Oppenheim Research

Figure 3: SAP Product Portfolio

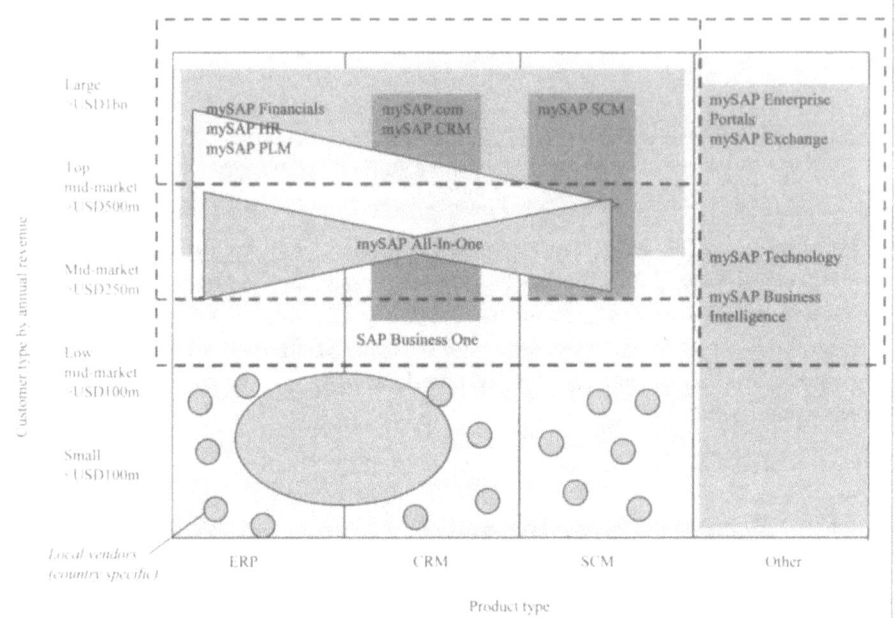

Sources: SAP, Oppenheim Research

3.3 Trends - Customers

Customer behavior has changed significantly over the last years, especially reflected by buyers' increasing power and a change in priorities. Industry experts talk about a shift from a sellers' market until the late 90s to the arise of a buyers' market. Two main reasons are often named for that: first, economic recession, and second, overinvestment during the last years. As a consequence of these influences, SAP like its competitors has identified four issues, which determine the customer's choice: quick return on investment, reduced total cost of ownership, protection of existing IT investments and finally optimization of existing IT infrastructure. This has led to a reallocation of scarce funds to the most mission-critical issues and longer sales cycles for software vendors.

Overinvestment was a result of the uncertainty about the future of information technology (Internet, e-Commerce etc.) as well as of the Y2K problem and the transition to

the Euro starting 1999. During that time, companies had purchased software licenses for more employees than necessary. Still having unused licenses, companies neither wanted nor needed to make new purchases, which led to a further slow-down in investment and extended the replacement horizon.

Finally, and especially important in the long run, potential customers are pushing down the average deal size, preferring smaller rather than large projects. This has a direct revenue effect for the software vendors. However, it might also have a positive effect in the long run, in particular, a positive impact on margins on software sales as well as on maintenance revenue due to less discounting by the vendor.

Changes in the distribution of market share at the beginning of the 21st century show that "generalists" such as SAP, Oracle, PeopleSoft and J.D. Edwards profited from the developments stressing integration over functionality, which has led to a lower total cost of ownership for the customers. In contrast, focused players such as Siebel, Manugistics and i2 Technologies face certain difficulties not being able to offer a readily integrated solution.

3.4 Trends - Employees

Globalization not only had an impact on the sell side of a software company, but it also offered the possibility of developing its product wherever it wanted to. Personnel costs are an extraordinarily cost position for software companies. Therefore, more and more companies move at least part of their software development to low cost countries like India. As SAP's CEO Kagermann pointed out in an interview in 2003, the movement of 1,000 developer positions to India could increase SAP's operating margin by as much as 1%. However, there is a trade-off between these pure salary costs and other influences like corporate culture, brand image and additional costs (e.g., resulting from high employee fluctuation), which arise due to dispersed developing centers.

4 Corporate History

4.1 Foundation: 1972 - 1986

When SAP was founded in 1972, one could hardly foresee how successful this software company would once be. In contrast, the myth goes that IBM did not believe in the vision of its five managers and saw no market for the product at this point in time. This behavior implied that a lot of doubts existed about SAP's future. Hasso Plattner,

Dietmar Hopp, Klaus Tschira, Werner Hector und Claus Wellenreuther founded SAP in Weinheim, Germany, with the vision of developing the first software for real-time data processing that would, in addition, finally integrate the different programs into one solution for the customers. The letter R, which stands for "real-time", would remain part of the brand names of the company's products for a long time. Historically, all other systems at this point in time were batch-based, so that one would enter the data and run the system during the night in order to get the data consistent and finally the desired outcome. The founders not only had the vision for the product, but they also had some unique new ideas about how to shape the architecture of these programs, so that they would be capable to run real-time and be consistent in order to work integrative.

Of the five founders, Dietmar Hopp was often considered to be the "business guy" with a strong focus on revenue and cost drivers, while Hasso Plattner was more known as the creative person with great ideas for the development of technology. Both of them had an enormous influence on SAP until the late 1990s, when Hopp left the board and the succession from the founders to the next generation was initialized. They ensured certain standards for their recruiting. Most many employees of SAP in 2003 still remembered having had recruiting interviews with one of the founders.

First customers of SAP included Dow Chemical and ICI, two large multinational chemical companies with a multidimensional organization and very complex processes. SAP worked extraordinarily intensively with these customers for a long time and focused on delivering on the needs of its clients. As Heinz Haller, former Global Business Manager Polymers at Dow Chemical, put it: "At that time, SAP was the only provider offering a fully integrated system. There was no other company offering a comparable solution to us that could model the entire value chain." SAP started with accounting software in 1973 (RF) and soon added purchase management, inventory management and auditing, already integrating it into one solution (RM). The sequence of developments was driven by the requests of the clients rather than by an internal master plan how the steps to a complete package should look like. However, the founders always took care to keep the software code generic so that it could be sold to other customers, too. SAP also ensured the independence of its software from a particular operating system, so that the switch from DOS to OS in 1974 succeeded in a smooth way.

Interestingly, SAP bought its first own computer no earlier than in 1979. Before that year it had used the computer center of its clients with their permission, especially when it was not used by the client itself, i.e. during night and on the weekends. SAP followed a strong policy of renting and leasing rather than buying equipment and buildings during this time. They moved into the first own building in 1980.

SAP grew from nine employees in 1972 to approximately 200 employees in 1986, while revenue grew from DEM 0.6 million to DEM 100 million during the same time period. However, SAP concentrated most of its efforts in Germany, becoming the dominant

player in this market, but resisting early temptations to expand abroad on a large scale.

4.2   Growth: 1986 -1998

After this first period of substantial growth, SAP had to face new challenges impacting the organizational structure, the ownership of the firm and the corporate culture. The relocation of the headquarters from Weinheim to Walldorf, Germany, in 1986 marked the beginning of a new period for SAP.

In the early years SAP had been a GbR (non-trading partnership). In 1976 SAP was reorganized in the legal form of GmbH (limited liability company). By 1988 the firm adopted the legal form of an AG (public limited company) and became listed at the German stock market in Frankfurt.

The shareholder assembly agreed to increase the nominal capital to DEM 60 million in 1988. For the purpose of the IPO, DEM 9 million were offered to new investors. During a press conference on October 24, 1988, the price of DEM 750 per share was announced. The stock started trading on November 2, 1988. By the end of the year the share was already listed at around DEM 800, giving SAP a market value of DEM 960 million.

Of the IPO proceeds, roughly DEM 40 million went to the firm, the rest to the founders. According to the official sales prospectus the proceeds of the IPO were to be used for financing the continuous growth of SAP. While reducing their combined share position to 76.4%, the remaining four founders (Wellenreuther had left the company in 1982) were still in complete charge of the firm and held all seats on the executive board.

Besides the financial aspects of the IPO the offering also brought along other changes. Through the listing the external view on SAP changed, the company was perceived as a "real firm" from now on. Internally, the perception changed such that now all employees could measure the success of SAP just by looking at the daily share price. The performance of the stock over the next decades was indeed impressive (see figure 4). Consequently, SAP was invited to become a member of the DAX-30 in 1995, the equity index of the 30 largest German publicly listed firms. By going to the NYSE in August 1998, SAP became a truly internationally registered firm.

Figure 4: SAP Stock Performance (log and normal scale)

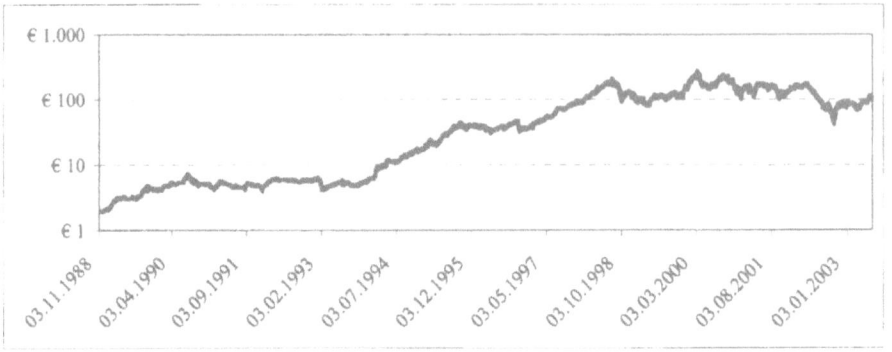

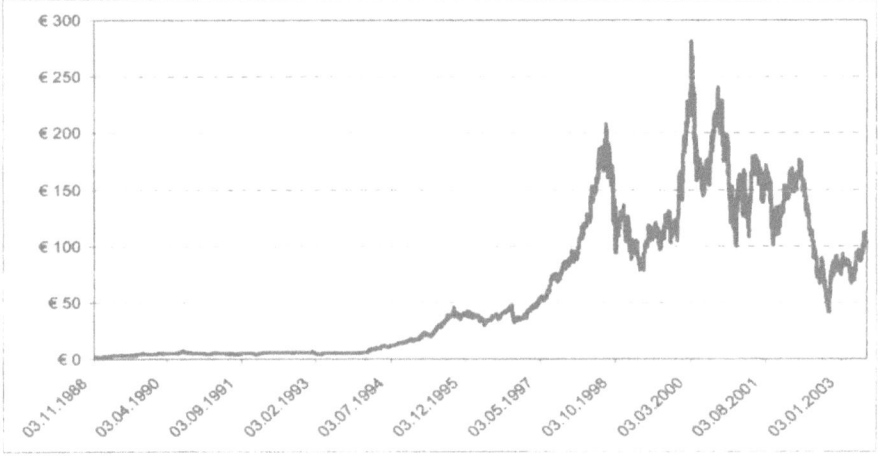

Source: Company Homepage

In 1984, SAP founded a new central office in Biel, Switzerland. This 100% subsidiary was supposed to manage the international expansion. The objective was to have a rather sales centric unit while the German headquarter continued to focus on developing.

By 1986, 11% of SAP's revenues came from abroad via an international sales network including subsidiaries in the Netherlands, France, Spain and the UK. However, the first steps abroad took place in a rather unconventional manner.

The very first customers of SAP were few large chemical firms such as Dow Chemical, that were looking for a way to improve the exchange of information between their

international subsidiaries. "SAP allowed us to link our different European divisions. Implementation of SAP was triggered more by our functional divisions rather than by the country managers", as Heinz Haller stated.

Being pleased by the performance of the software product, SAP's customers soon demanded installations in their other European core markets. After architecting the first solutions for non-German customers, SAP actually had already adopted to the different national environments, languages and other factors. Realizing that, SAP started to capitalize on those early investments. Soon after the first major projects had taken place abroad, offices were set up in the respective markets. Since 1986, the Swiss unit began to plan the upcoming international expansion more strategically by hiring experienced sales and marketing experts. A generic approach to enter new markets was developed: Being asked by a couple of major clients to serve their foreign unit in a certain country, SAP began to hire local sales people and a country manager. SAP would then officially enter the market by opening a first office. In case the country was very important or too large in size for a completely local approach, the entry was accompanied by German experts sent to the new office for a limited period of time. By leveraging the existing customer base of SAP the new subsidiary could soon report its first installations to the international sales unit. Eventually, the local SAP team used product presentations and marketing initiatives to further increase the local customer base.

The sales network was run in a decentralized manner. During the first period of local expansion, the new subsidiary could rely on the financial support of the mother. Within the new units a certain degree of autonomy did create some kind of start-up corporate culture. At the same the marketing efforts to potential clients benefited from the SAP brand and the image of being a German technology firm (see table 2).

Table 2: Opening of SAP Subsidiaries Abroad

1988	Switzerland, Austria, Netherlands, France, Spain, UK, USA, Denmark, Sweden, Italy
1989	Canada, Singapore, Australia
1990	Belgium
1992	Japan, Malaysia, South Africa, Czech Republik
1994	Ireland, Mexico
1995	Russia, Poland, New Zealand, Thailand, Philippines, China, South Korea
1996	Venezuela
1997	Hungary, India, Taiwan, Hong Kong, Indonesia
1998	Israel
1999	Portugal, Finland, Norway, Slovakia
2000	Greece, Bulgaria, Ukraine, Nigeria
2001	Cyprus, Turkey, Croatia

Sources: SAP Annual Reports

Naturally, the home market of SAP became Europe. Other major markets were North America and Japan, while China and India were considered as long-term strategic markets for SAP. By looking at the entry into the Chinese market one can identify many features of the typical entry strategy implemented. After giving product presentations in various major cities, SAP founded SAP Software Systems Co. Ltd. in Beijing in 1995. Quickly more than 20 employees were recruited. The first business orders

could be signed with Chinese subsidiaries of European firms or joint-ventures already present in China, examples included VW, Siemens, or Metro. The strong demand in China led SAP to open a second local office in Shanghai soon after.

In 1990, SAP started to run international graduate programmes by hiring non-German trainees. The new employees were intensively trained at the corporate headquarters in Germany and then sent to their particular home market to support and manage the local expansion. While in 1986 the ratio of international sales to total sales was 11%, it increased to almost 80 % at the end of 1998.

The major impact on the business development of SAP during the period of 1986 to 1998 came from the introduction and roll-out of R/3 in 1992/93, putting SAP in the position of being the industry leader.

The introduction of R/2 had already rendered former material requirement planning techniques absolute. R/2 was typically run on mainframe computers, e.g., the AS/400 series of IBM. During the middle and late 1980s, a hardware innovation paved the way for R/3: the emergence of the desktop as the core of a client-server-structure. By 1987, a customer of SAP had asked the firm to adapt the current software to be used on his new desktop-based computer system. This smaller client wanted to get rid of the large and expensive mainframe computers, but still take advantage of SAP software. While designing a single customer solution, SAP became aware of the structural design advantages of a solution centered around this new hardware set-up. These experiences directly contributed to the ongoing software development process for the product that was later known as R/3.

SAP had always been keen to remain independent in its developing approach. In order to outperform in-house software solutions, SAP needed to have a generic code and concept of software modules, which could easily be transferred and leveraged. Herewith, SAP was able to have a solution for the newly introduced NT-operating system in less than two months when it was introduced in 1994. The flexibility in the programming, e.g., of the language module, allowed SAP to have several language options of any product available for international customers early on.

By the time R/3 was introduced, SAP had a software solution, which was 1.5 years ahead of competition. Other potential ERP providers such as MNS lost most of their business mainly because they focused too long on mainframe solutions. In addition, industry solutions, e.g., a special package for the oil industry, were introduced by SAP during this period. Being of limited benefit for SAP in the early phase of the market introduction, the industry-specific solutions later turned out to be an advantage.

The role-out of R/3 became a big success. With R/3, SAP products now were also attractive to the middle segment of the market. Even firms with less than 25 employees began to install the software and ideas existed to even offer the software preinstalled on every new desktop delivered to a company.

His period was characterized by an even accelerating growth and still beeing internally referred to as the "happy R/3 days". But the growth also had a strategic decision element. Seeing the ERP segment as a "winner takes it all" market, even growing by 80% annually would in some regions mean losing market share.

4.3 Challenges: 1998 - 2003

By the time of the late 1990s, SAP had managed to expand internationally and had become a real global player. The number of employees had risen from 2,800 in 1991 to 19,000 employees in 1999. R/3 was still an extremely successful product and SAP's customer base had grown to 9,000.

In this situation, new challenges arose. The one with the most influence not only on the entire industry of enterprise software but on the whole business world was the emergence of the Internet. This new way of exchanging information had a strong impact on SAP's strategy and led to major changes in SAP's product portfolio.

SAP R/3's system architecture was capable to integrate the Internet already in 1996– but nobody at SAP regarded this as a significant feature that could be important to the customers. For a quite long time, this feature was not even communicated within the organization. As a consequence, SAP's image began to turn to that of a rather old-fashioned, complex and slow moving company, at least compared to most of its American competitors that aggressively marketed their online products. SAP only slowly realized that development. In a first phase that lasted about one and a half years, the company reacted confused to the changed business environment. Several projects were launched to deal with the Internet hype (e.g., eSAP and the acquisition of portals technology). SAP also acquired various smaller start-up companies, but its initiatives mostly lacked coordination. Smaller "best-of-breed" competitors, like for example Siebel in CRM software, nearly outgrew SAP in revenues in the late 1990s, although their software had a much narrower focus.

When Hasso Plattner himself in a speech to the employees in Walldorf in 1999 admitted that he had underestimated the impact of the Internet on the way business was done, he said that everybody at SAP should become clear about the fact that "the Internet is the future".

At that point of time SAP had learned the lesson that the Internet had changed the business completely and that the rules of this new game required a reformulation of the strategy. Several initiatives were started to secure the market leadership: On the one hand, SAP did still pursue strategic acquisitions of Internet start-ups whenever it felt that a certain company would complement its portfolio, but these activities became much better coordinated and focused on the new fundamental business requirements.

On the other hand, the company did increase marketing efforts (from 50.8% of revenues in 1998 to 57.3% in 1999) to establish a new brand image of being the number one enterprise software provider for every ambitious company. The new company slogan was: "The best run e-businesses run SAP". However, SAP still did not fully believe in this perception game. SAP's managers were convinced to have the best products to fulfill their customers' needs and kept marketing expenses at a reasonable level. They even let some of the customers switch to smaller "best-of-breed" competitors that marketed their niche products more offensively - always being convinced that customers would return to SAP and its fully integrated suite solution after realizing that they needed a full solution provider. This strategy worked out in most cases and after the first hype was over, SAP found itself with a bigger market share than ever before.

An additional problem that SAP realized during this period was related to its products. At that time its software was already offering too much functionality. The company's products could do more than the customers were asking for. This led to the situation that some customers who considered SAP's products "over-engineered" switched to competitors that offered a less sophisticated product for a lower price. The realization of the fact that functionality was no longer the most important criterion for a customer made the management of SAP rethink the company's strategy. Usability had been identified as the key technological requirement for future products and consequently, a new initiative of customer orientation was started, named "EnjoySAP". It was initialized in 1998 with the objective of redesigning the user interface of SAP's applications in a more user friendly way. The initiative led to the development of mySAP.com, a new easy-to-use version of SAP applications that combined latest e-Commerce solutions with the existing ERP software and was a fully web-based product.

In line with the surprising success of the Internet and the hype of the new economy, SAP entered again a phase of fast growth. Before the successful launch of mySAP.com in 2000, two external effects contributed to the fact that, despite the late start into the Internet business, SAP realized positive growth rates during this period of time: First, the fear of a software failure at the end of the millennium drove many companies to purchase a new enterprise software or a new version of their software earlier than planned, leading to increased sales. Second, the introduction of the Euro in 1999 as the common European currency had the same effect. It triggered an enormous increase in demand as nearly 20% of all systems were renewed in 1999 compared to about 10% during a "normal" year. Fortunately, the management had foreseen the exponential development of SAP's business model and therefore, SAP had the necessary infrastructure in place to support a large and growing number of customers. The only factor limiting the growth of the company during these times was the limited capacity regarding implementation. SAP simply had problems in finding enough qualified people that could implement the software at the customers' and accompany the implementation process. While it was a long term philosophy of SAP to outsource the very

last part of the value chain, implementation at the client, they also lacked enough qualified external partners during this period.

The burst of the Internet bubble and the following economic downturn that hit the IT industry at the beginning of the new millennium were the next hard tests SAP had to face. Since the foundation in 1972, tough markets had always been a good time for the company to gain market share. Managing costs was the most important challenge during these times. At SAP, cost reduction became an issue during the downturn of the economy that started in 2000. About 85% of the employees of the company had an academic background. These employees did identify with SAP to an extent that, when they saw that the market environment became difficult, they came up with over 1,800 different ideas to save costs in just one week. Their proposals ranged from starting to pay for the lunch that had been offered for free by the company (and still was in 2003, as the proposal had never been realized) to taking over a bigger share of the cost of the company cars. As a senior executive had once put it: "At SAP, people take over responsibility. This is because they know competence counts more than a title and that their ideas will be respected by the top management if they are good."

In the years 1998 to 2003, SAP faced another challenge in changing from the founder-led organization it had been for over 25 years to a company led by external managers. Mastering this challenge took place in two steps: In 1998, two of the remaining three active founders (Hector had left the company in 1996), Dietmar Hopp and Klaus Tschira, changed from the executive board to the supervisory board. Especially the changeover of Dietmar Hopp during this time of an unclear business environment left many employees with a feeling of uncertainty, as Hopp had been regarded as the "rational" business man, responsible for keeping the company on track and making the right decisions at the right time. The successor of Hopp, Henning Kagermann, became the new Co-chairman joining Hasso Plattner. He managed to resolve all doubts and became at least as respected for both his business skills and his understanding of the company's products as Hopp had been. The outstanding reputation that Kagermann built up in the years as a CEO also allowed Plattner to retreat from the board in 2003 without causing any turmoil inside the company or the financial markets.

4.4 The Future: 2003 and beyond...

At the beginning of the 21st century, competition in the business software industry had been increasing and consolidation had started. SAP was still the leader of the business software solutions industry and was determined to defend this position. To do so, the company had to fight against its existing competitors as well as to keep an eye on new rivals. Especially Microsoft, the by far biggest software company of the world (see figure 5), was eager to grab a share of the business software market by leveraging its experience and its undisputed market leadership in the consumer software market.

Microsoft had already launched a solution for small and medium enterprises (SME), which it was aggressively marketing. These developments required SAP to react appropriately, while not endangering its position in its core market.

Figure 5: Market Capitalization of Software Firms as of September 30, 2003

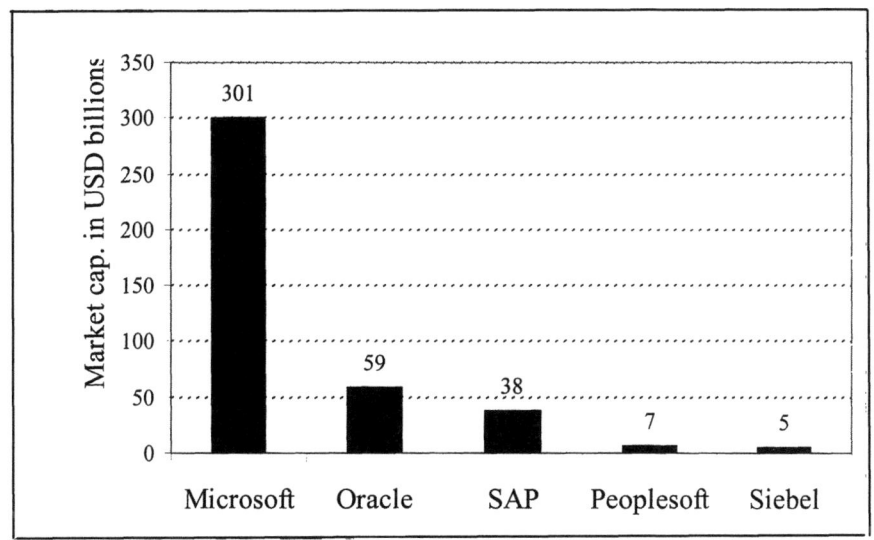

Source: Yahoo Finance, 2003

To differentiate itself from the existing competitors in ERP software and its segments (CRM, SCM, PLM etc.), SAP was constantly developing its product portfolio. In late 2003, SAP launched NetWeaver, a new integration and application platform designed to reduce switching costs of clients by allowing them to integrate their existing enterprise software modules, independent of their origin, into the NetWeaver interface. Herewith, SAP was for the first time able to target those clients that were previously bound to a competitor's product range by the specificity of their already acquired modules. Based on a graphical user interface, the software was designed for high usability. The launch of NetWeaver was a risky move for SAP, as it offered customers the possibility to combine SAP's products with modules of its competitors, thereby potentially reducing the revenue per customer for SAP. However, SAP's management explicitly decided to take this step, also in order to challenge their internal development department, as product managers of the modules could no longer rely on the bundling effect of a complete SAP suite solution, but had to compete directly with competitors' modules.

2003 was also the year during that the consolidation of the business software industry brought up the biggest take-over offer ever in this market. In an attempt to gain the critical size necessary to remain independent, PeopleSoft successfully took over J.D. Edwards in 2003. Soon after, Oracle launched a hostile take-over bid on PeopleSoft in order to improve competitiveness with respect to SAP in the enterprise software segment. In late 2003, the outcome of this attempt was still unclear. As an offer of this size happened for the first time in the enterprise software industry, the authorities watched it carefully. Both the European Commission as well as the US Department of Justice were examining the issue. SAP at that time seemed to be the lucky winner of the take-over battle. On the one hand, many customers, concerned about the uncertain outcome of the fight between Oracle, PeopleSoft and J.D. Edwards, switched to SAP products, regarding the company as a safe haven. On the other hand, industry analysts questioned the overall economic rationale of mergers in the software industry.

Another important development for SAP was the occurrence of Microsoft on the business solution software scene. SAP itself had launched its products for the mid-market segment, Business One and All in one, in 2002 and was counting on the SME segment for future growth. Although Oracle had also entered competition in this segment by launching Oracle Small Business Solutions in 2003, it was Microsoft that was considered the biggest threat. Although Microsoft did not have a long experience in the business software market, it had the resources to acquire the necessary skills (acquisitions of Great Plains and Navision) and many expected a showdown to come up rather sooner than later between the two giants of the software industry, SAP and Microsoft. The US-software company is about five times bigger than SAP in terms of market capitalization and has a cash reserve that is sufficient to buy the entire company. SAP's relatively low market capitalization was a result of the fact that its margins were significantly smaller than those of most competitors (see figure 6). Therefore, the board has given priority to the increase of operating margins in order to catch up with its competitors and has also been discussing potential cost savings initiatives, e.g., shifting software development to low-cost countries like India.

Overall, the increasing competition in the formerly prospering enterprise software market is a challenge for all players and forces them to rethink their strategies for the future.

Figure 6: Operating Margins of SAP and Major Competitors

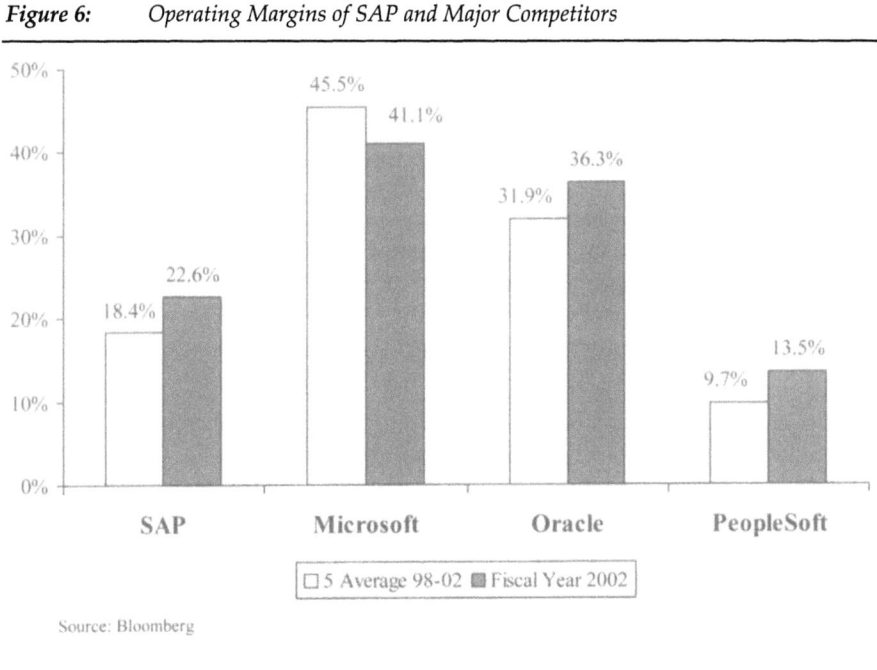

5 The Proposal

A message on his cell phone ended Jim's journey through the corporate history of SAP. Amazed by the findings, he decided to send his ideas to the board as soon as he would be back in Walldorf.

First of all, the concept would summarize the critical success factors of SAP since the company's foundation. In a second step, it would point out what he thought were the factors that would remain of crucial importance and whether the management also had to consider new factors for future success.

As a passionate sailor he knew that it was crucial to build on the experience acquired during past journeys. He felt that by looking back to the past of SAP, the management board would get a lot of insights on how to steer their ship to a successful future.

Maximilian Niederhofer

SinnerSchrader AG

1	Introduction	241
2	Company History	242
3	Market	243
4	Industry and Competitive Positioning	244
5	Business Model	245
6	Project Services	246
7	Media Services	247
8	Organization	247
9	The CEO's Perspective of the Problem at Hand	248
10	A Second Problem	249
11	The Problem at Hand – Functional Perspectives	249
	Appendix	251

1 Introduction

Matthias Schrader, co-founder and chief executive officer of SinnerSchrader AG, leaned back in his chair. On this day in early October 2001, he had been talking for over an hour and felt spent and rather irritated. From within his glass-walled office, he could see directly onto the busy floor of the renovated warehouse Oliver Sinner and he had made the company's avant-garde home. It had been a fast ascent, hard work and hard play, and up to this point he had enjoyed every minute of it.

Today, however, was not a good day. For a few months now, there was some intangible but omnipresent factor undermining morale among SinnerSchrader's employees. Both quantity and quality of the work done were declining. On the one hand, Schrader knew he had to right this thing, whatever it was, to keep the company's rapid growth on track. On the other hand, he neither knew where to begin, nor did he have the time to deal with these internal problems. His hand-held scheduler kept beeping to remind him of clients needing to be called and met with and his in-box was overflowing with messages that had one thing in common: the priority 'urgent' notice in the header.

"Best to delegate," he thought for the umpteenth time that year, "but then again, to whom?"

He had thus summoned the heads of SinnerSchrader's three functional groups to his office, people he informally called his chief consultant, chief engineer and chief designer. While he knew he had to get to the bottom of what was happening, he somehow felt that the three people in front of him were insisting on being a part of the problem. His gaze out of the glass walls of his office was as much an expression of the rising anger inside him as a question posed to his background in consulting: had anyone ever addressed this problem of a rapidly growing company theoretically? How do you deal pragmatically and quickly with this sort of behavior without alienating half of your employees? The chief engineer cleared his throat, bringing Schrader back to the confines of his office.

"So you realize," Schrader said to the three men in front of him, "that I consider this a serious problem. There are glitches in technical quality, delays in project completion, clients who are unhappy and don't even know who their main contact is. Last week, I got a call from a customer complaining that things were very different depending on whom he talked to. When I went down to speak to the people responsible, it seems that no one thought it was him. The engineers are blaming the consultants, the designers are blaming the engineers and the consultants are saying the 'creatives' and 'techies' aren't doing their work properly. When I asked an engineer yesterday what he had just completed, he barely knew the project name. It seemed like he just does what he's told, fires it out to another functional group and then forgets about it. Where's that team spirit we used to have?"

Maximilian Niederhofer

Schrader saw the three men shift uncomfortably in their seats.

"Well," said the chief consultant, "the point is that we have to promise fast deadlines because clients are pushy. And then, if stuff doesn't get done by the engineering group..."

"That fingerpointing is exactly what I was talking about!" said Schrader. "I want you three to sit down together and present me a workable solution plus implementation plan by the end of this week, something that is acceptable to all and incorporates your vision of where this company is headed."

2 Company History

SinnerSchrader AG, a consulting and service company for transactional websites based in Hamburg, Germany, was founded by Oliver Sinner and Matthias Schrader in early 1996. The two founders' initial project for Intershop, a software company, yielded €4,000, just enough to pay the deposit for renting the company's first offices. Organic growth was rapid and often only constrained by a lack of able employees. The company's 1996 projects included the development of two online shops for German retailers Görtz and Conley's, a distribution platform for IT wholesaler CHS and the marketing of the first-ever HTML-banner advertisement within the German internet universe.

By December 1997, SinnerSchrader had expanded aggressively, building several transactional online presences, among others for Hewlett-Packard (computers and peripherals) and Lingenbrinck (books). The management team had been enlarged to include two software specialists, Sebastian Dröber and Detlef Wichmann. Fiscal 1997 revenues were € 700,000, generated by the full-time equivalent of 12 employees (see figures 1 & 2).

Fiscal 1998 brought similar success, including new projects for Europcar (car rental), ricardo.de (internet auctions) and Transtec AG (hardware retailer). During the course of the year, the company also developed a tool for measuring online advertising efficacy, called AdTraction. For the Europcar website, SinnerSchrader received the Intel eBusiness Award for the "best e-business application in Germany". At the end of 1998, heavy recruiting had led to SinnerSchrader employing 26 full-time equivalents. Fiscal 1998 revenues had increased to € 1.8 million.

With the help of Michael Herz, a founder of coffee-retailing chain Tchibo, in early 1999 SinnerSchrader hired Thomas Dyckhoff, ex-DaimlerChrysler M&A officer, and prepared to go public to benefit from the general internet euphoria. On November 2, an initial public offering of 25% of company shares was listed on the Frankfurt stock exchange segment Neuer Markt. Over-subscribed 28 times and with an IPO price of

€12 at the upper end of the book-building span, the stock was first quoted at €22 and closed up almost 79% on the day. 1999 projects for Talkline (communications), ricardo.de and Lingenbrinck prompted a cascade of industry awards: two CeBIT Innovations finalist prizes, the Multimedia Award in Silver for the "most successful e-business newcomer of the year" and the TV Movie award 1998 for the "best shopping site of the year". Fiscal 1999 revenues were up sharply to €5 million.

2000 brought further rapid growth. Primary projects included a B2B platform for ricardo.de, a transactional website for Tchibo, a brokerage platform for PropertyGate.com (real estate), the development of tools for Deutsche Post (shipping), an online shop for Ipuri (fashion), the restructuring of the internet presence of Viag Interkom (mobile communications) and the online shop of Otto Versand (a catalogue retailer). Cash-rich from the IPO, the company acquired the German and US consulting and services company Netmatic AG, entered two joint ventures, established an international presence with SinnerSchrader UK and formed a strategic alliance with MediaTransfer to develop new marketing research processes. The company received three industry awards at the "Corporate Media 2000" trade convention. Oliver Sinner was named Hamburg's "Entrepreneur of the Year" by several entrepreneurial associations and the Hamburg Sparkasse. Fiscal 2000 revenues had increased to €14.7 million. By this time, 170 full-time equivalent employees were working for SinnerSchrader.

With the Neuer Markt index beginning to slide in the second quarter of 2000, a period of consolidation began for the industry as a whole. The growth forecasts for the most attractive customer segment, pure-play internet companies, were significantly revised downwards and SinnerSchrader's stock fell sharply from its high of €92 in March (see figure 3). Nevertheless, in defiance of the industry trend, SinnerSchrader managed to keep on expanding through to early 2001.

3   Market

Three factors favored SinnerSchrader's rapid expansion: the increasing penetration of the internet in Germany, the growing acceptance of online transactions as a medium for the interaction of customers and companies and the demand for integrated, one-stop-shop solutions.

At the time of SinnerSchrader's inception in 1996, Germany's market for online retailing was already larger than that of all other European countries combined. Not only did this make Germany the strategically most attractive market in Europe, analysts also anticipated that, in contrast to the United States, the country would continue to see high growth rates over the following years. Though subsequently revised in structure – less demand by new economy and more by old economy players – there was

little downward adjustment in the forecast of over-all demand for website services in Europe (see figure 4).

Up to this point, most businesses had been using the internet only as a means for one-way communication and public relations. With the potential of online transactions becoming apparent, companies were keen on interactive transactional B2C and B2B sites that were directly tied to company back-end systems. However, not only did internal IT departments not have the technical know-how, but company executives were not sure what applications to offer customers. Furthermore, there were little to no experiences in designing attractive graphical user interfaces for the internet. This induced demand for the integrated strategic, technical and creative consulting and services of architecture service businesses like SinnerSchrader.

Alongside the booming market for e-business solutions, the demand for online media services was growing at a breathtaking pace (compounded annual growth of 73%). Including banner advertising and different forms of direct marketing, this field of activity had been pursued by SinnerSchrader since its inception both through dedicated applications and the marketing of media space. SinnerSchrader's 5% market share in the online media services market resulted in purchasing conditions that had, in the past, yielded healthy margins.

4 Industry and Competitive Positioning

Though a very young market, the low barriers-to-entry for IT professionals-turned-entrepreneurs had allowed a multitude of competitors to flourish (see figure 5). In 1998, there were approximately 1,750 multimedia agencies, with the 50 largest agencies accounting for only half the industry revenues. The largest competitor at the time, Pixelpark, had a market share of approximately 8%.

However, in spring of 2000, consolidation set in. Industry flagships like Pixelpark and Kabel New Media announced financial difficulties. Fierce price competition had resulted from ever-more companies, like traditional IT providers and classical strategic consulting boutiques eager to expand business with existing clients, trying to grab market share. The resulting lower fees and capacity utilizations combined with relatively high fixed labor costs due to Germany's labor legislation wreaked havoc on the industry's margins.

Matthias Schrader believed a main competitive advantage to be the company's differentiated, "chameleon-like" positioning that resulted from its integration of the three functions, consulting, design and engineering (see figure 6). Competing with multimedia agencies like Pixelpark or Kabel on a project proposal, SinnerSchrader relied on

its technical background with award-winning application innovations. Confronted with the traditional IT providers like GFT or Iqena at a pitch, SinnerSchrader communicated its competence in consulting and creative design. Similarly, throughout the life of the company, SinnerSchrader's unique selling proposition changed. In the beginning a focus was placed on the integration of the conceptual and technical realization of transaction websites. From 1997-1999 the main competitors were multimedia agencies and the primary communicated USP was technological competence. During consolidation in 2000, competition from IT providers and consulting companies was more intense and the USP thus became SinnerSchrader's experience with graphical user interface (GUI) navigability and user friendliness.

5 Business Model

In 2001, Matthias Schrader described the company as "a strategic partner for the development, implementation and operation of end-to-end e-business solutions". The company's core value proposition was offering individually optimized e-business concepts in a one-stop-shop, undertaking all activities from the initial concept to launch implementation and the ongoing operational maintenance of the website.

While initially focused on pure-play internet companies, the end of the dot-com boom completely changed SinnerSchrader's customer profile (see figure 7). While in the second half of 1999 approximately 40% of revenues had come from internet companies like ricardo.de, fiscal 2000/2001 saw that figure declining to under 6%. The most important clients were now large, established brick-and-mortar incumbents like Deutsche Bank, Lingenbrink, Görtz, Tchibo and Europcar.

In analogy, the focus on core businesses also changed considerably over time. Before the company's IPO in 1999, the list of business activities had extended to "everything under the sun" connected to e-commerce and e-business. For instance, Project Services, Media Services and operations were all called core business activities of SinnerSchrader in its IPO prospectus, because in the absence of a clear strategy, these had become the most lucrative areas of business.

However, not all of these fields of activity retained their importance throughout the company's history. While Project Services remained the most important business in 2000/2001, Media Services and Operations had declined in both volume and value. In the early days of the company, the human resources constraint necessitated focusing on Project Services as the most attractive business, conferring a lower priority on Media Services and Operations during the boom. In 2001, the market for these services had then been captured by specialized niche providers, making them largely unattractive for SinnerSchrader.

In 2001, the Operations business (operating and maintaining transactional websites for clients) was discontinued, and the focus placed on Project Services and Media Services. In terms of revenue, the importance of the two remaining business continued to change significantly. While in 1997, Project Services had contributed 67% of Project and Media services revenue, they now represented approximately 85% of total sales.

6   Project Services

Project Services, the core business, are integrated consulting, design and engineering services resulting in the launch of a transactional website for which SinnerSchrader has developed both the front and the back-end.

On the basis of an extensive knowledge of an industry's market, competitive dynamics and the client's specific strategy, a consulting team consisting of experienced IT and marketing experts establishes what transactional needs a client may have. With the client's business model as a basis, an encompassing e-commerce strategy and implementation suggestions are developed from scratch.

If the strategy and implementation suggestions are accepted by the client, the consultants develop specifications for features of a transactional website, which are then passed on to both the design and engineering teams. Additionally, the design team receives information on the target segment and its internet surfing habits. The designers then develop a graphical user interface that combines attractive aesthetics with intuitive navigability. Often, an engineer will join the team to assure the technical implementability of designs. Upon completion, several design versions are submitted to the client for acceptance and/or improvement suggestions.

The engineers are responsible for implementing both the front-end and the transactional IT system. The processes here consist of continuous programming and simultaneous product testing. In more complex projects, a prototype is submitted to the client to assure the finished product's "usability". The technical realization of a transactional website by the engineers entails the integration of existing client IT architecture, standardized hardware and software components of leading original equipment manufacturers (OEMs) as Oracle, Sun and Intershop and proprietary SinnerSchrader software into one holistic solution that appears homogeneous to the outside user. SinnerSchrader's acting as a reseller for existing hardware and software products adds to the high reliability of the final solution and allows the company to offer lower prices than other architecture service companies.

The one-stop-shop approach of customization and integration in engineering has been *a significant factor for SinnerSchrader's success, because what has been done is gener-*

ally difficult to determine for an outsider. The resulting client lock-in, though not perceived as such by most customers, led to the establishment of a large and loyal client base, the large majority of which returns to request SinnerSchrader's services whenever an update or re-launch of a website is deemed necessary.

The pricing of projects was time-based throughout the establishment and rapid growth phases of the company. However, with market consolidation setting in during 2000, most projects were now being calculated on a fixed-price basis.

7 Media Services

Media Services are all forms of marketing to generate traffic for a transactional website as requested by clients. Past projects included online advertising and public relations campaigns, optimizing internet marketing operations as well as webmining. Services extend to banner advertisements, paid links, pop-up windows, sales alliances, etc.

Because this part of the business was constrained by resource limitations during the rapid growth phase starting from 1997-2000, specialized niche competitors emerged. Their increasing market clout, along with the ability to offer better prices than SinnerSchrader, had decreased the margins of Media Services. Furthermore, the end of the dot-com boom wrecked havoc on both the volume of advertisement requested, as well as on their contact prices per thousand. Furthermore, the effectiveness of online advertising has been increasingly called into question.

8 Organization

SinnerSchrader's organizational chart reflects its business model and the separation into Project Services and Media Services (see figure 7).

Within Project Services, the three value-adding processes – consulting, design and engineering – are organized into functional groups. Whenever a new project was acquired, it was staffed with consultants (often, it is also they who acquire the project alongside top management), designers and engineers. While paramount that the consultants have experience within the client's industry, the latter two are not usually requested to have industry experience. The responsibility for the project was generally delegated to a senior consultant, though top-level management tends to be highly involved in project management.

Maximilian Niederhofer

Media Services were not treated as a separate business, but staffed with consultants, engineers and designers according to need. Generally, requests for media services resulted from a given project or client, so a given project team would provide the service alongside their other work.

9 The CEO's Perspective of the Problem at Hand

The moment the three men had left his office, Schrader decided to jot down his thoughts on the problems facing the company, so as to be able to compare them with what the functional heads would come up with. He thought he was starting to have an inkling of what the source of the problem might be, though he did not yet think that he had found the answer.

"The main issue", Schrader mused, "is that three different cultures have developed within SinnerSchrader. There are the consultants, who have a more encompassing view of our business, are very experienced and well-paid, but who have a slight tendency to be arrogant when dealing with the others. Then there are the designers, typical creative people, more interested in the way things look than the way things work. They generally think of themselves as being cooler than the rest. And finally – perhaps most important – the engineers, called "techies" by everyone else, who care mostly for the technical solution and little besides that, and have their own subjects of interest and own hierarchy, and who don't seem completely at ease with the others."

"Different cultures by themselves would be fine," thought Schrader, "but what annoys me most is that these three groups often engage in fire-and-forget modes of work, with top management having to mop up the mistakes that are made. They rarely talk to one another privately, there's no team spirit. Worst of all, there's a lack of easy communication and a tendency to avoid taking joint responsibility of a project. When there's a problem, it comes directly to me. Everyone thinks his function is the most important one and that the company should be heading in that direction: to be a clear consulting boutique, a media design agency or an IT services business. None of the groups seems to really understand that our competitive advantage, the reason why people hire us and not the others, is that we're the perfect mix of strategic consulting, technical implementation and creativity."

10 A Second Problem

Schrader didn't put his pen down after he had finished this list. Instead, he took the latest financial figures out of his in-tray and examined them. He knew that there was a high uncertainty about the industry outlook in the short- to medium-term and, looking at the red number at the bottom of the income statement, his insides began to squirm.

While the company had grown right through the bursting of the tech bubble more or less profitably, Schrader thought that the worst might yet be to come. He had seen it happen to the most formidable of his competitors. In good times, they hired and hired, only to be hopelessly overstaffed when things turned sour. With the business model relying entirely on intellectual capital, capacity utilization figures of the industry as a whole were a key metric he followed closely.

"The real dilemma," he thought, "is that when the times are good, we lose huge opportunities because there aren't any qualified people looking for jobs. We've had to give up some very lucrative, phenomenally-priced projects because of manpower constraints. On the other hand, even if we don't hire as much as we could in the upswing, we've got loads of slack when there's downturn. There are fewer projects and these fewer projects have lower prices and it gets dangerous for the company as a whole. Vis-à-vis the financially stronger competitors, who have access to resources from their parent companies, this is a real disadvantage for us"

While Schrader was tempted to blame it all on Germany's infamously inflexible labor legislation, he knew he had to start human resources planning in the coming days. "I wonder how other consulting companies have solved this problem," he thought. "Maybe there are even lessons from companies in capital-intensive industries with high fixed costs and volatile demand." He also seemed to remember some models for retailers that had to buy inventory while demand was still uncertain. Could he adapt these models for SinnerSchrader?

11 The Problem at Hand - Functional Perspectives

The following day, the heads of the three functional groups sat down for their first meeting. While their teams did not get along, these three men had been with the company since the beginning, had seen the best and the worst of times and, as shareholders, were genuinely interested in seeing performance improve significantly.

"Well," said the consultant, "I'm not sure what the problem really is. My people complain about a lack of cooperation from both the engineering and the design teams, but over-all, they're happy. You know that we've basically organized ourselves so that the consultants stay in the industry they're familiar with. That gives them even more experience and they perform better than if we'd switch them around every time."

"That may work for you," said the designer, "but see, my people complain about the monotony of always working in the same industry. Because the consultants tend to speak to the designers they know personally, it just happens that several in the design team have been working in the same industry for three projects or more. And, frankly, they're sick of the transportation industry or communications. They want something new, like a B2C portal, something where they can indulge a little more. Creativity needs something different every now and then…"

"…something different is ok with me," the engineer said. "Every project is different for us, because the client's requests and their IT architecture are different, so I don't mind which way it goes. The only concern I have is that my people don't really enjoy working closely with the consultants because they've got such different mindsets. I'm sure that both sides have to compromise a bit. It would be a whole lot better if they got along, because most of the problems we have is miscommunication. Sometimes, I'd like to hire a translator to talk in between them!"

"You're right on," said the head of consulting. "I mean either, we bring them together and make them understand that they're working towards the same goal or we may as well keep them completely separate. However, that won't do the trick in the long term."

"Well," said the designer, "What do you think of this?", and started drawing on the whiteboard…

SinnerSchrader AG

Appendix

Figure 1: Revenue of SinnerSchrader (€, million)

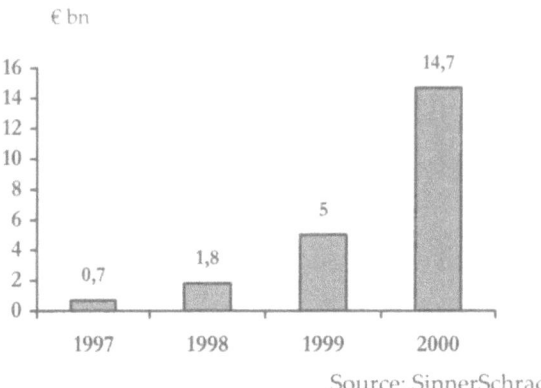

Figure 2: Workforce Growth (employees, full-time equivalents)

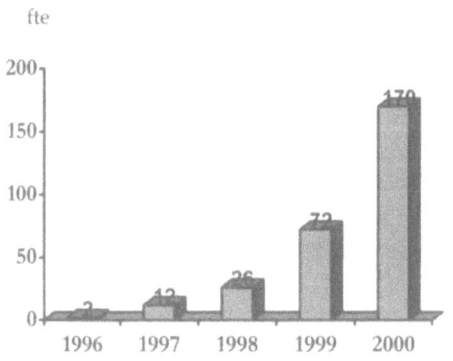

Figure 3: Development of SinnerSchrader Stock on the Neuer Markt

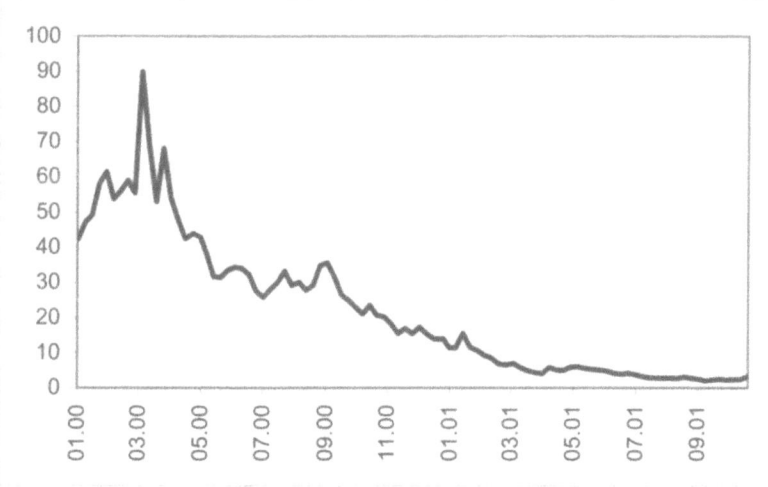

Figure 4: European Market for Website Services

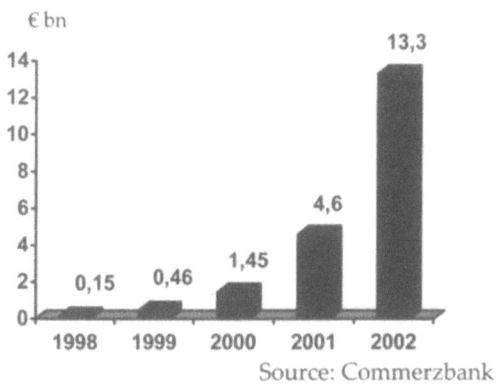

SinnerSchrader AG

Figure 5: Interactive Service Companies in Germany

1. Pixelpark
2. Concept
3. ID Gruppe
4. Artemedia/Lehr & Bose
5. Feldmann Media Group
6. More Interactive
7. Kabel New Media
8. BBDO Interactive
9. Fluxx.com
10. PopNet
11. AFIM
12. Eurotel New Media
13. Argonauten/Grey Interactive
14. Elephant Seven
15. bas Interactive
16. Antwerpes & Partner
17. Pixel Factory
18. Medialab Informationsdesign
19. United Media
20. SinnerSchrader

Source: Commerzbank

Figure 6: Distribution of Competences at Selected Competitors (% employees, full-time equivalents)

	Consulting	Design	Engineering	Media
GFT	3%	14%	64%	0%
Iqena	12%	7%	64%	2%
Pixelpark	13%	40%	29%	0%
SinnerSchrader	13%	26%	44%	4%
PopNet	20%	37%	14%	1%

Source: Commerzbank

Figure 7: Organizational Chart for SinnerSchrader

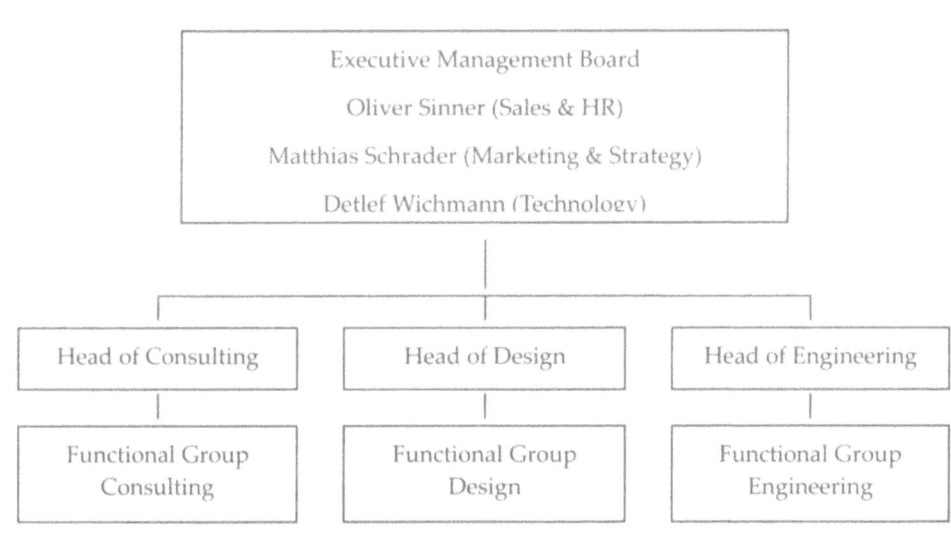

Source: SinnerSchrader, case author

Figure 8: SinnerSchrader Customers & Projects

Customers	1997 IV	1998 I	1998 II	1998 III	1998 IV	1999 I	1999 II	1999 III	1999 IV	2000 I	2000 II	2000 III	2000 IV	2001e I	2001e II	2001e III	2001e IV
Deutsche Bank	•			•		•									•		•
Görtz	•							•							•		
Lingenbrink			•				•						•				
Europcar		•								•	•						
ricardo.de				•						•	•						
Talkline						•								•			
Tchibo											•	•			•	•	•
OTTO												•				•	
VIAG Interkom													•			•	
Bertelsmann													•	•			

Source: SinnerSchrader, Commerzbank, case author

Eric Adler, Christoph Frehsee, Florian Kreuzer and Tim Kunde

Sushi Factory

1 Introduction 257
2 Founding Team 258
3 Sushi and Kaiten Sushi Bars 259
4 The Sushi Market in Germany 260
5 The Sushi Factory Business Model 264
6 Operations Management 269
7 Marketing 271
8 Human Resources 273
9 Controlling 274
10 Investor Relations 274
11 Growth Options 275

1 Introduction

Autumn, 2003. It is a chilly evening in a restaurant in the northern German city of Hamburg and the customers were writing on the walls: *"The best sushi bar in town. If I could I would move in here!"* "日本にいるみたいだ！" *"Congratulations to 5 years of great sushi and service"*. It is a revolution of sorts—not the fact that customers were writing on the walls, on canvases put there to celebrate the restaurant's fifth anniversary, but the concept of the Sushi Factory itself.

Nearly six years earlier, the company's general manager and co-founder, Bodo von Laffert, left a secure position at a top consulting firm to start the restaurant chain. Together with three friends, Oliver Greiter, Silke-Susann Otto and Steffen Sajonz, he developed a business plan with the ambitious goal of introducing the novel concept of Japanese *kaiten* (literally "revolving") sushi bars to Germany and becoming the leading German sushi chain, with 120 restaurants by 2006 (see initial rollout strategy in Figure 1). They incorporated the Sushi Factory (legal identity Pretty Good Food GmbH & Co. KG) in April 1998 and opened their first restaurant in Hamburg in October of the same year. The Sushi Factory began offering delivery service in 1999 and opened a second restaurant in January 2000. The second restaurant was bigger than the first, and it also housed a central production site for seafood and rice preparation. Encouraged by the win of Wirtschaftswoche's Start-Up Prize in 2001, the Sushi Factory started B2B operations and began providing sushi to caterers, selected groceries stores in Hamburg, and airlines such as Lufthansa. In March 2002 they opened a third restaurant in Bremen, supported by the production site in Hamburg. In 2003, the Sushi Factory opened a traditional sushi bar in an established restaurant in Hamburg and began trial production of frozen sushi for grocery stores.

Eric Adler, Christoph Frehsee, Florian Kreuzer and Tim Kunde

Figure 1: Initial Sushi Factory Roll-Out Strategy

By 2003, the Sushi Factory had become a successful and profitable business with annual sales of €2.7 million, over 80 employees, and significant potential for growth and expansion into the B2B sector. But looking back at the company's initial strategy of opening 120 restaurants, von Laffert was wondering. Had Sushi Factory's growth been too conservative? Was now the right time for a rollout and, if so, how should he identify opportunities and leverage the Sushi Factory's core competencies?

2 Founding Team

The Sushi Factory's founding team included Bodo von Laffert, Oliver Greiter, Silke-Susann Otto and Steffen Sajonz, with von Laffert responsible for the Sushi Factory's operations. After graduating from WHU, one of Germany's most renowned private business schools, he had spent three years with the Boston Consulting Group before leaving his well-paid job in order to start his own business. During his studies at WHU, von Laffert spent an exchange semester in Japan and worked as an intern in a Japanese company, where he got to know the Japanese mentality and culture. He still has many friends in Japan and is able to communicate fluently in Japanese.

Oliver Greiter also had experience in Asia. He did a vocational training in foreign trade and spent about four years working in Hong Kong and Japan. Already having started another successful company, Greiter had entrepreneurial experience but de-

cided to contribute only 30% of his time to the Sushi Factory. He is in charge of the IT support and import activities for the company.

Silke-Susann Otto is the only woman in the team. She had got to know von Laffert while writing her doctoral thesis on controlling in Japanese companies at the Center of Japanese studies at the WHU. With a university degree in Japanese studies as well as in management, she had spent two and a half years in Japan. The others were no novices concerning Japan, but she certainly was the most experienced. She helped set up the company's first restaurant. From the beginning, however, she intended to gradually reduce her efforts for the Sushi Factory and started to work for McKinsey & Company.

Steffen Sajonz, finally, an industrial engineer with a degree from the Technical University of Darmstadt and an MBA from the Kellogg School of Management, had started a consulting career together with von Laffert at the Boston Consulting Group. He supported the start-up phase of the Sushi Factory with 60% of his time, and reduced his efforts to **5%** in the beginning of 1999.

3 Sushi and Kaiten Sushi Bars

Sushi is the pinnacle of Japanese culinary art. Its origins date back to the 7th century. All sushi contains rice flavored with vinegar to make it smoother and tastier. It usually includes a piece of fresh raw seafood, but certain variations use vegetables, egg, cooked seafood, or other ingredients. The two most well-known and popular forms of sushi are *nigiri* (meaning "pressed in the hand") and *maki* (meaning "roll"). *Nigiri* consists of oval balls of rice with seafood on top. *Maki* consists of rolled rice and seafood which is wrapped with seaweed and then cut into bite-sized pieces.

Highly regarded for its healthy attributes, sushi contains the nutritional value of typical Western European food but significantly less fat. Fish oil helps to prevent heart and circulatory system diseases. Fish and shellfish contain taurine, which is known to lower cholesterol levels. On top of that, the consumption of rice in its original unprocessed form—contrary to complex carbohydrates such as sugar and bread—results in a slower increase in blood sugar levels. As a result, the filling effect lasts longer, which reduces the temptation to snack between meals. This is one of the reasons why few overweight people can be found in Japan.

Sushi became Japan's most popular dish through the accessibility created by kaiten sushi bars. The business model of kaiten sushi bars is based on the "what you see is what you eat" concept. Customers are seated around a small conveyor belt serving numerous types of sushi on small plates. As the sushi comes by, customers simply take

Eric Adler, Christoph Frehsee, Florian Kreuzer and Tim Kunde

the type of sushi they want. Sushi chefs traditionally work in the middle of the conveyor belt, assembling the sushi directly in front of the customers. Besides being efficient by eliminating ordering and preparation time, this adds entertainment value to every visit. Carefully observing consumption, the chefs produce sushi in batches and continuously replenish the belt themselves. The pricing policy is unique in terms of transparency, simplicity, and flexibility, all of which serve to attract and retain a wide variety of customers. Payment follows a simple principle: the plates have different colors representing the different price categories. The customers simply pile up the plates and pay accordingly at the exit ("what you eat is what you pay").

In Japan kaiten sushi bars are a €2 billion business, with over 2,700 restaurants. They have started gaining popularity outside Japan after a London-based entrepreneur opened YO! Sushi in 1997. Outside Japan, the direct contact with the product on the belt greatly reduces the consumption barrier for a relatively unknown product and encourages customers to try new types.

4 The Sushi Market in Germany

Despite several years of enormous growth, in 2003 sushi is still generally regarded as exotic by Germans. The first sushi bars in Germany opened in the early 1990s and the concept quickly spread to all major metropolitan areas. By 1997, about 100 sushi bars competed for a steadily increasing customer base. In 2003 over 240 establishments offer sushi (see Figure 2). But in 2002, the sushi market's sales of €124 million still constituted only 0.07% of the overall German food market (2002 sales of €187 billion). The overall food market, however, shrunk by about 8% in 2002, while sushi enjoys high levels of popularity. The market grew at a rate of 25% a year in 2002. This growth was especially strong in retail sales, catering, and B2B. The market share for sushi is therefore expected to reach 0.46% in 2011.

Figure 2: Number of Sushi Bars in Selected Cities (1997 vs. 2003)

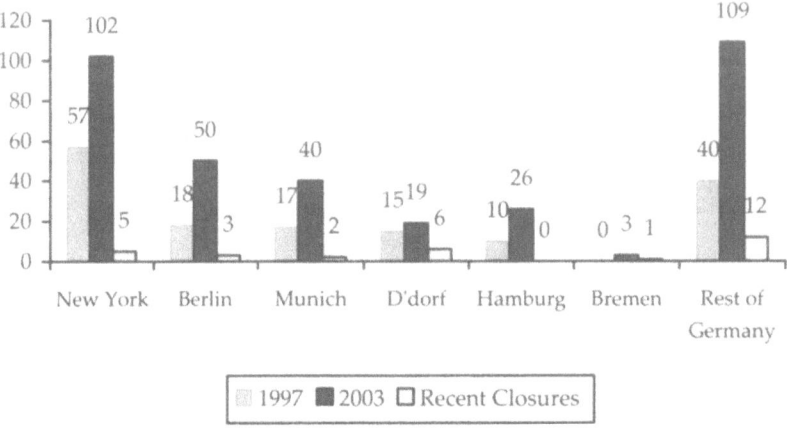

Consumers

While the first half of the 1990s saw decreasing numbers of patrons at restaurants and dance clubs, the second half of the decade saw a resurgence of outside-the-home entertainment. More people ate outside their home more often (see shifts in consumer trends in Figure 3). Going out was not limited to weekends any more, with sales becoming more evenly distributed over the week. This was especially true for young, unmarried couples. Sushi restaurants profited from the trend since they perfectly met the clientele's demand for fast, high-quality food in a fashionable surrounding.

Figure 3: Shifts in Consumer Trends, 1991-1996

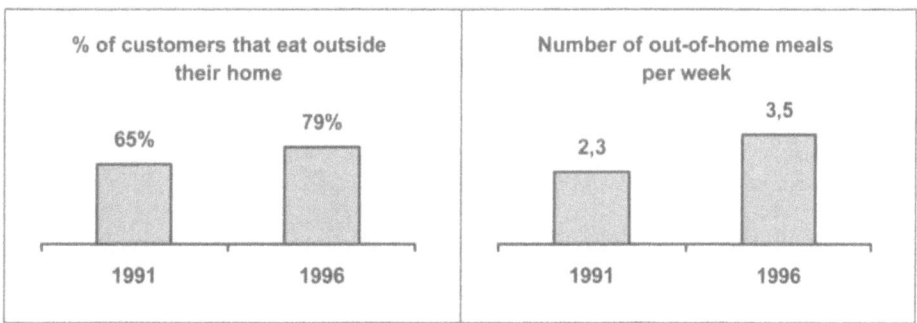

The typical customer profile for sushi restaurants in Germany changed quite substantially over time. In the early 1990s, only Asian immigrants and trendsetters went to sushi bars, but the bars soon became popular for yuppies and increasingly attracted a more mature, wealthy crowd. By 2003, sushi was still exotic to large numbers of Germans but attracted a wide range of customers. Although, according to von Laffert, *"The Sushi Factory's kaiten bars were visited by anyone from high school students spending their pocket money to 70-year old retirees,"* a typical sushi customer in **2003** was between 28 and 40 years old (Figure 4), well-educated, worked as a "creative" freelancer or white-collar employee with significant income, lived in a metropolitan area and showed an open and cosmopolitan attitude to life. Always short on time, he or she looked for healthy, creative food that was nevertheless served quickly. Consumers spent approximately 25 to 40 minutes in a sushi bar and paid about € 20 on average per person (€ 16 for food, € 2.50 for beverages, and the rest for service).

Figure 4: Sushi Customer Profile

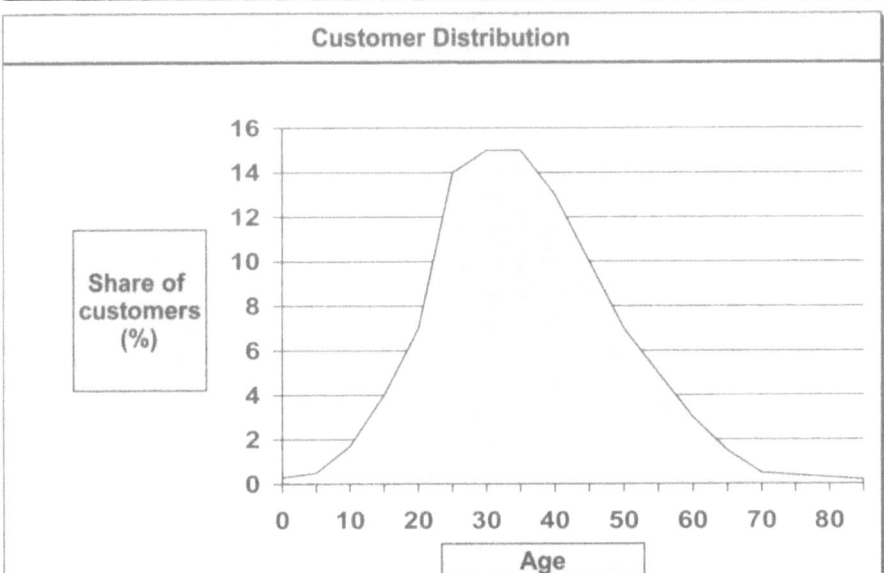

In the past, sushi restaurants benefited from the demographic trends in Germany. An aging population created a wider range of customers with more disposable income. This effect will probably be less strong in the future.

Competition

The restaurant market in Germany is highly fragmented, with restaurants competing for customers at the local level. Due to their business idea of serving excellent exotic food, sushi restaurants and bars compete with a diverse group of competitors. These range from traditional fast food chains to high-class fashionable Asian restaurants.

No sushi chain dominated the market either in 1997 or 2003. The Sushi Factory is said to be the market leader in 2003 with a market share of a mere 1.7%. Competing business models exist. Most restaurants are single-location, family-run Japanese restaurants often positioned at the upper-end of the price scale. Certain companies, however, are also focused on creating kaiten sushi bar chains.

Frankfurt-based Sushi Circle was founded by Andrea Godon, an investment banker at J.P. Morgan, who had learned about kaiten sushi bars while working in London and realized the market potential in Germany. Sushi Circle opened Germany's first kaiten sushi bar in downtown Frankfurt in 1997. Due to Godon's business relationships with

various venture capitalists, Sushi Circle was able to finance a quick nationwide expansion. By 2001, Sushi Circle had ten restaurants in Frankfurt, Hamburg, Berlin, Munich, Cologne and Wiesbaden. *"Sushi Circle got into trouble because they lacked experience with the Japanese culture and knowledge of the product,"* said von Laffert. *"The company faced massive problems retaining its Japanese cooks and experienced quality problems because the management was too far removed from restaurants operations."* Sushi Circle had to close several restaurants and was finally bought out by a group of ex-managers from REWE, a large German retailer, in 2001. In 2003, the company operates six restaurants (two in Frankfurt, two in Berlin, and one each in Hamburg and Munich). It realized a significant net loss in fiscal 2002. Apart from its restaurant business, Sushi Circle offers take-away service in its restaurants as well as sushi cooking classes.

In 2003, FAI Sushi operates three restaurants in Stuttgart, Karlsruhe, and Berlin. It offers take-away and catering service. FAI Sushi experienced problems similar to Sushi Circle when it initiated a nationwide rollout. Six of the nine bars it operated in 2001 failed and had to be closed.

Suppliers

The most important ingredient in sushi is undoubtedly the seafood itself. Rather than sourcing their seafood directly from fisherman, sushi restaurants in Germany normally turn to Japanese trade companies and a diverse group of international fish suppliers. In order for sushi bars to offer fresh and healthy fish, it is important for them to be close to the main seafood distribution points. Proximity to the ocean itself is not important, as seafood normally comes by airplane or truck rather than by ship. The largest fish distribution point in Germany is still the port of Bremerhaven, 180 kilometers from Hamburg. Large seafood buyers are able to exploit market power over suppliers and obtain substantial price reductions. The large number of potential suppliers results in relatively low dependence on suppliers.

5 The Sushi Factory Business Model

The Sushi Factory's Strategy

"Sushi Factory outlets will become the most successful, most popular and best known sushi restaurants in Germany, Europe, and worldwide." Sushi Factory mission statement, 1997

The Sushi Factory's business model is based on the "what you see is what you eat" concept of kaiten sushi bars. The founders intended to create a restaurant chain that provides healthy food quickly and simply and meets the needs of fitness- and wellness-conscious consumers. Restaurant chains (i.e., centrally-controlled groups of restaurants operating under a strong brand name and offering standardized quality) have been successful in the United States (e.g., Red Lobster, Chang's) but were still in their infancy in Germany in 1997.

The Sushi Factory's founders originally considered setting up a "McSushi" style chain that would offer sushi as quickly and cheaply as fast food chains such as McDonalds or Burger King. They soon realized, however, that this concept would be difficult to achieve because sushi-specific personnel requirements and raw material costs made low price points impossible. Additionally, the lack of consumer familiarity with sushi made intensive promotion necessary. Consequently, sushi had to be positioned as an upscale/lifestyle product. This contrasts with the kaiten sushi model in Japan, where sushi is sold as a commoditized version of the more expensive traditional sushi. The modified business plan, developed at the end of 1997, provided a strategy for a European-wide rollout of kaiten sushi bars. After setting up eight fully-owned sushi bars in Hamburg, Munich, Düsseldorf, Cologne, Frankfurt, and Berlin by 2001, the Sushi Factory intended to expand throughout Europe via franchising. By 2007, the Sushi Factory planned to operate 120 bars throughout Europe with a strong focus on Germany. To generate economies of scale, it wanted to establish regional sushi production centers that would serve all of its restaurants within 50 kilometers. A typical restaurant was expected to become profitable from year three onward, generating yearly revenues of €700,000 and operating profits of €170,000. In addition to the traditional bar business, the Sushi Factory wanted to offer take-away service, a higher-priced delivery service, and business to business services (e.g., delivering standardized lunch boxes to supermarkets and gas stations). The Sushi Factory was to be positioned as a high quality provider of fast food (see market positioning in Figure 5).

Figure 5: Intended market positioning of Sushi Factory

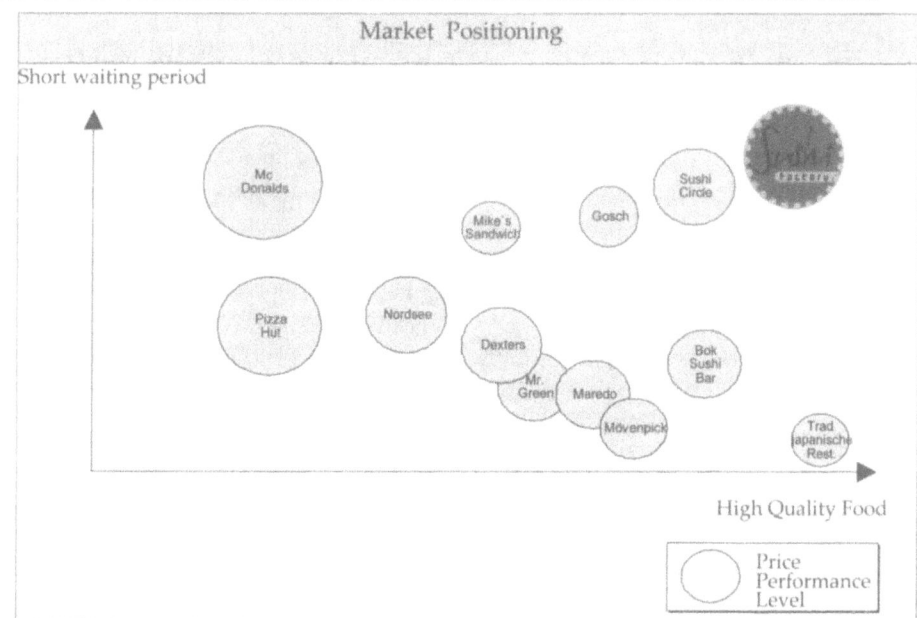

B2C Segment

Although the Sushi Factory's revenues grew by an average of 40% from 1999 to 2002, the company remained far behind its original objectives with respect to restaurant development. By 2003, Sushi Factory has set up three sushi restaurants: two in the Dammtor and Grindelhof neighborhoods of Hamburg and a franchising partnership in Bremen, in which Sushi Factory holds a share of 30%. A central production site located at the Grindelhof restaurant assures quality and supplied the three restaurants with the necessary daily sushi quantities. B2C sales (i.e., the sushi bars, take-away service, and delivery service via telephone and Internet) were still the dominant part of the Sushi Factory business model, contributing significantly to the total revenues of €2.7 million in 2002.

"The Sushi Factory's per square meter revenues exceed those of McDonalds" von Laffert claims. Nevertheless, the profitability currently still varies considerably between the restaurants. Although the sushi bar at Grindelhof is three times larger than the one at Dammtor, it generates significantly less revenue, a fact von Laffert attributes solely to the location.

B2B Segment

In order to generate additional revenue streams and make the best use of available production capacities, von Laffert sought new distribution channels by focusing on the B2B segment, which offered attractive growth rates. The Sushi Factory has entered into partnerships with hotels and restaurants, is involved in the catering business, and supplies sushi boxes to large food retailers.

The Sushi Factory's partnerships with hotels and restaurants contribute a single-digit percentage to overall revenues. Due to difficulties producing sushi as an additional menu item as well as the Sushi Factory brand as a quality "seal of approval", restaurants and hotels use the Sushi Factory as an outsourcing option. The Sushi Factory's partners can choose between two different options: delivery of finished sushi nicely decorated on a traditional sushi board or training sessions for the restaurants'/hotels' cooks in combination with a subsequent delivery of prepared sushi ingredients. With the second option, the restaurant's clients can watch the final sushi preparation.

An innovative B2B relationship is the creation of a sushi bar within Bistro Lambert, a stylish restaurant in Hamburg offering French and Mediterranean cuisine. Sushi Factory runs the bar and supplies the food. Customers can order from the bar and Bistro Lambert's existing menu. This combination of sushi and classic French food is considered unique. Being the first of its kind in Hamburg, the opening received strong press coverage.

The Sushi Factory has also entered the catering business. In 2003, this segment is expected to grow at a rate of 30%. The company offers on-site preparation of sushi by its Japanese chefs all over Germany, as well as delivery of sushi anywhere within a 200 kilometer radius of Hamburg or Bremen. In 2001, the Sushi Factory extended its catering business to airlines and secured contracts with Lufthansa and others to supply their airport facilities and provide sushi for other special occasions. Also in that year, Aramark, the third largest caterer in the world, approached von Laffert and asked the Sushi Factory to provide sushi for the VIP lounges at Hamburg's AOL Arena.

In most cases, the Sushi Factory did not initiate the partnerships. Rather, it was the Sushi Factory's reputation for product quality, professionalism, and credibility that attracted partners.

Finally, the Sushi Factory has begun to deliver Sushi to food retailers and delicatessens and to create so-called "shop-in-shop" concepts. The initial full-return policy offered to retailers led to huge losses during the first year of the program, since the unsold and returned sushi had to be scrapped. To remedy the situation, the company discontinued its return policy even though this meant losing a large number of clients. It succeeded, however, in building up a new client base. In 2003, 15 retail outlets are supplied by Sushi Factory. These outlets include five subsidiaries of the large German food retailer Spar and four delicatessens, including one in the large Galeria Kaufhof in downtown

Eric Adler, Christoph Frehsee, Florian Kreuzer and Tim Kunde

Hamburg. Besides volume effects, these B2B relationships increase the name recognition of the Sushi Factory brand and its overall popularity. Recently, the Sushi Factory has entered the frozen sushi market in cooperation with Icelandic, a large frozen food company, which sells combination boxes of sushi. Though a still very small market segment, von Laffert expects demand for frozen sushi to grow by 300-400%. Von Laffert made a conscious decision not to market frozen sushi under the Sushi Factory brand. Icelandic sells the frozen sushi in standard-sized boxes under their own brand name.

Product Range and Pricing

In its restaurants, the Sushi Factory offers a broad variety of sushi. Its in-house menu card lists 39 different types of Sushi in 5 different price categories. The items range from € 1.70 for simple creations such as *kappamaki* cucumber rolls to up to € 4.80 for more complex offerings such as *ikura*, which contains caviar. The plates come in five different colors, representing the different price categories. Daily sushi specials, depending on the season and climate conditions, complete the menu. Besides the standard offerings, the company also allows customers to special-order food such as yakisoba noodles, sashimi and even Häagen-Dazs ice cream. It also offers a variety of alcoholic and non-alcoholic beverages, although the favorite among customers is the traditional green tea. In the market, Sushi Factory is considered the price leader and competitors often have to match its low prices.

The menu has undergone only slight changes since the company's foundation. In 1998, it had begun with three different price categories (DM 3.90, DM 5.40 and DM 7.60) and a more limited number of products. The Sushi Factory carefully observed client preferences and tried to meet them by increasing the number of variations of the most popular types of sushi. From time to time, B2B customers expressed special requests, which the company then included in the restaurant menu.

The take-away service offers four different boxes - small, medium, large, and "party" - ranging in price from € 8.40 to € 65. The delivery service pricing and menu includes both the four different sizes of sushi boxes as well as a more traditional and complex menu of individual sushi offerings. The Sushi Factory offers rebates for online orders and requires minimum order amounts between € 10 and € 40 depending on the distance from the center of the city. In 2003, most sushi restaurants in Germany do not offer an online ordering system at all. Many competitors, such as Sushi Circle do not deliver orders of less than €50 and don't offer online ordering either.

6   Operations Management

Sourcing

Sushi's main ingredients are rice, fish, seaweed, vegetables and extras such as soy sauce, wasabi, and ginger. The Sushi Factory sources the seaweed, rice, and extras directly from Japan through exporters. *"Our knowledge of the Japanese language helped us quite a lot when it came to dealing with Japanese exporters,"* von Laffert remarked. Vegetables such as avocados and cucumbers are bought on the wholesale market in Hamburg.

One of the more challenging aspects of the business is the sourcing of fresh seafood. Assuring the highest possible quality requires that the restaurants be supplied daily. By 2003, Sushi Factory purchases over one metric ton of salmon per month. After switching to a multiple sourcing strategy, the Sushi Factory has been able to obtain 20-30% lower procurement costs than its rivals. Unfortunately, the levels of quality varies, which sometimes makes certain types of seafood unavailable.

Central Production

Every morning, the fresh seafood is delivered to the 180 square meter production center at the Grindelhof location. Chefs predict the demand and are also responsible for specifying the order quantities. While the Sushi Factory's management monitors this process with a database, the chefs' estimates have become quite accurate.

After receiving the fish, the two Japanese cooks and one assistant first scale and then clean it. For the previous two years the Sushi Factory has used scaling machines, but some of the cooks still prefer to scale their fish by hand. After that, the cooks cut the fish into sushi-sized pieces and place it in boxes for delivery to the restaurants. Craftsmanship, a high level of knowledge, and years of experience are needed to be able to filet the fish and judge its quality. This first step of the production—particularly the art of filleting—is the most crucial to ensure high-quality sushi. Only the most experienced and the most knowledgeable chefs from Japan dare to take that responsibility. Others joke that there are only some who want to start working every morning at 5 a.m. At one time, the Sushi Factory had a German cook specialized in seafood on the payroll, but he was not able to continuously reach the same level of quality as his Japanese colleagues.

Another ingredient prepared at the production center is the rice. The rice is washed and then cooked in special ovens, before it is seasoned with vinegar and cooled. According to von Laffert as well as the chief chef Hinohara, this process is quite difficult

and only a few players in the market succeed in achieving a consistent level of quality. The chefs then prepare the *nigiri* rice balls using a robot brought from Japan. They then place the *nigiri* rice in boxes, which are delivered to the restaurants along with the unpressed rice. The automated pre-production saves time at the sushi bars and makes the final assembly very efficient. All other ingredients are prepared and assembled in the restaurants. Restaurants receive shipments of raw materials twice a day.

Von Laffert believes that automation results in up to a 15% savings in total production costs. Rice robots, however, cost between € 20,000 and € 30,000. Under the existing set-up, the Sushi Factory can produce as many as 20,000 pieces of sushi per day. Daily production, however, varies between 10,000 and 20,000 pieces depending on the day of the week and special catering jobs. Von Laffert and Hinohara made the difficult decision to buy the robots, but not all chefs are convinced that this is the right way to produce sushi. For them it was like asking a painter to become a photographer.

Final Assembly and Restaurant Operations

In the middle of each restaurant's conveyor belt, two to three chefs prepare the sushi and arrange it on small plates. Their judgments about spot demand for each type of sushi are usually quite accurate, leading to a scrap rate of lower than 1%. The chefs always produce sushi in batches of 8 plates (i.e., between 16 and 32 pieces of sushi) and make sure that at least 100 plates are on the belt at any one time. No sushi runs on the belt for more than 30 minutes. Special customer orders, however, are prepared immediately. The "live" sushi preparation creates entertainment value.

Aside from the chefs, the restaurants require a shift manager and two to three employees per shift. The shift manager ensures a smooth flow of operations, coordinates the delivery service with the three drivers, and fills in for employees where necessary. The employees seat people, act as a cashier, serve beverages, prepare the wasabi and place it on the belt, clear and clean the tables, and wash dishes. Each restaurant operates in two shifts, the first from noon to 7 p.m. and the second from 7 p.m. to 1 a.m. Von Laffert has written a 200-page manual, which regulates all operations.

Quality Management

In order to provide excellent sushi to customers, an ongoing quality management system is indispensable. The continuous quality management at the Sushi Factory includes two steps. The incoming raw material quality is ascertained by the Japanese chefs at the production center. The restaurant chefs then check the quality again during the final assembly. Additionally, a system of ongoing quality checks has been im-

plemented. Together with a food scientist, the Sushi Factory developed a total of 80 process checklists to prevent any kind of poisoning. Not all of them are used on a daily basis. The most important ones include regular employee medical examinations, periodic supplier auditing and sending fish samples to laboratories. A risk assessment listing possible dangers has also been created for every ingredient, from seaweed to shrimp. This was a very important process for both the management and the chefs. *"We all learned more about our product and we realized that producing high quality sushi is far more complicated than we thought,"* von Laffert explained.

"Our quality management really pays off," says von Laffert. *"Last year a magazine tested sushi for health risks in various restaurants nationwide, and I'm very proud of our excellent results!"* With the lowest bacteria levels of sushi bars in Hamburg, the Sushi Factory ranks among the best restaurants in Germany—far better than its fiercest competitors, Sushi Circle and FAI Sushi.

7 Marketing

Advertising

The Sushi Factory drew its marketing knowledge both from Nicola Kreuzer, who is in charge of the Sushi Factory's marketing activities, and von Laffert. Kreuzer had worked for the marketing department of Beiersdorf before coming to the Sushi Factory. Von Laffert had concentrated on marketing during his graduate studies and was involved in several marketing projects in his consulting days.

In the past, the Sushi Factory benefited greatly from strong public relations. Winning the start-up award from McKinsey in 1999 led to press coverage on television and in several newspapers and magazines. *"The first press reports created a snowball effect,"* remarks von Laffert. *"After we won the award, a lot of people started calling us."* The Sushi Factory soon gained a strong reputation - especially with B2B clients – and by providing excellent quality, it did not disappoint its new customers. Since then, press coverage has come in waves, with journalists often feeding off from other articles. While at the beginning, the company relied heavily on advertisements in cinemas and posters, the Sushi Factory's marketing activities have shifted towards image-related activities such as event sponsoring and other goodwill actions. In general, von Laffert estimates the acquisition cost of a new customer to be around €5 in 2003.

Intensive B2B marketing has not really been necessary, since the Sushi Factory got a steady stream of inquiries from potential clients. The company is often unable to re-

Eric Adler, Christoph Frehsee, Florian Kreuzer and Tim Kunde

spond to the number of requests it receives. It also benefits from free advertising, when supermarkets use the Sushi Factory logo in their advertisements.

By 2003, Sushi Factory has become the most well-known kaiten sushi bar in Hamburg. Its name recognition stood at 28%, with its closest local competitors, "Sushi for Friends" and "Sushi Circle," lagging behind at 13% and 7% respectively.

Customer Relationship Management

Because of the novelty of sushi in Hamburg and the local nature of the restaurant business, the Sushi Factory has not been able to access an existing market. Instead, it had to create a customer base from scratch and utilize customer relationship management tools to cultivate and maintain interest in its restaurants.

One of the first tools that the company employed was customer education, which had been explicitly requested by customers. The restaurants offer three-hour courses, at a price of €75, on how to make sushi. They also sell a special Sushi Factory cookbook, which explains how to prepare sushi at home. The company's website provides information on everything from the history of sushi to the intricacies of wasabi.

In order to retain customers, the Sushi Factory management utilizes basic but critical CRM tools. Their customer comment cards ask questions such as how the customer liked the service, as well as how many times the customer has eaten at the Sushi Factory and how many times the customer has ever eaten sushi before. The feedback allows the management to gauge the penetration of sushi at each location and to get a better picture of the customer base. The Sushi Factory has also begun to award its customers "Sushi Miles". With a purchase of €7 and over, the customer receives a scratch-off card with a random number of miles. Customers can then redeem the miles for rewards ranging from sushi meals to the Sushi Factory cookbooks. Finally, the Sushi Factory promotes customer loyalty with its unique "Last Minute Sushi" offer. Customers who live or work near the restaurants are notified by e-mail of excess sushi at bargain prices.

8 Human Resources

Japanese Cooking Chefs

Initially, the Japanese chefs were a real attraction. People were amazed with the fact that the chefs had come all the way from the other side of the world in order to roll together some rice and fish. At first it was hard to find the right people and to motivate them to come to Germany. *"I am sure that without my experience in Japan and my language skills as well as those of other team members, we would never have been able to get these people to work for us!"* von Laffert is convinced. *"People can taste the difference and they appreciate the quality. This is well worth the high salaries and the expenses necessary to find the right chefs."* Interestingly, it was not only the high salaries that motivated chefs to stay with Sushi Factory. The majority of cooks were so impressed by the situation that they even brought their families over to Germany, enrolled their children in schools and kindergartens and motivated their wifes to take part in German language courses.

Finding professional and highly skilled chefs has become much easier since the Sushi Factory was placed on a list of the best employers of sushi chefs outside Japan. Thereafter, it was not necessary to travel to Japan and talk to the people directly any more. Despite the fact that the chefs stay with Sushi Factory only two to three years on average, the relations between the Japanese chefs and the German management are very good and based on mutual respect. In 2003, 70% of the company's chefs were Asian, although not all were from Japan.

Restaurant Support Staff

The situation is somewhat different with the restaurant staff. Finding people is not too hard, since these jobs are not very demanding. But keeping the personnel has been a real challenge. Over the lifetime of the company, about 450 people have been employed and the staffing level in 2003 is 90 employees. The support staff account for most of the personnel turnover. In the words of one manager, *"I really don't see why and how we should keep these people. Most of them loose motivation quickly; some of them even steal or commit fraud."* Despite the presence of organizational instruments such as the company's mission statement and the company values expressed in the operations manual, these types of problems persist and amplify the turnover problem.

Eric Adler, Christoph Frehsee, Florian Kreuzer and Tim Kunde

9 Controlling

Knowing the cost of each product is vital for pricing. With this in mind, von Laffert has created a cost accounting system that calculates the cost of each product based on detailed information about the cost of ingredients, labor, and overhead. *"I am sure that none of my competitors knows its costs as well as I know ours,"* von Laffert states with a slight smile. With this cost information, the company is able to adjust the prices of sushi to generate a reasonable profit margin on each product. The Sushi Factory's management has deviated from this system in only a few cases, which usually involved reaching a higher margin for types of sushi that were cheap to produce but in high demand by customers.

Apart from this very detailed cost accounting, Sushi Factory does not run a financial controlling on a regular basis. Rather, it consists of aggregating the relevant information at the end of each accounting year. It is difficult to perform these calculations more frequently because von Laffert does most of it himself. But by doing the calculations once a year, von Laffert feels he has a good idea about how the different parts of the business contribute to the success of the Sushi Factory. It is, nevertheless, hard to calculate profitability, since the B2C and B2B operations share common resources such as the production centre. Von Laffert is, however, able to say with certainty that the restaurant in Hamburg downtown was the most profitable in 2002, with a profit margin of about 20%, whereas all other businesses, including the Grindelhof restaurant, were at about 10%.

10 Investor Relations

The Sushi Factory was started without bank money by using personal funds and money invested by friends and family. The founding management was able to raise the necessary capital from 14 different shareholders to open the first restaurant. The plan was to get to know the business, to optimize processes, and then to expand geographically. After the success of the first restaurant, a second financing round allowed the company to open its second restaurant at the Grindelhof location. This time, the management decided to take on a substantial amount of debt because the business was running well and had sufficient cash flow to settle the outstanding interest and principal payments. As a result, von Laffert and Greiter together still hold the majority of the Sushi Factory shares in 2003. Von Laffert and Greiter thus effectively control the company and the 12 minority shareholders have relatively little influence. The shareholders have been quite satisfied with the development of the company so far.

It had always been clear to the founders that a rollout strategy could not be financed solely with private sources or cash flows from existing restaurants. Von Laffert estimates that he had spent about 20-40% of his time dealing solely with venture capitalists, without any success so far. It seemed that no venture capitalist would give them the necessary capital under appropriate terms. Somehow, sushi is not something that people perceive as a very exciting business, especially in times of the technological hype. This hype is over now, but people still don't seem to realize that it makes sense to invest in a stable but growing business. Moreover, von Laffert feels that venture capitalists' time horizons were too short. *"They're always thinking about what they'll get from the investment in two years, as if two years was the kind of time horizon within which all the steps necessary for a nationwide rollout can be taken."* Investing in a sushi chain requires a longer-term perspective. The investments will only pay off after eight to ten years.

11 Growth Options

Despite its moderate growth, Sushi Factory management has not given up on a nationwide rollout strategy, which was reinforced in its 2003 business plan update. Management still favors an aggressive scenario with up to 90 restaurants in Germany, supported by 8 production centers, within the next 6 years. Another, more moderate scenario suggests 30 restaurants. But is growth at that rate really necessary? Or is it something the founding management brought into the business plan to catch the investor's attention? Right now, there is nothing to complain about. The Sushi Factory is profitable and moderate internal growth is possible, while competitors like Sushi Circle and FAI Sushi are currently in trouble. Does the Sushi Factory need to pursue its ambitious plans?

Obtaining the capital needed to grow, however, has not become easier over time. Von Laffert still argues with venture capitalists about the appropriate valuation. *"The Sushi Factory's valuation not only depends on its current revenues but also on factors such as the reputation of its brand, its management ability, and its long-term potential for growth,"* von Laffert remarks. Sometimes he wonders if all the time he has spent with potential investors has been worth it. Obviously, the venture capitalists know nothing about the business. How else could they expect von Laffert to accept such bad conditions! Of course he wants to grow, but he is not going to squander everything that he and his colleagues have created.

Eric Adler, Christoph Frehsee, Florian Kreuzer and Tim Kunde

Franchising

Franchising would allow the Sushi Factory to leverage its brand and expand without a significant infusion of equity. Sushi Factory has, for all intents and purposes, franchised the location in Bremen through part ownership. It could easily expand to other cities in Germany by establishing new production centres and restaurant clusters based on the existing model. As Howard Schultz of Starbucks once said, *"After a while, opening a store was like switching on the espresso machine."* The Sushi Factory has not yet reached this point, but it is possible that it might reach it some day.

In the early days, von Laffert and his founding partners were convinced that the franchise model would enable their nationwide roll-out. Over time, however, von Laffert has become sceptical. For him, franchising equates to losing control, especially over product quality. Franchisees might not have the cultural heart beat needed to run a Sushi Factory bar successfully. How can he be sure that the franchisees really understand what the Sushi Factory stands for? How can he be sure that franchisees maintain the high standards of quality that the Sushi Factory has come to be known for? Von Laffert is horrified with the idea that some care-free people destroy all the reputation he has built up in the past. After all, this is about sushi—not about flipping burgers. Care and dedication are required.

B2B and Frozen Sushi

New restaurants are not the only possible path to growth. The B2B channels provide additional revenue. The supermarket business is new. Although the Sushi Factory is just starting with frozen sushi, the company's arrangement with Icelandic looks promising and the market is growing at extraordinary rates. Despite initial problems related to branding and design, the market entry has been a success. With all the problems related to expanding the restaurant business—particularly regarding financing—frozen sushi and regular B2B relationships may the future of the company. With long-term contracts, the business would be stabler. The Sushi Factory could increase automation. Savings in personnel costs would further increase profitability. By concentrating its activities in the B2B sector, the Sushi Factory could also concentrate on production and would not have to worry about the intricacies of the restaurant business.

Von Laffert has come to a crucial crossroad. Soon, he will have to take important strategic decisions determining the future development of his company. What have been the key success factors of the Sushi Factory in the past and how can he leverage the company's established core competencies? Von Laffert also wondered where his customers will be writing on the walls on the Sushi Factory's tenth anniversary. Will it be in restaurants all across Germany or still onto the same walls in Hamburg and Bremen?

Mehr wissen – weiter kommen

Wie bewertet man Wachstumsunternehmen richtig?

Wachstumsunternehmen – ein neues Phänomen? – Traditionelle Unternehmensbewertung – Unternehmensbewertung mit Kennzahlenvergleichen – Ökonomie des Internet, der Biotechnologie und der Medizintechnik – Kennzahlen zur Bewertung spezieller Wachstumsbranchen – Kundenwertmessung – Rationale Bewertung von Wachstumsunternehmen

Die Kursentwicklung der am Neuen Markt notierten technologieorientierten Unternehmen zeichnet sich durch eine hohe Volatilität aus. Eine zuverlässige Aussage über den tatsächlichen Wert dieser Unternehmen erweist sich in der Praxis daher als äußerst schwierig.

Markus Rudolf und Peter Witt gehen in ihrem fundierten Buch auf die verschiedenen Bewertungsanlässe und die spezielle Bewertungsproblematik von Wachstumsunternehmen ein. Sie stellen alle wichtigen traditionellen und innovativen Bewertungsmethoden vor und zeigen detailliert deren Voraussetzungen, Stärken und Grenzen auf. Dabei gehen die Autoren der Frage nach, ob die neuen Verfahren wirklich besser dazu geeignet sind, einen realistischen Unternehmenswert zu ermitteln. Reale Fallstudien vertiefen auf anschauliche Weise das Verständnis für die komplexen Zusammenhänge.

Markus Rudolf/Peter Witt
Bewertung von Wachstumsunternehmen
Traditionelle und innovative Methoden im Vergleich
2002. XXII, 311 S.
Br., EUR 34,90
ISBN 3-409-11877-2

Änderungen vorbehalten. Stand: Januar 2005

Gabler Verlag · Abraham-Lincoln-Str. 46 · 65189 Wiesbaden · www.gabler.de

More Knowledge for a Better Performance

State of the Art of Innovation Management

International authors of different fields look at technology and innovation management from several perspectives: in 27 articles they discuss aspects of their disciplines focussing on innovation management, ultimately presenting an interdisciplinary crossing-over into all other functional areas within the realm of business.

The book is divided into 6 parts:
- Innovation and Strategy
- Innovation and Research & Development
- Innovation and Marketing
- Innovation, Controlling, and Finance
- Innovation, Foundations, and Universities
- Innovation and National Economic Performance

Furthermore, some authors devote themselves to new topics such as venture capital, virtual stock markets, and futurology.

Managers, students and professors of business administration gain new insights and various impulses for research and its implementation.

Sönke Albers (Ed.)
Cross-functional Innovation Management
Perspectives from Different Disciplines
2004., XIV, 518 p.
HC, EUR 59,90
ISBN 3-409-12627-9

Gabler Verlag · Abraham-Lincoln-Str. 46 · 65189 Wiesbaden · www.gabler.de

MIX
Papier aus verantwortungsvollen Quellen
Paper from responsible sources
FSC® C105338

If you have any concerns about our products,
you can contact us on
ProductSafety@springernature.com

In case Publisher is established outside the EU,
the EU authorized representative is:
**Springer Nature Customer Service Center GmbH
Europaplatz 3, 69115 Heidelberg, Germany**

Printed by Libri Plureos GmbH
in Hamburg, Germany